From SAS to Blood
Diamond Wars

We are the Pilgrims, master; we shall go
Always a little further; it may be
Beyond that last blue mountain barred with snow,
Across that angry or that glimmering sea.

Inscription on SAS memorial clock tower taken from James Elroy Flecker, 'The Golden Journey to Samarkand'.

Conflict diamonds (sometimes called blood diamonds) are diamonds that originate from areas controlled by forces or factions opposed to legitimate and internationally recognized governments, and are used to fund military action in opposition to those governments, or in contravention of the Security Council.

UN Definition

From SAS to Blood Diamond Wars

By Hamish Ross

with Kauata 'Fred' Marafono

Pen & Sword
MILITARY

First published in Great Britain in 2011 by
Pen & Sword Military
An imprint of
Pen & Sword Books Ltd
47 Church Street
Barnsley
South Yorkshire
S70 2AS

ISBN 978 1 84884 511 4

A CIP catalogue record for this book is
available from the British Library

Typeset in 10pt Palatino by Mac Style, Beverley, East Yorkshire
Printed and bound in the UK
By CPI

Pen & Sword Books Ltd incorporates the Imprints of Pen & Sword Aviation,
Pen & Sword Family History, Pen & Sword Maritime, Pen & Sword Military,
Pen & Sword Discovery, Wharncliffe Local History, Wharncliffe True Crime,
Wharncliffe Transport, Pen & Sword Select, Pen & Sword Military Classics,
Leo Cooper, The Praetorian Press, Remember When, Seaforth Publishing and
Frontline Publishing

For a complete list of Pen & Sword titles please contact
PEN & SWORD BOOKS LIMITED
47 Church Street, Barnsley, South Yorkshire, S70 2AS, England
E-mail: enquiries@pen-and-sword.co.uk
Website: www.pen-and-sword.co.uk

Contents

Foreword

Our country is rightly proud of its military forces, not least our elite SAS. But what happens when these well trained and highly motivated men and women retire from the regiment? What do we expect them to do back in civvy street? Hamish Ross's book charts the path taken by one of these remarkable pilgrims.

A couple of years after I left Sierra Leone as British High Commissioner and had retired from Her Majesty's Diplomatic Service, my daughter went out to Freetown for a while to help at the Blind School there. By now peace and democracy had been restored. But this being Africa you could never be certain what lay around the corner, so before she left I gave Catherine a telephone number and one name – Fred. I told her that if there was any trouble at all just ring Fred and I was sure that he would help her. Such is the confidence, trust and admiration I have for this remarkable man – one of those unsung heroes who emerge in conflict situations like Sierra Leone. Fred Marafono is one of those people who 'cross the river' for you, to quote the SAS saying. I am very pleased therefore to write the foreword to this book.

How times change! Twelve years ago I was reprimanded by my government and pilloried in the press for having contact with so-called 'mercenaries'. Nowadays private security firms are a vital part of the British Government's efforts in places like Iraq and Afghanistan. But even back then some of us, not least the Sierra Leone people themselves, already knew what a vital and positive role the private security firm Executive Outcomes had played in fighting an insurgency and protecting the population. This book reveals how a force of just 200 trained and disciplined men achieved what a subsequent force of thousands failed to initially. What EO achieved in Sierra Leone was down to the likes of men like Fred Marafono; however, even amongst his colleagues, Fred was special.

But this book is as much about Chief Sam Hinga Norman, a man that both Fred and I crossed the river for. He was another African in the Nelson Mandela mould who fought for the cause of justice, peace and democracy. Sam Norman's arrest, detention and untimely death remains a huge blot on the Sierra Leone story. Hamish Ross's book reveals much of the real truth of the man, very little of which emerged in his shameful trial as a war criminal by the Sierra Leone Special Court. In the eyes of most Sierra Leoneans he is a national hero.

However, perhaps the real heroes of this book are the 'ordinary' Sierra Leoneans who sacrificed so much for the cause of peace and democracy – the countless thousands who lost their homes, their limbs, their loved ones and their lives. It was their courage and sacrifice which prompted people like Fred Marafono to cross the river.

Peter Penfold

Acknowledgements

Many of those whose input I wish to acknowledge gave their time and effort because of their regard for Fred. First of all, therefore, I want to thank Fred for calling on his wide network of old comrades and friends and for ensuring that our collaboration worked so smoothly.

His former comrades: Alan Hoe, Pete Flynn, Simon Mann, Roelf van Heerden, Tshisukka Tukayula De Abreu, Cobus Claassens, Tijjani Easterbrook and Alastair Riddell all gave support. I particularly want to thank Juba Joubert for his sustained input.

The Secretary of the SAS Regimental Association was most supportive and is greatly in my debt. I am also indebted to Doug Brooks, Rick, Jim Hooper, Tim Spicer, Michael Grunberg, the Rev Alfred SamForay, Gregor Ross and Ewan Ross. Special thanks are due to Peter Andersen, whose excellent online archive has been a valuable resource.

I would like to thank Rudi Bruns for writing an account of his experience as a hostage of the RUF and also Dr Joe Demby, who gave permission to quote his report on the autopsy of Chief Sam Hinga Norman. I wish to thank the Norman family for giving me access to the diaries and notebooks their father wrote in prison, and especially to Florence Norman and Sam Norman Jr for their support.

Finally, I am most grateful to Peter Penfold for his contribution to this work and for writing its Foreword.

Part I

Chapter One

The Master's Company

Stirling was a master of that art and it got him good results.

Blair 'Paddy' Mayne, Journal, Montevideo, 20 December 1945

It all began with a phone call. One Friday evening in May 1985, Ian Crooke, Second in Command of 22 SAS, rang Fred and told him they were going to meet someone in London the next morning; he would pick him up between 7 and 7.30 am, and, as an afterthought, told him to bring a tie. Travelling in civvies on a job was not unknown for Squadron Sergeant Major Fred Marafono MBE; during his twenty-one years in the SAS it had happened before. Fred was not his given name though, it was Kauata, and he was born on the Fijian island of Rotuman. Instead of pursuing his intention of studying veterinary science, first at Navuso Agricultural School and then continuing it in Australia, he was attracted by a recruiting drive on the island, and made the decision, as had his father before him during the Second World War, to serve in the British army.

Not until they were about to join the M4 at Swindon on Saturday morning did Fred asked Ian whom they were going to meet.

And he said, 'We're going to meet the Colonel.' I said, '*the* Colonel?' And he said, 'Yes, *the* Colonel.' I said, 'Boss, I feel very honoured, I don't know what to say.' And he said, 'Fred, be yourself. You'll like the old man. He's very easy to talk to.'

Ian was right. When they arrived at 22 South Audley Street, David Stirling, founder of the Special Air Service, put Fred at ease from the start: he looked him in the eye, spoke to him as an equal and was in no way condescending.

We sat down around his lovely old wooden desk, it was a lovely desk with a big black panther statue – the statue was beautiful, all the muscles were rippling. And David Stirling offered us cigars and a glass of wine. And then he started to explain to me why I was there. He said that Ian Crooke would explain to me the whole reason why I would be involved. 'Ian and a few of you are due to leave the army shortly and Ian and I talked about forming a security company to provide employment for some of the men who are leaving the Regiment. Recruiting will be selective and Ian told me that you can do the job.' I was very honoured and lost for words and only managed to say, 'Thank you.' Cigars were lit and we drank a toast to its success before Ian continued to explain the company's philosophy and objectives and the part that each of us would play in it. My role was to find the recruits for the new company – KAS. And that was the beginning of me landing in the world of security after being in the Regiment.

From that beginning, Fred was to go on to develop a second military career and achieve an outstanding combat record in Sierra Leone's blood diamond wars. Recruited by Simon Mann for Executive Outcomes, the classic private military company that stopped a war, he would progress from ground force commander to gunner in a helicopter gunship, culminating in supporting the SAS in Operation Barras.

Fred's journey, however, from SAS through KAS and on to West Africa is not a gung-ho tale of intervention in a war-torn former British colony: his pathway was to become intertwined with that of Chief Sam Hinga Norman, a champion for democracy; it would run up against the cost of commitment to good men when political expediency dominates; and his record along the way raises issues about professional private military companies in conflicts where the western democracies are loath to risk their soldiers' lives.

But first there was a learning curve to be navigated in the ways of private security companies. Fortunately, David asked Alan Hoe to be a consultant to KAS. Alan had served in the Regiment, and after he left and gained experience with International Risk Management (IRM), he set up his own company, which specialized in kidnap and ransom situations, particularly in South America and Italy. In the light of that background, he was able to offer advice; and eventually, after he got to know him better, he went on write the biography of David Stirling.

He asked me to look at his company and, being brutally honest, I thought that the future looked gloomy. Whilst he had some superb guys there: he had Ian Crooke, Sekonaia Takavesi (Tak), Fred Marafono, Peter Flynn and Andris Valters – all of whom had enjoyed good careers in the SAS; they were still soldiers, very enthusiastic soldiers and they all worshipped David Stirling. But there was no business experience and David himself was never a particularly shrewd businessman. They were trying to be all things to all men instead of looking at the market, deciding on their product and then selling it.[1]

Opportunities were seized if they came their way. Images of a ship on fire, explosives in the hold, abandoned by its crew and adrift in the English Channel, appeared on television. Alan Hoe prompted them on the sequence they had to go through: Lloyds' Register to find out the ship's owners; contact the owners; Pete Flynn, who was also a pilot as well as ex-unit, to charter a helicopter; obtain advice and quotations on best type of fire-fighting equipment. The plan was they would abseil on to the ship, extinguish the fire, and Fred, who had been in the Boat Troop, would sail the vessel to port. They were slow, however, compared to the salvage crew that succeeded in beating them to it and towing the ship away. Alan Hoe's view was that it could have been done, if they had been quicker off the mark.

They chased and won several small contracts like a Bulgari jewellery exhibition. But it earned the company very little, and they probably overspent on their endeavour to win it. The team lived from Monday to Friday in the top floor of 22 South Audley Street, or the penthouse, as they called it, and they earned a salary of £15,000 a year.

In theory at least, David Stirling's fame would have brought kudos to a company that contracted with him and ought to have attracted clients. But it did not seem to work out that way.

David had some hugely potent contacts but he rather scared them off, I think, because they could not really get a handle on what he was trying to do. He would talk about starting a mercenary company one day, and the next he would be offering bodyguards and then looking after high value species the day after. He had good contacts like Margaret Thatcher, William Whitelaw and Dennis Healey as well as many influential business friends but he got little out of them because, I think, he frightened them off.[2]

One contact he did not frighten off was Prince Bernhard of the Netherlands, who was the first president of the World Wildlife Fund (WWF). It was well-known that elephant and rhino were endangered as a result of poaching for tusk and horn. The poachers and hunters did not make much from a kill, but the ivory and horn was finding its way along a route that led through the Middle East to the Far East. It was suspected that at least one Asian embassy was behind the trade: rhino horn was in high demand in Asia as a traditional medicine. Stirling spent years in central and eastern Africa, and had influence in some quarters. Alan Hoe was involved in setting up an infiltration operation.

I went over with Ian Crooke on one occasion to meet Prince Bernhard to discuss the proposition. We spent the best part of a day with the Prince talking about the project, and into the equation he brought John Hanks, who was a senior executive within the WWF, and was very much in favour of the project.[3]

Funding for what became known as Project Lock came from the WWF and, it was believed, from a department of the South African government. The operation was aimed at all parts of southern and central Africa 'where the survival of rhino was threatened by poaching,'[4] A small team, including Ian and Fred based itself in South Africa; there was an office in Johannesburg and another in Pretoria.

And it was very, very enjoyable. We were attacking at two levels: one group was to do the training with the game wardens in a park in Namibia. That was our first operation, to know the animals, to know their habits and everything. And then the other group were stationed in a base and had to try and get to the people who were actually dealing in these endangered animals. The decision was made that since I look like a Malay, and I could speak Malay – there's a very big Malay community in South Africa, in Cape Town –, my background was that I was to be a Malay from Woodstock, overlooking the harbour in Cape Town. That was the cover.

But you cannot operate in South Africa without the approval of the South African government. Whether you like it or not that is the reality. We had two very nice business people who were very helpful. One of them ran a security company, and the other played a supporting role. The one who ran the company used to work for the South African intelligence service. He was very helpful; he was the one that made it possible for me to get into the network. He had the connections for me to get into the security company network. I eventually went across to Zimbabwe.

The thing was that before you could be accepted by these people, you had to be ready to show that you were interested in the endangered species, the rhinos and the elephants. And an English couple that ran the reserve for King Maswadi III were very helpful in showing us the different types of species: the white rhino, the black rhino. We learned a lot about the animals, we'd see them and learned what to do and what not to do. We then had to find out the people who were wanting to buy these animals, and go and try and make a deal. And I would be the seller.

For my first deal in selling a set of black rhino horn to a Chinese man in Manzine, we recced a site suitable for a team to set up a covert hide to photograph the whole operation. The car boot was rigged up with a covert microphone and the position where I was to stand forced the client to face the cameras. And it was a Chinese man who owned a restaurant. At the end of the deal I was supposed to collect the money. But of course, that was the thing, nobody goes around carrying a big wad of money. So he said, 'Come to the restaurant to collect the money.' What do you do; do you say no? I said that I'd come that evening. And I went back and I told the others. I was given a right telling off: that is risky, you'll never get the money back. But a promise is made, I had to go and get the money; you have to carry it through; you just don't turn around – whatever it is, it is.

I went, but the plan was that Nick Bruce (one of the team) would cover me in. He was to check out the place, looking for any suspicious signs, order a meal and when I came in half an hour later, if everything was OK, we were to make eye contact. I was to go to the bar, order a drink and ask for the boss. If things looked suspicious, Nick would cough when I was at the bar before he paid for his bill and left the restaurant. Nick was to go back to base and wait for my return.

So the boss man came. We shook hands, and he said, 'Come to the kitchen and meet my family.' So I met the family. Then he said that this was the amount we agreed but there was slight damage to the commodity – to the rhino horn – so instead of X amount he would deduct 7%.

That was the beginning. And then we were to go to Swaziland, Botswana and Zimbabwe.

Although KAS was beginning to get into the illegal marketing at this level, what it was not providing was conclusive evidence of the source promoting the poaching. Before they could refine and develop their approach to penetrate a deeper level of involvement, the whistle was blown on them. Not by embassy officials who may have felt they were being accused, but from inside the WWF. It was discovered that the WWF was funding mercenaries.

There was a lot of criticism bandied about when the media got hold of the story. John Hanks lost his job, a chap who had been an ardent member of WWF for many, many years. Prince Bernhard took a lot of criticism over it, but I don't remember the press ever giving a fair, unbiased view. But these things happen in life. If you've got the name David Stirling linked – you've got controversy and the media rake over old ashes.[5]

President Mandela of South Africa later set up a commission headed by Judge Mark Kumleben to investigate the smuggling of ivory and rhino horn. The commission confirmed that 'the covert unit operated against smugglers in Zimbabwe, Zambia, Namibia and other southern African countries.'[6]

However, David Stirling would not have achieved what he did in 1941, founding a unit in the North African desert that was destined to have a such a distinguished history throughout its first seventy years, if he had been deterred by the Jeremiahs of this world.

He had expectations of the men he recruited for KAS from their counter-terrorist experience in the Regiment, and through his contact with a leading figure in a key industry, he floated the idea of presentations to company executives on strategies to prevent terror attacks. Some of the team carried out surveys, and did a risk analysis. The result was that senior, hard-nosed executives, in spite of their disbelief, were forced to listen to presentations from, what they privately considered to be, a couple of madcaps depicting terrorist threat. Indeed, in the 1980s, such scenarios (which will be passed over here) might have sounded like some fantasy for a film script. They would not be reckoned improbable today.

A great plus factor in a small security company comprising former members of the SAS, combined with Stirling's style of management, was that they were able to express and develop forward-looking ideas that Stirling, through his contacts, could bring to the decision-maker level. Ian Crooke, for example, explored with like-minded retired members of US Special Forces the idea of a joint UK/US operation, whereby either government, or indeed any other approved government, could – if they had on their hands limited intensity conflict – avail themselves of a mercenary force that was composed of ex-US and ex-UK Special Forces soldiers.[7]

However, this was not to be a covert force designed to carry out the kind of work often attributed to the CIA in the past of destabilizing a government that was hostile to US interests in a particular region. This idea, which was prescient, was for limited conflict situations – of the kind, as we shall see later, in Sierra Leone – where there was a threat to an established government on the one hand, and on the other, a sympathy and a willingness by the west to give support, but a reluctance for political reasons to risk US or British soldiers' lives. The idea got as far as White House level: David Stirling and Pete Flynn went to the States. Stirling met President Ronald Reagan; Pete was not present at the meeting, but he met Vice President Bush.[8]

Nothing came of the idea at the time. Yet only a few years later, a private military force was founded in South Africa of the same sort of calibre as the KAS concept; Fred was a member of it, and it stopped a rebel war at the request of the recognized government of Sierra Leone.

After Stirling died, new ownership took over the company. Fred and most of the team left. Fred's hallmark is his loyalty, a loyalty that came to him naturally, from his heritage; such was his attachment to David Stirling that when the SAS Regimental Association held its memorial ceremony in honour of its founder, at Ochtertyre in Perthshire, Stirling's home area, Fred flew especially from Sierra Leone to attend.

It was to be in this country that he would perform some of his best work, fighting insurgency in conflict diamond regions.

Chapter Two

The Chief

Pike Bishop: When you side with a man you stay with him.

from the film *The Wild Bunch*, directed by Sam Peckinpah

The team of six, led by Project Manager Alastair Riddell, formerly a senior officer in the Parachute Regiment, touched down at Lungi International Airport, Sierra Leone at around 9.30pm on 31 October 1994, looking forward to food and drink and a bed. But they found that, here, transfer to the hotel was tediously slow: there was a thirty-minute bus ride to Tagrin Ferry Point; a two-and-a-half-hour ferry trip to Government Wharf Ferry Point in Freetown; and finally a taxi to the Mammy Yoko Hotel, which they eventually reached at around 2.30am. They were contracted to provide security at the Omai Gold Mine and Golden Star Resources concession at Baomahun. For Fred, the contract was to open one of the most important periods of his life – a period in which he would form a deep friendship with a Sierra Leonean Chief, and one that would see him in combat again.

Soon after their arrival though, Fred had an introduction to the deceptions and graft that were common in everyday life. At the end of their first day, as they were having a meal by the hotel pool, a group of girls appeared and asked if they could join them. The girls said that they were refugees from the war in neighbouring Liberia, that they were all living rough in a tiny room and had to sleep on the floor. Fred and his colleagues felt sorry for their plight and offered them food. However, if they were to allow them to share their rooms, Fred knew that because of colour, his five colleagues would be compromising themselves in the eyes of the white community and the client company, whereas he would not. And so, on the understanding that it would only be for one night, Fred let the girls spend the night in his room; the girls slept on the bed; he on the floor, using his belt order for a pillow.

Next morning he left for work. But when he arrived back at the hotel at 5pm, one of the girls was still in his room. In response to his asking her why she was still there, she said, 'You promised to pay me $100'. Realization dawned on him; he was being taken for a patsy, and in a flash of anger he said, 'What $100? I never promised to pay you'. His room was on the third floor and he opened the window and told her that he was going out. And he said, 'But when I come back, if you're still here, I'm going to throw you from the window'. He took 10,000 leones (SLL) and put them

on the table and said, 'That is it finished'. Fred learned later that the girls were not
Liberians but local girls working a racket with the hotel's security staff.

That incident seemed to take on new life in expatriate folklore in Freetown,
because more than four years later, in January, 1999, a British journalist in the, by
then, war-torn capital wrote, under the headline, *Street Life: Freetown: Mercenaries,
prostitutes and other hotel guests*, a sensational, heightened account of it and why it
took place, as though it had just recently happened.

> Fred, 58, took seven prostitutes up to his room the other night.... the adrenalin
> of dicing with death seems to make everyone hungry, thirsty and rampant.[1]

To be sure, the insurgency situation in the country had deteriorated to such an
extent by 1999 that the journalist's use of the word mercenary had resonance then
that it would not have had four years earlier. Even so, at the beginning of November
1994, security was a key issue for the mining concerns in Sierra Leone.

The government of the day was a military junta, the National Provisional Ruling
Council (NPRC), headed by Captain Valentine Strasser. From 1991 an insurgency
war was being waged in the eastern part of the country, allegedly fomented by a
warlord, Charles Taylor, from neighbouring Liberia. His protégé in Sierra Leone
was Foday Sankoh, a former Sierra Leonean soldier-turned dissident who learned
his tactics at a guerrilla training camp in Libya. Sankoh was attempting to take
control of the diamond rich areas of the country. His pillaging was notoriously callous
and barbaric: he had a 'pay yourself' policy for his followers of the Revolutionary
United Front (RUF), encouraging them to kill, loot and rape with impunity.

Alastair Riddell had been contacted by Golden Star Resources who wanted to
develop their operations into and across Africa.

> I was asked if I would head up a team to develop the exploration site, and I was
> authorized to hire a small team. Fred was first on my list, for I knew he had just
> come back from Guyana, as we kept in constant touch. He readily agreed to join
> me.
>
> We deployed in October 1994, and went to work with gusto, carrying out a
> recce of the mine, fortunately on the day of a Board meeting, when we were able
> to report the success by SATCOM from the site. This was a huge step forward,
> as the country was mired in inefficiency and lack of direction: authority was
> questionable, and corruption was endemic with all the associated difficulties. We
> made huge progress, much of it with Fred's help always covering my back as
> we went from negotiation to negotiation with government ministers (all about
> 30 years old), the army and the police.[2]

As the newcomers in the business, the team that Fred was part of had to establish
an office in Freetown and a base in Bo where the concession was located, while, at

the same time, trying to ensure that they were not treading on the special preserves of established companies. They took over a large walled compound in Bo and two other properties; they tried to find out the best airfields and the best hospitals for medivac, if they took casualties; they took advice on the routes to take and the routes to avoid; they read up on the regulations that applied to the mining industry in Sierra Leone; and they found out what other companies paid their people.

One particular meeting stands out for Fred. It took place at a rutile mine. The head of security at the mine was a Briton who lived in South Africa,

> He gave me the impression that he 'knew it all' and ignored me completely, which was very rude I think. Regardless of what he thought of me and my ability, at least he should speak to me instead of ignoring me completely and only speaking to Roger England, our medic, who was ex-Rhodesian Army Medical Corps, whom Alastair recruited because of his medical and African background. The British guy, the head of Security, was saying that if you do the security job properly, you'd have about sixty pairs of eyes to give you the information on what is happening. He said that if anything was happening within a hundred miles around he would know about it from his intelligence.

That boast was soon to be put to the test.

Over the following weeks insurgency activity intensified. Most of Fred's company returned to the UK for Christmas. Fred stayed behind; his job was to monitor the situation. And it was during this time that he began to get to know Regent Chief Samuel Hinga Norman, a Mende. It was in his chiefdom, in Bo, that the mining concession was sited; and Chief Hinga Norman was liaison officer to the company. Alastair had formed a very favourable impression of him, right from the start.

> This was when I met Chief Norman who was my local adviser. He was former British army, and the impression I got was that was indeed a wonderful man, so pro his country that he once said to me, 'What we need is the British back to sort out this mess.' Prophetic words indeed in the light of what was to come over the next few years.[3]

Fred too observed their liaison contact closely: he tended not to wear western dress; he held himself erect; he walked quickly with a walking stick; and his shoes were always highly polished. That intrigued Fred, because from his experience, someone whose shoes were always highly polished was likely to have been an officer. And such was the case with Hinga Norman: he had served in the British army, had trained as an officer at Mons Military College and for a time was stationed in Germany. After Sierra Leone became independent, he served as the first ADC to the commander of its army, Brigadier Lansana. However, it was the character of the man that made an impact on Fred. When you engaged with him, he looked you straight in the eye.

And it soon became obvious to Fred that he was not motivated by self-interest – his concerns were the wellbeing of his people.

About this time, the RUF rebels attempted to take over the town of Bo. Armed with AK–47s and RPG–7s, they made a dawn advance towards the headquarters of a local defence militia, the Special Security Division. Now there was also in Bo a detachment of the Sierra Leone army stationed in the west of the town. The rebel incursion, though, was towards the town centre via New London junction. Fred was in Freetown at the time and so the situation was reported to him later. The Sierra Leone army unit made no attempt to leave its barracks, but the people of Bo were not prepared to give up their town to the rebels. There is a large student population in Bo; and Chief Norman, dressed in white, assembled a group of civilians and students. Armed with sticks and clubs or whatever weapons they could get their hands on, and with Chief Norman at the head, they massed and confronted the rebels. This confrontation between a group armed with automatic weapons and rocket propelled grenades and a motley assortment, whose strongest weapon was moral force, had a strange outcome: the rebels backed off and withdrew. The Bo youths then set up checkpoints to control movement into the town. Only at this stage did the army make an appearance, suggesting to the civilians that they should leave the security to 'the professionals'.

A newspaper's headline summed up the people's frustration with the army's lack of convincing response, 'Enough Was Enough'. It is true that the Sierra Leonean army was beset with deep-seated problems that only reform and professional training could resolve. Its complement had been enlarged at such a rate that its recruits were inadequately trained. To boost numbers even convicts were allowed to join. Underlying all that, soldiers were paid a pittance and had to forage for themselves as best the could. Against the background of increasing terrorist activity, and the RUF leader encouraging his followers to pay themselves, the allegiance of military personnel could not be relied on. Hence the term *sobel* was coined: soldier by day, rebel by night.

On Monday 2 January 1995, six days after the rebels' attempt to take the town, Fred drove back to Bo. He sat in front with his driver. The security company was not authorised to carry weapons – if they had been armed, most likely, they would have been shot at by the Sierra Leonean army. Working in this situation where rebel activity was becoming bolder and incipient anarchy loomed near, Fred carried twenty-one years of SAS experience to guide him. He was prepared to balance risks and act on split second judgement; and in the months ahead, he was going to have to train and motivate men who lacked his zest for action.

He began with his driver. There was the likelihood that as rebel groups moved westwards they would set up Illegal Vehicle Checkpoints (IVCP) in the country areas. Anticipating that, Fred explained to his driver what he wanted him to do.

Slow down, as though we're going to stop, release your door catch, put the vehicle in second gear and drive as close to them as you possibly can. And when I say

'GO' kick the door wide, put your foot on the accelerator and drive like mad. The door will open unexpectedly on the nearest of those manning the IVCP and hit them; and I do the same with my door – I kick it open so that both doors get those manning the IVCP.

That was the hope. And his response to the man's unspoken scepticism that they could come through alive, 'Otherwise! It's better to die trying than to die like a sheep'.

That afternoon, as Fred was been driven back to the mining concession, the rebels attacked and burned the village of Buyama, about 12 miles from Bo. What would be their next move he wondered? He had been booked into the Sir Milton Margai Hotel, and, when he checked in, he made a point of telling them that he would be staying about a week or ten days. When he met some of the mining company's workers on site he gave them the same story. But he was ranging over other options.

Throughout his time in the SAS, Fred had extensive training in counter-terrorism, had fought insurgents in several countries and therefore had insights into how insurgency worked. He assumed that although the rebels had been baulked in their attempt to intimidate the citizens of Bo they would not give up. Foday Sanhok, leader of the RUF, had been trained in Libya; he had probably been briefed on Mao Tse-Tung's dictum that 'the guerrilla must move amongst the people as a fish swims in the sea.' Some of Foday Sankoh's RUF would be mingling among the local people, probing for vulnerable spots and easy targets. Until they made their move, though, it was not possible to determine friend from foe. However, there was one likely target – Chief Hinga Norman. Hinga Norman had motivated and led the town's resistance to the rebel incursion the previous week; he was also the mining company's liaison officer, and he lived in a house in the city. With these thoughts in his mind, Fred went about his business for the remainder of Monday and again on Tuesday, paying close attention to what was happening around about; but on Tuesday he invited Chief Norman to his hotel for dinner that evening.

They had a convivial meal and Fred voiced no concerns about Hinga Norman's safety. However, he had observed him closely over the few weeks they had been together and he made some shrewd deductions: Hinga Norman's insistence on appearing in public wearing highly polished shoes was a carry-over from his officer training in the British army; he was likely to be just as fastidious about punctuality. And so after they finished their meal, Fred invited him to join him for tapas at the hotel the following morning at 10am sharp.

Next morning Fred left the hotel with his driver after 9am; however, he returned to it just before 10am. Next, he told the driver to wait in the car, and he went into the hotel, with his radio handset to his ear. As he was walking across the foyer to Reception, he put the phone away, went up to the desk and said, 'I've just had a call, and I'll have to go back to Freetown. Could you give me my bill please?' As he was paying the bill, the hands of the clock on the wall in Reception were pointing at

10 o'clock; Chief Norman arrived and Fred took him by the arm and led him straight to his waiting vehicle. No observer watching Hinga Norman's movements could have had an inkling that he was about to be moved out of Bo.

Fred's execution of his one-man operation was worthy of his years in the SAS: patient, low-profile observation to begin with; emergence of a clear, simple plan; then skill and timing in extracting the Chief without resources or back-up. Indeed that morning, on the drive to Freetown, memories of some of his operational experiences returned. It began when his acute inner warning system was reactivated. This was an extraordinary faculty he discovered he had when he was on SAS operations – and it was of proven efficacy.

That morning it was triggered again. They were about five miles from Bo and were passing the burnt out Salcost crushing plant. Salcost was an Italian road construction company that was building a road with Italian government aid to Sierra Leone. Heavy plant, bitumen mining machines and burnt out trucks scarred the quarry site. Fred had been commenting that if the rebels destroyed the plant it would be a tragedy, not only for the company but for Sierra Leone. Whatever was Hinga Norman's response, it was lost on Fred, because the road, at this point, went through a cutting, and suddenly the hairs at the back of his neck felt as if they were rising, and he had the overpowering feeling that they were being watched.

Images from past SAS operations returned as he remembered when he had had that feeling before. In 1965, his Squadron was in Borneo, and neighbouring Indonesia was sending insurgents across the border to destabilize the local situation. Indonesia, though, denied responsibility for the attacks and the British government, for its part, could not take overt action against that country. But the SAS were covertly penetrating its borders, tracking down the raiders' bases. Once, Fred's patrol was well inside the Indonesian border watching a track that was used by Indonesian soldiers. There were three army camps situated some distance from each other, roughly in the form of a triangle; and the routine was that from these three camps, in the morning, the soldiers would send civilians to check out the tracks. If they were clear, a shot would be fired from each camp at around 0900hrs. Traffic would then move between camps.

> On this occasion, Lou Lumby and myself were to watch the track, lying alongside an old log a few metres from the track, camouflaged with our face veils and cream. We heard the sound of boots on hard compacted sandy track – a sort of *toom, toom*. Lou signaled to me with the thumb down and about 5 minutes later, a patrol of Indonesian soldiers passed by. Away and out of sight, we could hear them talking and the first thing that came to my mind was as if one soldier said to another, 'Hey, did you have that feeling that we were being watched back there?'

Later that year, however, there was nothing whimsical about the way Fred's inner sense took over: it saved his life. It happened on the 29 May 1965 in the Republic of Yemen. An initial contact took place in Wadi Sharkah at a place code named Crow. An SAS patrol came across a group of terrorists sleeping by a stream and a firefight took place. The patrol won the engagement but took two casualties and the remaining terrorists fled taking their wounded. The following morning the SAS checked the area for signs of blood, and Fred's Troop found some heading towards a rocky outcrop above their own position.

Two of us, covered by our Troop Commander, followed the blood trail. Suddenly we lost the trail and on doing a cast, we found the track, but this time it was heading towards a little village below. I was on the left hand, sidewalking on the lip of the re-entrant and Ken and the Boss were on the right hand side. Suddenly, I sensed that there was something wrong and I stepped back off the top of the bank. A shot rang out. We hit the deck at the same time and as the other two fired, the bullets came over my head. I shouted to them to stop and to guide me to where the shot came from. I threw a rock and they told me to go left a bit. The second rock seemed to be in the right area, and I followed it up with a phosphorous grenade. When it exploded, I stood up and as the smoke cleared, I saw a figure in a little hole in the bottom of the re-entrant. I was just about to run down but then I realized that all he had got to do was to look up and put a bullet through me. Training took over and I double-tapped him at the back of his head. His black hair rose up and bits of brain spattered everywhere. It was horrible. But war is too. You either kill or be killed!

After searching the body, they buried it with rocks where it lay. Fred took from it one Rial note of The Arab Republic of Yemen; he wrote the date on it – a sombre memento of obeying instinct and choosing, in a split-second, who would live and who would die.

Yet again in Yemen, when he was in the role of the hunter, his extraordinary sensitivity alerted him that he and his friend were no longer the hunters – they were the prey. And his anticipation of his enemy's next move saved both himself and his friend. It happened in the district of Sheikh Othman. One terrorist tactic was to mingle in a crowded area and then lob a grenade at a patrol of British soldiers as it crossed a road junction. A variation on this tactic was for a terrorist to infiltrate the busy souk on the look out for a soft-centre target, an off-duty soldier buying trinkets to take home, and shoot him at close range. The terrorist weapon of choice for this type of assassination was the Czechoslovak Vzor 7.65 pistol. It fitted neatly into the hand, was easy to conceal and deadly at close range. Over the period, these tactics accounted for the death of about 13 British soldiers.[4]

In response to this danger, two-man teams of SAS soldiers, not in uniform but in Arab dress, and usually enhanced with make up, went out after dark to mingle in crowded areas, armed with a concealed 9 mm pistol in a shoulder holster. They were tasked to observe for signs of an assassin stalking his victim and then take him out. One particular evening, Fred was partnered with his friend Paddy Byrnes and they were approaching the junction they had to cover. Men assigned to this role had not only to look the part, they had to act the part and normally remain mute as they performed it. And so this evening, as Arab men quite often do in public, Fred and Paddy held hands as they made their way towards the junction they were allocated. They were approaching it when a patrol of the Parachute Regiment came into sight; as it was passing, one Para shouted to his mate, 'Look at the queers!' Of course the man had no idea that he was referring to two under-cover soldiers of his country's army; but even if he had, it might have made no difference to his comment. However, the taunt was too much for Paddy and he muttered a few expletives in a low voice to Fred. Whether the expletives were heard more widely, or whether it was the body language of an 'Arab' in response to abuse in English that did it, something alerted another hunter, one armed with a 7.65 pistol. But then, he too, in his zeal to stalk them, betrayed his intentions. And Fred's instinct picked it up.

How? His eyes were everywhere. On us and away from us, but most of all, his hands were in a footer pocket, a pocket almost like the sporran on a kilt. I told Paddy to keep an eye on him too. Next minute we lost him! Then suddenly, the hair of the back of my head seemed to stand up and when I turned around, there he was right behind us with his hands in the pocket of his footer. I started to scratch my left armpit where my 9mm was in a shoulder holster and he pulled out his hands holding a box of matches and walked away.

Fred has no doubt: the man was an assassin. Even to this day when he recalls it, he comes out in goose pimples.

Hence on the morning of Wednesday 4 January 1995, as he and Chief Hinga Norman drove through the cutting in the road by the wrecked Salcost plant, Fred had no doubts that his life-saving sixth sense was still operational. It was probably becoming clear to him too that he might soon be called on to take up a combat role again.

The mining Company put up Chief Hinga Norman in one of the rooms of a stadium in Freetown. And as he thought over what he had done in Bo, extracting Hinga Norman from a vulnerable situation, Fred realized that he was forming a commitment to the man. He responded to Hinga Norman's integrity. He felt that Hinga Norman took his responsibilities as a chief very seriously and that his first priority was the well-being of his people. For example, the concession paid a small percentage to the local authority of the area in which it was sited, and that authority was the traditional tribal chiefdom; and Hinga Norman saw to it that the money went to the people – it was not to feather his own nest. In his political views he was forthright: he wanted parliamentary democracy restored to Sierra Leone.

Hinga Norman too was becoming aware that a bonding was developing. He and Fred often met for a meal together and one evening Hinga Norman questioned him about it.

He said, 'Fred,' and he looked at me for a long time, and he smiled and he said, 'Fred, you have a country, you don't need to get involved in this sort of situation; you have a country that you can go to. Why do you get involved?' And I said, 'Chief, if I was to turn my back on you, every time I heard something about Sierra Leone on the news, especially you fighting the war, I would feel very guilty for leaving you when you most needed me. I would carry that burden for the rest of my life and I would rather not.' We both laughed and never talked about it again.

That was the way that Fred described it to Hinga Norman, but at a deeper level he was committing himself to an action, which in the SAS, is called 'Crossing The River'. Crossing the river is when someone – whom you have trusted with your life and who has trusted you with his – is in need of your help, you do not turn your back on that person, and that decision is irrevocable.

Rebel activity was continuing and getting bolder. On 18 January, apparently in an attempt to intimidate foreign companies, they attacked a rutile mine belonging to Sieromco (Sierra Leone Ore and Metal Company) and took hostages: five expatriates, including the company's security officer, and three Sierra Leonean senior management. Rudiger (Rudi) Bruns, Honorary Swiss Consul-General to Sierra Leone, was in his office at the mine that morning. Three auditors of KPMG were checking the annual accounts, and two British computer consultants were cleaning the company's computers. When they finished they left and drove to Bo, Rudi's secretary, Brimah, going with them. Brimah then returned to the mine, and, as he approached it, rebels ambushed his car and he was killed. About lunch time Rudi and the Managing Director, James Westwood, were preparing a presentation for their board of directors at head office in Zurich, when they heard gunfire. As it came nearer, the Sierra Leone military and paramilitary who were guarding the mine fled. In a nearby residential compound were the living quarters, where there were wives and children.

When the gunshots came closer to our works' compound, I had already packed my briefcase with documents, some cash and personal items, for example, my Nikon F3 camera – which I saw later in the hands of Foday Sankoh! I rushed in my company car, a Citroen 2CV, to the main gate to enter our residential compound, just next door, to support my wife. Too late! Groups of RUF 'boys' with red headbands, firing gunshots into the air, were blocking the main gate. What to do? Back to the office! Within a few minutes, about eight of my colleagues assembled in my office, probably because my office was the last one of the whole block and considered to be safer.

Suddenly, it was dead quiet. No voices, no shooting, no birdsong. This continued for approximately ten minutes. These minutes were terrifying; no way to escape; no place to hide. We had heard stories of RUF burning houses while people were inside, committing atrocities or just killing innocent civilians. Then we could hear the noise of breaking doors by force – we had wooden doors. It started at the other end of the office block. They were coming closer, door by door. There was no screaming or shouting! My wife called me from the residence, asking what to do and what to pack. 'Just keep calm and pack what we enjoyed most, and things to remember.' She did very well. My office door split within seconds. We were expecting the worst. In came a boy of about 15 years, an AK-47 in his hands and obviously surprised to meet so many people in the room. We immediately raised our hands and whispered 'surrender'. The boy looked at us and replied, 'Don't be afraid, I am your friend. Please come out and join me.' This was the beginning of a ninety-two-day journey across Sierra Leone of about 250 miles, walking in the shoes I was wearing, mainly at night over long distances for 12 hours or more with no rest.[5]

During his time as hostage of the RUF, Rudi saw at close-hand the effects on children who had been abducted and brutalized, becoming boy soldiers with a Kalashnikov.

I tried to escape twice, hiding in the bush, but I noticed that two SBUs (Small Boys Unit) were taking personal care of me. No chance! I remember one boy saying, 'Please Papa, don't do it again.' It also became clear to me that these SBUs had lost their childhood. The gun was the family. One of my 'caretakers' found a little toy car in the village; he looked at it for a few minutes, and then destroyed the toy.[6]

After his eventual release, it took years before Rudi felt he could put on paper his experiences without revisiting trauma. Fortunately, however, his friendship for Fred was the deciding factor, and as this work was in process, he wrote for it a fascinating account of being a hostage. It appears in full as Appendix I.

A week after the attack on the rutile mine, the RUF took seven Roman Catholic nuns hostage. The Sierra Leonean army response to the RUF was quite ineffective. At one point Chief Hinga Norman, through the channel of the British High Commission, wrote to the Queen asking for British military help. This was quite a logical move, for until 1961 Sierra Leone had been a British colony and was a member of the Commonwealth. However, there seemed to be no official response to this appeal. The stumbling block for the British government was that Sierra Leone was ruled by a military government.

However, the Economic Community of West African States (ECOWAS) had earlier established a non-standing military force, ECOMOG, which intervened in a peace keeping and security role in Liberia in 1990, and now, with the worsening situation in Sierra Leone and at the behest of the NPRC, a contingent of its Nigerian troops based themselves in Freetown.

As a consequence of intensified rebel actions, the Omai Mining Company discontinued its activities and withdrew its personnel from the country, leaving

Fred behind to monitor the situation and report back if there was any improvement. Fred saw Hinga Norman quite often, and he discussed with him a very successful model the SAS had used in Oman in the 1970s. There, the SAS pursued not only a hearts and minds campaign, they also set up small training teams – and Fred was in one of them – to train cohorts of loyal local people, warriors in their own right, in proven military tactics and the use of modern weapons. And they moulded them into a highly effective fighting force that helped stem communist insurgency. The idea came to Fred when he was with Hinga Norman in the company of a cadre of local hunters that Hinga Norman was very close to, the Kamajors. The Kamajors were more than hunters however, they were a warrior cult, and they were characterized as being extremely loyal. Fred felt that a modified version of that SAS training in Oman could be made to work in Sierrra Leone, and that the selection and training of small numbers of men from the 149 chiefdoms could be carried out by a private military company, some of whose personnel would be ex-SAS. Hinga Norman was interested in the idea. But how would such a scheme be funded? The only possibility seemed to be by the government of the day, the National Provisional Ruling Council, headed by Capt Valentine Strasser. And Hinga Norman had the standing in the community that could bring about a meeting with Strasser to discuss the idea.

First of all though, its feasibility had to be explored, and so Fred flew to the UK and contacted his old Squadron Commander of SAS days, John Moss, who now worked for the private security company, Control Risks. Fred also wanted Alastair Riddell to be part of it.

> Fred and I would have made the same committed team that we had always been. He believed, and he was prepared to commit with very little support. He wanted me in, but I could not keep pace with him and his absolute disregard for structure. He led and others followed in this situation. We visited John Moss. He knew Fred; I did not know him.[7]

Fred persevered, and persuading John Moss that this could be a good project for the company. A modified version of the original Omani model was worked out for the situation in Sierra Leone and priced. They would train a force of some 750 local fighters, drawn from all the chiefdoms of Sierra Leone. Each chiefdom, depending on its size, would provide between five and ten men, who would be put through a selection process. Training would last for nine months. The force would be divided into four troops: the Boat troop, the Land Rover troop, the Helicopter troop and a Heavy Weapons troop. With arms and equipment, which would include scout helicopters, that could be used as medivac, Land Rovers, four tonners and 81mm mortars, the overall cost was in the region of £2.5 million. John Moss agreed to fly with Fred to Sierra Leone and stay for five days during which time a meeting with Valentine Strasser would be arranged. If they were given the go-ahead, Fred and

John Moss would then return to the UK and recruit a small team to carry out the training.

On 2 March, the pair arrived in Sierra Leone. Arrangements for a meeting were made through the good offices of Hinga Norman, and on Friday 10 March, John Moss met Valentine Strasser. But when he came back from the meeting John was not impressed: it seemed as though Strasser was high on marijuana. He was said to be a user. If he was, it was almost understandable that he sought refuge in a hallucinogen, because it was commonly believed that he was the accidental Head of State. He had been an army officer engaged in fighting the RUF, but in frustration at lack of support and non-payment of salaries to them, he led a group of soldiers to Freetown with no more ambitious an aim than to protest. However, on learning of their approach, the President panicked, deserted his post and fled the country; and Strasser, at the tender age of twenty-six, found that it was Buggins' turn to be leader. Neither he nor his council, military though they were, had any real strategy for defeating the RUF. Whether or not Strasser took in the details of John Moss's proposals, his body language suggested detachment. He was wearing dark glasses in a semi-darkened room; he would look up every now and then from his desk at John and then back to his desk. The conclusion of the meeting was that there was no money to pay for the training or the equipment. He said that there was not even £1.5 million to pay for the training of the Sierra Leonean army. So the following day, John left for the UK.

However, there was an attempted follow-up to this proposal that Fred did not know about until fourteen years later. The SAS invited Fred to the camp at Hereford on 6 June 2009, to a function celebrating the forty-fifth anniversary of the reforming of 'B' Squadron after its disbandment at the end of the Malayan campaign. Because of his seniority, Fred found he was sitting at the top table next to John Moss. After the meal, the two discussed Sierra Leone and the lost opportunity. And John filled in the outline of what happened on his return to the UK on 11 March 1995. At Control Risks they felt that they had invested some time in working up a proposal that sounded both feasible and worthwhile, so they reviewed it, revamped it and priced it at £10 million. They then put the proposal to the MoD with a request for funding. The MoD turned them down. But as Fred put it, the MoD would have to pay a lot more a few years later to support the government of Sierra Leone.

Thwarted at official level, in March 1995, ideas about training and supporting local fighters had to go on the back burner for Fred, but a new assignment came his way; and he seized the moment, because it meant that he would be paid again. When the RUF kidnapped personnel from the Sieromco mine in January, they took them deep into the bush. Nothing was known of their whereabouts and no ransom demands were made. Eventually, however, the rebels made initial contact by radio with the Freetown office of Sieromco. The rebels had quite a sophisticated radio communication system, for Foday Sankoh had originally trained as a radio operator with the British army. One of his hostages, Rudi Bruns, took note of how Sankoh used his communication system when he was in the RUF leader's base at the time, Camp Zagoda.

> Foday Sankoh was in regular contact at specific times with his commanders. His radio station, powered by solar panels (probably stolen from SierraTel transmitter stations), was not far away from our huts and we were able to listen to his communication. We even heard him one day talking to Charles Taylor. He was using an old British military code system when he was giving commands and instructions. His strategic military chart was a Shell Road Map of Sierra Leone, available in most book shops. Coloured stickers marked the position of his troops. The same Shell map with coloured stickers I was to see later in the office of the Nigerian ECOMOG commanders at 1ˢᵗ Battalion Wilberforce Barracks in Freetown.[8]

As a result of the radio contact, the company contracted Control Risks in the UK to carry out negotiations with the rebels. Negotiations were expected to be protracted, so Control Risks deployed two negotiators, who would work in rotation over a two-week cycle. They had to have security; as he was already in the country, Fred was asked if he would protect the negotiator. He accepted with alacrity. The first negotiator on duty was Jonathan Atkins. In addition, a team of British police negotiators was sent out to give advice. Dialogue with the rebel group, however, was conducted by a Sierra Leonean.

Fred was impressed by the professionalism of the British negotiators. In the background, they stressed the importance of writing down all that had to be said on each radio call; they briefed on how to manipulate dialogue so that the rebels had the sense that they were in control, whereas they were really working to an agenda set by the team. Permission was given to speak to each hostage, so it was established that all the hostages were in the one place; and as each conversation with the rebels was finishing, confirmation of the timing of the next radio call was always pushed for. All the time, a picture was being built up. It seemed that Foday Sankoh had control of the situation and that the hostages were unharmed. And it was through this patient work that the Red Cross became involved. For some reason, Foday Sankoh trusted the Red Cross and was prepared to have a dialogue with one of its representatives.

The representative of the International Committee of the Red Cross (ICRC) was Primo Corvaro. With his arrival, the balance of responsibilities changed: the negotiators now worked directly to Primo, and dialogue took place between him and Foday Sankoh. Having raised the profile of the RUF, Sankoh gave indications that he would adopt a humanitarian approach with the hostages. Negotiations reached a delicate stage. Then came the breakthrough. On the evening of Sunday 16 April, after his conversation with Sankoh, Primo told the negotiation team that he thought they should fly to neighbouring Guinea the following day in anticipation that Sankoh, in the next few days, could release the hostages at the border. The Control Risks negotiator on duty was uncertain about this and asked the advice of the British High Commission and police team. Both counselled against it, advising that they stay in Sierra Leone. He then asked Fred what he thought:

> I said, 'Jonathan, are we working for the British government, or are we working for the client?' He said, 'We are working for the client.' I said, 'If the client says go, he wouldn't ask us to go without a good reason.'

Jonathan made his decision and a senior manager of the company Sieromco, Joe Blume, arranged for a helicopter to fly them to Guinea the next day, along with the luggage of their hostage personnel in the bush.

When they landed at Conakry, the Guinean authorities were very difficult: at first they would not allow the team to get off the helicopter; after discussion between the Guinean government and the Red Cross, they were allowed to disembark; then the helicopter was held at the airport for about four hours before it was allowed to return to Sierra Leone. The next obstacle was passing through Customs. Fred, Primo and Jonathan had the hostages' luggage on a trolley. The officials wanted them to open the baggage. Fred took his job seriously and he refused, saying that it belonged to people out in the bush. Then the officials wanted to open Fred's cell phone, but he argued that they needed it on duty. At this point, a sympathetic woman official on duty took charge and allowed them through.

The speed of their move to Guinea meant that no preparatory work had been done for their reception, and Fred found that his job description became pretty elastic. He and Jonathan first went to the office of the British Consul for assistance. The Honorary British Consul, Val Treitlein, was in London, but her daughter gave them her car and was very helpful, guiding them round the system and making arrangements for them. This particular contact was to turn out to be very important for Fred two years later. Sieromco, the mining company, liaised with a bauxite mining company in Guinea which provided a compound where the hostages could be received.

> My job was to organize the reception, isolate a certain area, clear the area and occupy it in readiness before the hostages arrived.

All these arrangements had to be made very quickly, for in Primo's opinion the release of the hostages was imminent. And sure enough, the following evening, which was Tuesday, after his discussion with Foday Sankoh, Primo said, 'They're releasing the hostages on Wednesday.' So they drove to the border to receive them.

The remainder of the negotiating team, who had advised against going to Guinea, were still in Sierra Leone, and they now undertook a mad scramble to get to Conakry. Meanwhile, Primo and the team met the hostages at the border, took them into the care of the Red Cross, and then drove to a half-way house to spend the night there. As it turned out, among the hostages was the rutile mine's head of security, the same head of security who had had such a condescending attitude to him when Fred first met him on his early fact-finding tour of mining sites.

And when he came in, I looked at him, and he looked at me and bowed. And the thought crossed my mind – 'anything that happens within a hundred miles I know immediately.' But then I thought back to when I was a kid; I was told to fight like an Englishman: when he's down you don't kick him. When he's down you pull him up.

The hostages had indeed been through a rough time in the three months they spent in the bush. Rudi Bruns was glowing in his praise for the Red Cross.

The ICRC is a very thoughtful organization. My highest respect! Being in the bush for three months, not thinking of women apart from our wives, no beer or other beverages, what did we find in the ICRC vehicles which took us to Conakry? Lady drivers, soft drinks and beer in the boot. I immediately placed myself in the front seat. A beer can was passed on to me and, thanks to the efficient air conditioner of the vehicle, within a few minutes we had our first cold beer in three months. Everybody was happy.[9]

That evening, though, they were able to talk to their families by satellite phone.

Then there had to be a period of re-orientation before the expatriates were handed over to their embassies; and Fred's new role, and that of the negotiator, was to stay on in the country and help in the process of the hostages readapting to normal life. For a brief period Fred organized trips to one of the islands and they went swimming. Then the hostages were handed over to their embassies. Sieromco's manager Joe Blume had already block-booked a number of seats with various carriers: KLM, Air France and Sabina.

The world's press seemed to be waiting at the front gate of the bauxite compound, from where a fleet of cars could be seen lined up. But at the back gate of the compound, out of sight, were also one or two vehicles; and it was in these, from the rear of the compound, that the German Ambassador led a small convoy, taking the hostages to the airport.

Two days later, on 7 May 1995, Fred left for a break in the UK. He had hardly been home three weeks before a means of fighting the rebels in Sierra Leone returned to the front burner: he was contacted by Simon Mann and offered the chance to return to Sierra Leone and take on a job which opened the way for him to have a combat role with one of the most effective private military fighting units in the world.

Part II

Chapter Three

Executive Outcomes

From the Gadites there went over to David at the stronghold in the wilderness mighty and experienced warriors, expert with shield and spear, whose faces were like the faces of lions, and who were as swift as gazelles upon the mountains.

1 Chronicles, Chapter 12, 8

Executive Outcomes (EO) stands out above all other private military companies for the effective and efficient way it defeated an insurgency, and so enabled democracy to be restored to a country. A South African, multi-racial company of highly experienced combat veterans with years of counter-insurgency operations in southern Africa behind them, it was contracted by the Sierra Leone government who, by now, had come to accept that the country's military lacked the capacity to defeat the RUF. With no help forthcoming from the western democracies, the government hired a private military company to do what the state was unable to do. The Sierra Leone government initially intended to fund the cost out of treasury receipts, which would have included tax receipts from mining concessions as well as other internal sources. And the contract stipulated that in the first year EO would deploy between one hundred and two hundred men.

Yet, as we saw, only a few months earlier the head of government, Valentine Strasser, had told John Moss that they were unable to fund a training scheme based on an earlier SAS model, which would have been delivered by ex-SAS personnel. What had changed in the government's fortunes in the meantime? Essentially nothing had changed, which suggests that Strasser, who, after all, was the head of a military regime, had no intention of arming and training a militia as an alternative force to the army, and simply fobbed off the training proposal with lack of funds as an excuse.

Fred had been recruited to provide training for the EO contingent in jungle warfare. On 8 June, he arrived back in Sierra Leone, and learned that Executive Outcomes were already in the country and in action.

It turned out to be quite an interesting day because that was the day, when I arrived, there was a battle going on – on the ground in Sierra Leone. Executive Outcomes were shaking themselves out in their formations and so forth and they were ambushed at this village just outside Waterloo. They were ambushed from both sides: in other words they were set up. Somebody in the Headquarters must have been passing information. The rebels were waiting for them. Unfortunately for them, Executive Outcomes were very well trained, very seasoned troops. And they beat the attackers, and they regrouped themselves. The only casualty they had was one of the commanders had a small piece of shrapnel in his eye. And that was the only one. Otherwise they beat the rebels. They regrouped and spent the night there, and they extracted themselves and regrouped; they debriefed the following day and went over what were the weak points. But they regrouped brilliantly.

Treachery, then, was very much a factor within the Sierra Leonean army. It is not difficult to see why: some people, it seemed, were hedging their bets, for the rebels had penetrated so far west that they were in the outskirts of Freetown. Every morning, in the capital, their radio call-sign, 'House of Culture' could be heard. Soon after he arrived, Fred saw for himself the extent of their deployment only about 15 kilometres from Freetown outside Waterloo, where the ambush had been sprung on Executive Outcomes.

Later on, in group search, we were to find a very big base camp just outside Waterloo that could hold 600–800 men, including sick bay; and it was a well-stocked camp. The question was how come they could build a big camp like that without anybody knowing. And the answer is very obvious – with the connivance of some of the people in the army, because they would not be seen on the map. When we eventually found the camp we discovered that it was only about five kilometres away from the ambush. But of course when they got beaten by Executive Outcomes they were cooking the food, and they fled and left everything. They only carried what they could carry. After that we spent the night there in the camp and destroyed everything that needed to be destroyed and then we pulled out.

Before he became part of the combat unit, however, Fred was to have provided it with jungle warfare training. He was highly experienced in this field; when he was in the SAS, he had been an instructor in jungle warfare in Brunai. And so on that basis, and also because he knew some of the country, he was approached by former SAS officer, Simon Mann, and contracted with Branch Energy, a company which was part of a group that included Executive Outcomes.

Men who have had a lot of combat experience are able to size up potential comrades very quickly; and when Fred met the EO personnel, he recognized their calibre.

I arrived and I saw these guys sleeping downstairs in bunk beds with mosquito nets and a shower outside. And I thought to myself, can you imagine getting a group of British people to sleep like that? I soon realized that there was nothing I could teach these people. And second, the last thing you want to do is to confuse people: they had a very good, very well-oiled machine; they were a very disciplined and well-trained force and very successful. Why change them? That was when I volunteered to join the fighting unit.

The commander of Executive Outcomes in Sierra Leone at that point was Brigadier Sachse, who was ex-South African Defence Forces (SADF). Because Brig Sachse had had Fred recommended to him by Simon Mann, he readily agreed, and Fred joined the fighting force.

Executive Outcomes had an impressive capability, underpinned by a clear understanding of the guerrilla war they were fighting: the company was self-sustained and did not have to rely on local back-up; it had a Boeing transport plane to bring equipment and supplies from South Africa; it had helicopter gunships, the formidable titanium-plated Mi-24 and Mi-17, bought from former Soviet bloc countries after the fall of communism; it had a mortar section and armoured vehicles complete with transporters; it had night vision equipment; and it had sophisticated intelligence.

Its first operation was to clear rebel forces from the area around Freetown. This the company achieved in a matter of days and it was during the operation, when Fred was with them, that they came across the now deserted base camp from where the rebels set out to launch their ambush of EO, as a result of what looked like a tip-off from army HQ. Having cleared the Freetown area, EO now prepared for the larger operations into the country.

The commander of these operations was Colonel Rudolph (Roelf) van Heerden, who had an extensive military background, with combat experience going back to the 1970s. He had served in the war in South West Africa in 1978 in the 102 Battalion; then he transferred to South Africa and became the Senior Operations Officer in 82 Mechanised Brigade, and was on operations in Angola. After his staff college course, he was transferred to covert collection in army intelligence. When that directorate was closed down due to political pressure, he was among the first members to be recruited to Executive Outcomes, and he worked with the company as Operations Officer in various countries. And for the forthcoming operations in Sierra Leone, Roelf was prepared to use Fred as one of the front men.

He was recommended by Mann, Simon Mann; Simon and also my previous boss, Brig Sachse. He was recommended to me: I was told that he had some knowledge of Sierra Leone areas and the local population, and that we should use him. And we did.

I met him right there at the beginning. He was a friendly face. Well OK, he was not part of the planning phase but, when we started the operations, he was clearly a front man there.

This was our second operation after signing the contract with the government. Having driven the RUF rebels from the outskirts of Freetown, which was very successful, we planned to take up the second phase of the operation in taking over the diamond area of Kono. We were 64 men from EO with about 10 men from the SLMF (Sierra Leone Military Forces) and Fred.[1]

While EO was contracted to carry out a combat role, one of its other main functions was to train and support the Sierra Leone army. And this was to turn out to be an opportunity for Fred to draw on the depth of his own experience. Fred thought highly of his EO commander.

The planned move was that we'd have two armoured vehicles, Russian armoured vehicles for troop carriers that we had, that were to be loaded on to a low-loader; and then we were to move the low-loader up to a point, off-load them and then drive the rest of the way to Kono. So that was the move. And the Commander for that move was Colonel Roelf (Rudolph) van Heerden A very well seasoned leader of Executive Outcomes' fighting force and Tom Nyuma, the Sierra Leonean, who was also the Deputy Defence Minister. That was the move.

On 24 June, they formed up on the shooting range of the Benguema training centre for their move on Kono. But their first priority was to watch on TV the South African national rugby team, the Springboks, play New Zealand in the final of the Rugby World Cup, which was held in Johannesburg. The Springboks won 15–12, and President Nelson Mandela, wearing a Springbok shirt, presented the trophy to the home side. Post-apartheid, South Africa had come back into international sport. It seemed to augur well for the operation.

Col Roelf deployed Fred 'running right up front with the front guard.' This was a position that Fred relished.

We drove up to Makala and then off-loaded the vehicles and we drove by road. I was in the Executive Outcomes' vehicle leading, as I knew the country. Everybody wanted to be in the first vehicle, and so the first vehicle was overloaded. And if that was not bad enough we had a fuel problem – so start and stop. And at one of the check-points, I looked behind and there was this vehicle that had an anti-aircraft gun. So while a mechanic was repairing our vehicle, the Executive Outcomes' land rover, I walked over to the Sierra Leonean driver, a sergeant, and I said, 'Excuse me, who's the Commander?' And he said, 'I'm the Commander.' I said, 'You were the Commander, now I'm the Commander.' I said 'This is Sierra Leone, I want you with me in front, we'll take the lead.'

As part of its support for the Sierra Leone army, EO was asked by senior officers to look out for shortcomings in the training and tactics of their country's military, and to make recommendations for improvement. From the start of the move on Kono, Fred saw that the local soldiers were inexperienced in convoy movement and fighting off an ambush.

> I briefed the people how they should sit, about observation, and, when we stopped, de-bus and all-round defence. And every time we stopped, the same drill. They did very well; it was only a matter of teaching them and showing them. The driver said, 'Come and sit with me in front.' I said, 'No my friend, it's not in the front the fighting is done but at the back. You don't sit in the front, you sit in the back with your fighting men and fight the action at the back. You must be there with your men to make sure – if something happens.' I briefed them and discussed with Col Roelf and Tom Nyuma that if we should come to a cutting in the road, I would accelerate and if the rebels took me on, that would be a warning to everybody, and the main party could give me covering fire and then clear the objective. Then we would move forward. And that was how we moved.

It did not take Fred long to spot some fundamental weaknesses at the leadership level in the army, weaknesses of a kind that would undermine the commitment of men fighting in this type of warfare. But these were weaknesses that could be addressed.

> This is the sad thing about the leadership: normally, when they fight, and this is what the army asked us to find out, the wounded are left behind. And that is the fear of any soldier – that you are wounded and you are going to be left behind. And I was to prove it later on when the group took Gandorhun, when we cleared ten miles, twenty miles all around, up north and east.

On the first day of their advance, Col Roelf recalls, 'We encountered little drama along the road.' They had helicopter top-cover and thanks to their capable pilots, who warned them of ambushes ahead, they were easily able to roll them up. But at times, Col Roelf had to restrain Fred's style of leadership.

> I had to call him back on a number of occasions, as he was to break contact with the men and put himself at risk. What Fred showed to me was his disrespect for the enemy and he really wanted to overrun them. Fred showed to me that he has no fear, and I had to ask him to take it slowly, as he was then very much older than my average guy. He was a pleasure to work with – a horse I had to keep the bridle pulled on.[2]

They spent the first night at Masingbi at an old school that was burnt out by the rebels.

From the appearance of the school, it must have been a secondary school and a big one at that. I sighted the defensive positions for 2 armoured cars covering the main road and the rest was all round defence, which the soldiers took up automatically.

On day two they carried on along the road again; their second stop was at a military camp at Bumpe – less than a 1000 metres from Yengema Airfield and Sefadu (the town is known as Sefadu or as Koidu and sometimes written as Koidu-Sefadu). Col Roelf's plan was to rest there for the night, start early, and move to Koidu-Sefadu and clear and establish a firm base. Fred gives a glimpse of that night that shows Executive Outcomes as a well disciplined team, working together, familiar with their proven tactics, preparing to deliver maximum impact.

So we spent the night at Bumpe, and the commanders of Executive Outcomes covered all the vulnerable points: they set the mortars up; the team silently ready at the mortars; and the rest of us in all-round defence.

That very morning, early in the morning, the rebels came and attacked the camp. I don't think they knew who were there; they were firing at the camp, a normal stand-off attack. And when they finished – we never returned any fire, because we wanted to follow up –, when they finished, they all went back on the road; they didn't know that we were there; and in the meantime, everyone got from stand-to to ready, and we followed. And when we came over the little rise we could see them going in two ranks with their weapons on their shoulders; and we hit them, and they ran and we followed all the way up to Yengema; and we cleared Yengema airfield and then from there we moved on to Sefadu and cleared the centre of Sefadu. And the rebels had never come across anybody that chased them like that.

Col Roelf's summary of the last twenty-four hours of their advance on the Kono district neatly sums up the effectiveness of EO's strategy and tactics.

When we reached Yengema, we found only a small contingent of the SLMF, now very much relieved. The plan was to attack the town of Koidu the next day and to drive out the rebels. Very early the next day the rebels did an attack on our position; and we killed 9 rebels that morning, and did an immediate follow up of the enemy. Within an hour we had taken the Yengema airport with little resistance; and by midday we had the town of Koidu under control. The rebels could not stand the momentum and withdrew from the area.[3]

In one of the villages EO cleared, women and children and elderly people, who had been unable to flee the area, told them of their treatment at the hands of the rebels. Word of the company's presence got around, and over the next two days, as they cleared the Kono district, local people came out to cheer them, hailing them as liberators and heroes, calling them 'Bafana Bafana', which was the name of the South African national soccer team. The rule of law was re-established, and the presence of Sierra Leone troops with EO helped to restore people's confidence in the army.

The next operation that EO undertook was to Gandorhun, south east of the Kono district; on this operation, Fred was involved from the planning stage, when it was decided that he would lead the ground assault force, as Col Roelf outlines.

We had some rebel incursions. So I planned this operation with the Sierra Leonean Army, with top guys like Tom Nyuma; and Fred was part of the operation. We planned it over a few days – 3 or 4 days – and assembled all the forces, of which the ground force was all Sierra Leonean Government troops. The EO contingent were airlifted by helicopter and put on high ground and they did the shelling with the mortars and they did some strikes with the helicopter gunships.

And Fred was put in charge of the Sierra Leonean troops. There was a captain in charge; but I mean Fred was more energetic and knew more, had more knowledge; he had more drive; he was not a scared man, not at all. It was very difficult for me to sort of hold him back, because it was bordering on unnecessary exploitation of a soldier. I've never done it that way: I use the indirect method of scaring off my enemy and chasing them into the bush, back into the bush.[4]

Operations Officer for this attack was Col Renier Hugo; Jim Hooper, a military journalist, who knew some Executive Outcomes personnel from their previous contract in Angola was given access to the company's forward base and eventually accompanied Col Hugo with a mortar team to high ground overlooking Gandorhun. He later wrote an account of the operation for military journals, and then covered both the Angola campaign as well as the Sierra Leone actions in his book, *Bloodsong*.

The original plan called for air strikes in support of the ground assault force, but the weather closed in and heavy rain and low cloud prevented any flying. Instead, it was decided that whenever the helicopters could operate, they would airlift the mortar team to higher ground and the Mi-24 gunship would support with rocket attacks. Fred was to be the professional leader of the assault force, and, on that understanding, the Sierra Leone officers assembled the troops. Then Fred took charge.

So the first day we left by road and we left late; and I knew the first place we would come to – we had been there before –, I told them, 'Look that is likely to be an ambush place.' Which it was.

There was a dip in the road leading up to a narrow path, overlooked by a very good ambush position. Immediately after that, the ground opened up to a lovely killing field of fire from the scrub to the right of the track under the mangrove trees. As if this was not enough, the rebels left the body of an old man right on the road as a bait – for when everyone automatically moves closer for a look. There and then they sprang the ambush, and 4 of our soldiers got hit. We took casualties but beat off the rebels.

At EO's forward base they received a radio message from Fred that that his force had been ambushed but had cleared through and were advancing towards the nearby village of Woama. They stayed the night there.

As darkness fell, the Sierra Leone troops became nervous: trying to boost their morale, they would occasionally fire their weapons at nothing at all, thinking it would scare off the rebels from attacking.

What they did not realize was that they were showing that they were ill-disciplined and scared too. Johnny Moore was the Sierra Leone captain in charge. I said to him, 'Tell your troops to save their ammunition because tomorrow we are going to be hit.'

Fred impressed on the men that nobody would be left behind, they would carry their wounded and dead with them, and when the weather cleared they would be airlifted out. Fred's leadership, however, amounted to more than depth of experience and personal courage: he was able to imbue these men with a sense of their own worth and their own proud heritage. During the Second World War, Fred's father had fought with the British army in the Burma campaign; so also had British West African units of the 82nd (West Africa) Division. He said to them, 'You are the same people that fought in Burma with honour.' Given the depths to which morale in the Sierra Leone army plummeted during those years when it was shown not to be a credible force against the rebels, it is doubtful if these soldiers had ever before been reminded of the military tradition to which they belonged.

At first light next day they assembled, and moved out.

Five hundred yards out of our camp we got hit; we were ambushed. Eventually, at the end of the day we had one dead and ten wounded. And they were carried to the next place. And the local soldiers, at first they were just like fish – when you see the fish swirl in the water –, but when they realised that nobody was going to be left behind, they stood firm and everybody wanted to get in there. The enemy dead, we just searched the body, but nobody was to mutilate, ever. We are who we are. Discipline must be maintained.

When they reached their next objective, Gbekidu, Fred radioed EO's forward base that they had been hit and taken casualties. And that was as far as he got before the radio batteries went flat on him. At EO's base, Jim Hooper, the military correspondent, was aware of the frustration the team felt because the weather kept the helicopter grounded. They were not concerned though.

Everyone was confident of Fred's ability to keep his troops together and see off any rebels. But it was time to get the mortars in position to support him.[5]

Jim Hooper lent a hand, loading the helicopter with ammo crates of 120mm and the 82mm mortar bombs. At daybreak, if the weather lifted, the mortar team were ready to leave.

Night closed in swiftly and silently on Gbekidu. Fred made the troops stay in the same room as the dead. They did not like that: they were superstitious. He told them, 'That's nonsense.' No one demurred; and no sound of moaning came from the wounded – although the unit had no morphine with them.

In the morning, the cloud base lifted and the helicopter arrived. Fred had briefed the troops that when the helicopter landed, they would unload the ammunition first then load the wounded and the dead.

> And there were some young kids that were part of the group that lived there; and I told them to stay at one side, and after the dead and wounded were taken on board, when I gave the signal, this group of five or six kids went straight into the helicopter. I signalled the helicopter to close the door and it took off. And that was it: no one else could jump into the helicopter.

After the helicopter took off, the ground assault force left Gbekidu and headed for their objective, Gandorhun; Fred was with the lead troop. This time there was no contact with the rebels, who, they knew from the previous day's fighting, had taken losses. When they entered Gandorhun, Fred could see that there were very good firing positions that gave excellent cover for view and fire and would have cost the assault force heavily. Then as they took over the town, a few mortar rounds began to fall: the mortar team had been airlifted to higher ground. However, because his radio's batteries were flat, there were no communications between the ground force and the EO team, and so Fred put down yellow markers on the ground for the helicopter pilots to see. On the higher ground, Col Hugo was already with the mortar team and the journalist, Jim Hooper, had been allowed to join them.

> Through his binoculars Colonel Hugo could see armed troops in Gandorhun. Knowing how frightened the rebels were of helicopters, he immediately deduced that Marafono and his men had already taken the town. At this point the Mi–24, having been rushed through its scheduled maintenance, screamed past us before making a low pass over the town and verifying what Hugo suspected. 'We have a visual on Fred,' the radio crackled.'[6]

Gandorhun was in government forces' hands again. What the operation had shown was that although, in the past, there were instances of Sierra Leone troops being reluctant to engage with the RUF in combat, here, with the support of Executive Outcomes and under good leadership, they could acquit themselves well.

The net effect of what Executive Outcomes achieved in a matter of months led to changes taking place in the country's political climate. Its impact for the good was out of all proportion to its numerical strength: during the first three months it had 114 – 116 men in the country; when its Angola contract came to an end, that number rose to between 180–190.[7] The large concentrations of rebel forces that had threatened Freetown had been pushed back to the east; the diamond-bearing areas of the country were becoming safe for companies to work in again; and politicians were beginning to think in terms of elections for a re-established democracy. However, there was some way to go yet: guerrilla warfare continued; and a military regime still ruled the country, but in principle agreement had already been reached that at a suitable time, power would be relinquished to a democratic government.

Until that happened though, there was an authority vacuum at district level. Many of the local chiefs, the traditional source of authority, had fled to Freetown; and as Executive Outcomes cleared areas of the rebels, interim, ad hoc, authority would rest with military personnel, whose integrity and professionalism could be questionable. With that in mind, Fred returned to Freetown and contacted Chief Hinga Norman.

> Having cleared the area we established a rule of law – no more harassing of people and so on. And as we established in Kono and it became safe, I came back to Freetown and I saw the Chief. And I said, 'Chief could you arrange for me to meet the Kono chiefs?' Because what I didn't want was the military to rule the civilians. I wanted the chiefs to go back. And the Chief organized it so that I met the Kono chiefs, six of them; and we met at my house on Wilkinson Road. It's the same house that Branch Energy with the mining company use now – it was my house then. The Chief organized it so that I met them. I asked them, 'Please could you come back to Kono to look after your people?' And the question they asked was, is Kono safe? And I said that Kono was safe, safer than Freetown, there was no harassment, no looting or anything; the rule of law was very strict. Unfortunately, I think there were certain fears on their part and it never came about.

Other chiefs did return and some had never fled, and they were to be very useful to Executive Outcomes in helping to flush out pockets of RUF rebels in the Gandorhun area. Fred arranged for Col Roelf to meet Chief Hinga Norman.

> There were a number of chiefs from various districts, one of whom was Regent Chief Hinga Norman, who played a major role in bringing these guys together. I think they all had a sort of political agenda in helping Kabbah [later President

of the restored democracy] come into power; and in the war at that level as well. I met Hinga Norman there with the help of Fred; and we became friends, Hinga Norman and I, we became good friends.[8]

It seems that Chief Hinga Norman was giving thought to whether, in the longer term, the Sierra Leone army could hold on to the gains made by Executive Outcomes. Kamajor, in the Mende language, means hunter, and the society of hunters known as the Kamajors probably existed from time beyond memory. More recently, however, it was developing into a chieftaincy-based militia.

Hinga Norman asked me how we could use the Kamajors, how we could utilize them. Which I did, and I went into the Kono district and I met a guy by the name of Randolph Fillie-Faboe; he later became a Minister in the SLPP [Sierra Leone People's Party]. And we used the Kamajors to a very great extent, and very, very positively. And we had very good results with the Kamajors in working with them, supporting them on their level; and they were giving me vital information. And a number of my operations, with specific reference to the Gandorhun area, came from the Kamajors. They brought me information on a daily basis; and Fred and I were always co-ordinating on this; and he always said to me that we should use the Kamajors more and more, to make them figure prominently as a local militia as they had support from the local people and so on.[9]

At the same time, as commander in an area, 'Roelf worked hard to build trust with the local population.'[10] He ordered the removal of anti-personnel mines that the Sierra Leone army had planted; he established a clinic and combined local administration council.

Executive Outcomes had also the task of supporting and training the Sierra Leone army. As a result Fred's role broadened: he was asked to show army personnel how to organize and take a food and fuel convoy which would travel from Masiaka up country to Bo, Kenema and Daru. Dealing with convoy ambush had been part of the jungle warfare course he had been responsible for in his past life, so he was the ideal man to instruct the Sierra Leone army.

By this time, Simon Mann, who put Fred up for Executive Outcomes, was receiving a lot of feed-back on his performance, and wrote to him on Tuesday 11 July 95.

Dear Fred
I am very sorry to have been unable to see you since you started – I have been 100% entangled first in Luanda and now London. All reports are that you have done a great job, as I knew you would, and are the man for that job.
The bearer of this letter is an old hand in this game, and he can explain to you. We are all working hard to think thru the SL situation. To this end can you please

trust R —— [the bearer of the letter] entirely and allow him to debrief you fully on <u>all</u> aspects of the operation.

R —— has a non-disclosure strategic brief from Tony and myself, and, in the course of talking to him, it is likely that changes and developments to your role, should you be interested, will raise their head. Please accept this letter as a note from me that you can develop this line of approach should you wish: Tak sends his best:

All the best from me and many thanks again

Yours Aye
Simon Mann.[11]

Although the major threat to Freetown had been lifted, the nature of the guerrilla war meant that there were rebel units scattered around the country, in touch with their headquarters by radio. And so frequent were the attacks on convoys between Masiaka and Mile 91that it became called 'Ambush Alley'. Fred was tasked to organize the convoy and take it along 'Ambush Alley' to Mile 91. At Daru, the ultimate destination of the convoy, there were stationed some units of the Guinean army, whose government had sent them as a token force to show solidarity against the RUF.

Systematically Fred set about the assignment. He wanted backing from the top and so he met Tom Nyuma, Deputy Defence Minister in the military government. Civilians would drive the convoy vehicles, and Tom Nyuma arranged for Fred to meet the chairman and the committee of the drivers' union. Fred outlined his requirements: the committee should select the drivers who were to take part in the convoy; the number of vehicles should be not more than fifty – which meant it was a large convoy –; all the vehicles were to be road-worthy; they should have a minimum of six good tyres; they must not be overloaded; and Fred made plain that he would inspect each vehicle. When he later met the drivers who were allocated to the convoy, he briefed them that if there was a breakdown, everybody would stop – no vehicle was to be left.

And I told them that if we should come across an ambush what I wanted them to do. 'First of all, switch the engine off, and leave the vehicle keys in the ignition. If the ambush is from the right, de-bus from the left and move away from the vehicle, get down.' We would sort the ambush out and then when we finished we would organize and move on again. The reason why I didn't want them to take the vehicles' keys – and I was proved right – was that if they came to start the vehicles and there were no keys, they would run.

In addition to the fuel and food trucks there were three four-ton trucks with soldiers, two Land Rovers, two vehicles with 12.7 anti-aircraft guns and recovery vehicles. There was also an Executive Outcomes helicopter, an Mi-17, not a gunship, to fly top-cover.

Finally, the day came for the convoy to line up. From past experience Fred anticipated that sod's law would kick in when the convoy assembled. He was not wrong: they were late in getting off, and at the last minute the Guinean army contingent turned up with their trucks full of supplies for their own troops.

What I didn't know at the time: they were doing business – all these trucks were loaded with goods – they were doing business up country. But worst of all, before we set off, these people were drunk. They were all big talk; they wanted to be in the lead.

The low opinion that Fred formed of Guinean officials when he was involved in the release of the hostages a few months earlier was now transferred to the military of that country. However, he had to step lightly too: the Guineans were overall under the control of the Sierra Leone army but their men took their orders from their own officers; and there was the *lingua franca* problem – Guinea is a francophone country, and French was the second medium for communication. Over and above that, there was a heavy hierarchy of Sierra Leone officers to relate to: the army sent one colonel, three majors and six captains. It was not a case of Fred being outranked, he had no rank; but he was the professional leader of the convoy and the over-representation of officers was so that they could learn the principles involved.

The convoy lined up with the Guinean contingent further back, and Fred gave the signal to start up the vehicles. The helicopter was in the air, and the convoy moved off. It was not all that long before they drove past the site of an earlier ambush: the roadside was littered with burnt out trucks, bloated bodies and partial skeletons of victims. When the front of the convoy reached the top of Magbosi hill, Fred received information that one of the rear vehicles had a puncture. He ordered the rest of the convoy to the top of the hill; they de-bussed and the protection team formed an all-round defence; and they waited while a wheel was changed and the rear group caught up. Then the convoy moved off again.

Further along the route, gunshots suddenly rang out from among the vehicles. Fred stopped the convoy and asked who was firing. He was told it was the Guineans. He ran to their position, demanding to know who they were firing at. One of them said, 'The rebels.' Fred was on the point of losing his cool. Angrily he faced them, 'If there were rebels, I would be the first to fire.' The effects of drink were still apparent on the Guineans; it could have turned nasty at this point, but suddenly Fred's radio crackled into life; it was the voice of the EO helicopter pilot, Chris Louw, asking about the shooting.

I told him it was the stupid Guineans. The cloud base was getting low and I also thanked Chris Louw and told him to go back to base. He was reluctant, but the cloud base was getting lower and to fly the helicopter at low speed would be risking both the helicopter and lives of the crew. As I was speaking to Chris, one of the Guinean officers signalled to me that everything was OK.

So tension relaxed, and they carried on without top-cover or further incident until they reached Mile 91 around 7pm. There the convoy passed to the control of Colonel Carew of the Sierra Leone army. Their task completed, and fortified with a cool soft drink, Fred said that they would set out on the return journey. The Guineans were surprised at this decision; they thought they were to stay overnight at Mile 91. That denied to them, they wanted their vehicles to be in the centre of the small returning military convoy. Fred refused that request, telling them that with their two armoured vehicles their place was at the rear.

The return was uneventful until they were not far from Masiaka where they came upon one of their convoy's food vehicles broken down, the greatly relieved driver sitting alone in the dark. His truck had broken down soon after the convoy started and it seemed that no one wanted to tell Fred and delay the convoy. The recovery vehicle was hitched up and the truck was taken to Masiaka and turned over to the local army unit and the police.

Inducted into the management of convoy movement, the Sierra Leone army officers who had accompanied Fred were supposed to be ready to take the next one on their own. Fred's job for this convoy was to organize it up to the point of departure. He followed the same procedure with the drivers' union. All the officers had been with Fred on the first convoy; the colonel was in charge, and one of the majors was deployed at the front, one at the back and then there were the captains.

When I set them off, I realized that at the front they were driving like mad, but I was only with my driver, nobody else at that time. So what I did was after the last vehicle set off – I couldn't leave them like that – I had to chase the convoy. My driver and I, we drove like fury and caught up with the convoy quite a way on when they stopped at this village. So I reassembled all the vehicles and I said, 'No, you cannot do that; who is going to protect the rear? You've got to go as a group and fight as a group.' I nearly went on that convoy. I nearly joined the convoy but my driver would have to drive back on that road by himself. I looked at him and he wasn't very happy. I said, 'Don't worry I'll come back with you.'

On the way back to Freetown, they passed through Masiaka and got as far as Waterloo when Fred received word that the convoy had been ambushed. He turned and headed for Masiaka, intent on mustering reinforcements from the local military unit and carrying on to relieve the convoy. He knew that this time the Executive Outcomes' helicopter could not be spared: it was in service, ferrying food and supplies from the transport plane that flew in from South Africa once or twice a month and kept EO self-sufficient. So they could only relieve the convoy by road.

He reported to the local Maskiaka military commander, a major, who agreed to provide some men. Exasperated by the sight before him, Fred silently contrasted the professionalism, dedication and discipline that went into convoy-ambush exercises at the jungle warfare training centre in Brunai with what he was presented with.

The major was in flip-flops, a pick-up truck of ten to twelve men, some with only one magazine for their weapon. I said, 'How are you going to fight a war?' And an old colonel, a nice old boy, stepped forward and said that he would come with me.

So this motley assortment, more like Fred Karno's army than a group of professionals, set out in the pick-up truck. They drove only about six or seven miles when they had a puncture. There was no spare wheel. Fred had every right to despair, 'It was a right Mickey Mouse convoy relief.'

But they went back to Masiaka where Fred phoned Tom Nyuma and pleaded with him – could he not send a helicopter. Tom Nyuma responded on the instant that he would come by road with reinforcements. He did not take long and arrived with four Land Rovers loaded with soldiers; and they drove to the scene of the ambush at Magbosi.

When we arrived it was getting dark. The rebels were still there looting: they took two of the tankers and started to siphon the fuel. So we got out and walked down and cleared the ambush area and stayed there. And what we did, we set up a group at the front and a group at the back and then we held the ground there. And what was incredible, as we were clearing the area, we saw the body of this old lady the rebels had killed; and you know it was horrible, with this big stick stuck in her. So we covered her up and when the operation was finished we buried her with dignity. That was the rebels!

The following day, they held the ground and cleared the area. And from what they discovered it was obvious that local people had been in cahoots with the rebels. The locals benefited from ambushes. Fred and the soldiers found a warehouse where the loot was stored. That indicated the likelihood of a rebel base quite near, so Executive Outcomes mounted an operation, located the camp, and cleared it.

In this way the war continued to be fought, with Executive Outcomes seeking out rebel camps in the bush and taking the fight to them, not allowing the RUF to determine where encounters would take place. On many operations, EO were aided by information from groups like the Kamajors; sometimes the Kamajors took action themselves against the rebels.

As the year came to a close, talk of elections for a restored democracy was in the air. The military government, though, started dragging its heels; there was internal dissention, and in February 1996, Strasser was ousted as head of the ruling elite by his deputy, Brigadier Julius Maada Bio. However, there was overwhelming support from the people for the restoration of democracy. That elections in Sierra Leone were being planned only months after the capital city was on the point of being taken by the RUF was possible only as a result of the operations of Executive Outcomes. As the first President of the restored democracy would later put it,

> Executive Outcomes was the only credible and dependable military outfit opposing the rebels.[12]

But what would happen in the future when the company's contract came to an end? The RUF was still a force to be reckoned with; there had been no miraculous transformation of the Sierra Leone army; and the Kamajors were in reality a militia. There was still a case for training and arming them.

Fred had been thinking about the problem for some time, and he came up with a clever, self-funded scheme to raise money to train, equip and arm a force of Kamajors under the leadership of Chief Hinga Norman, by setting up a company to trade in diamonds and sell them abroad. He discussed it with Chief Norman, who liked the idea but cautioned first of all, that neither he nor Fred knew anything about diamonds – although he knew people who did; and second that he did not want to be closely involved, because diamonds tended to destroy friendship – and he would rather have friendship – , but he would help a company that Fred was part of.

Next Fred contacted his old friend from KAS days, Pete Flynn, and invited him to Sierra Leone. Pete, it will be recalled, was not only ex-SAS, he was a pilot; and he, in turn, got in touch with Simon Mann, who was working with a security company called Ibis. The company did not have a presence in Sierra Leone, but Simon Mann thought it would be useful if Pete went there as a foot on the ground to assess the possibilities for security work with a flying capability. And on that basis, Pete Flynn joined Fred. After assessing the situation, though, Pete felt that there was no useful role for airmanship, but recommended to Simon Mann that a better use of his time would be to help establish a scaled-down version of the model for the training of a local force that could stand up to and defeat the RUF.

The diamond fields of Sierra Leone were one of the country's main resources. Its industry appeared to be regulated but in reality there was wide-spread corruption and exploitation: an illicit market operated with people stealing them from a mine and secreting them, or finding them by searching in a river bed. But at this point the thief, or the finder, had a problem, which Pete outlines.

> Then they used to try and sell the diamonds; and the only way they could sell the diamonds was to the local dealer – they were Lebanese mainly, quite a cross-section, Dutch even. But they used to rip them off: you'd get a $25,000 diamond and they would give them maybe $50 or $100 for it. So we said if we could get in with those people down near Kenema, we could buy the diamonds at a fair price

and take them over to Antwerp, sell them, get the money and bring the money back and give the money (not all the money) to the Chief – because we needed working capital. The basic principle was to give them a certain amount and then they could buy weapons to set up what Fred was setting up and also buy rice and tools and all the rest of it. So basically they'd be able to fund the setting up of that. Which was right. [13]

They cleared the idea with Simon Mann and his partner Tony Buckingham. Then Fred and Pete set up a company, Inter-Afrique, whose business was mining and general trade; they registered it in Freetown, under the Business Registration Act, on 5 March 1996[14]; and they took on two local partners: George Jambawai and Humphrey Swaray, who was the manager of the international airport at Lungi. Pete put up $25,000 as working capital and Simon Mann put in a similar amount. There were five shareholders: the four partners and Chief Sam Hinga Norman, each holding 15% share in the capital of the company, with 25% assigned to the company. The Commissioner of Income Tax assessed the company's tax liability for the tax year at SLL 960, 000, and Fred paid over a cheque for SLL 251, 475 in payment for 1995/96.

However, on the political front momentum was gathering for the forthcoming elections, and on 22 March, Chief Norman wrote to the company secretary:

Due to my possible involvement with the elected government of Sierra Leone, I hereby relinquish any rights or benefits offered by the company, Inter-Afrique (SL) Ltd, and authorize you to transfer my shareholding back to the company free of charge.

Signed this 22nd day of March 1996.[15]

Operational responsibilities in the company were allocated along the lines that Fred would obtain a dealer's licence, and Pete was to become familiar with appraising uncut diamonds.

So they sent me off to Antwerp to do a familiarization course to get familiar with appraising rough, uncut diamonds so that I could assess them. So I had to learn as much as I could about diamonds. Then I could assess, pretty well, uncut diamonds – not cut ones, I wasn't interested in that – look at the size, the colour, the clarity and all that.[16]

Fred, meantime, had to go to the UK but before he left, however, he completed and signed the requisite documentation, along with a photograph, applying for a diamond dealer's licence and left it with their partner, George Jambawai, to register.

On Saturday 27 April, Pete arrived back in Sierra Leone from his familiarization course, and they decided to start buying right away. But one detail niggled Fred: when he returned from the UK, he found the dealer's licence was made out not in his name but in that of their local partner, George. There was some story that he was more familiar with diamonds. It should not really have mattered since they were partners in the enterprise. However, Fred's acute sensitivity to potential threat was triggered.

On 1 May they went from Bo to Kenema where they leased a small aircraft at the airport for $1,500 to fly them to Freetown with the diamonds they hoped to buy. Word got around like wildfire that they were there – paying fairer prices –, and they did a brisk trade. Content with their efforts, they headed for the airport to fly to Freetown. But as they approached the airport, they were intercepted by the police; and Fred sensed instantly what was going to happen.

> I knew straight away. Because when I asked the guy, our partner, George, 'Are you coming to Freetown?' He said, 'No.' And he was the only one whose name was on the licence.

So the trap was sprung on them.

> In retrospect we realized we'd been stitched up. We left the little place that we'd been buying the diamonds in; we had the diamonds and a bag of money, literally a bag of money; loads and loads of leones – I mean hundreds of thousands of leones, worth may $10,000 US. So Fred had the bag and I had the diamonds; we came back and getting near the airport, I think Fred's sixth sense kicked in. As we approached, the police intercepted us and they found the diamonds and they found the money; and they said, where is your dealer's licence? And what was our story? George has got it. Where is George? He is not here, he's gone, he's not far away. And we had a bagful of money. And I said, 'Fred, give them some money.'
>   And he said, 'No, we've got to make a stand.'
>   I said, 'Fuck that, just give them some fucking money. Why don't you just give them some fucking money?'
>   And Fred said, 'No we've got to stop this corrupt stuff.'
>   So they arrested us, and they put us in the back of the Land Rover. And they're all cheering as they drove us away – they've got these white men. And then they put us in this little prison, tiny little place, just like a hole really.[17]

Eventually they were released on the promise that they would fly to Freetown, retrieve the company documents for Inter-Afrique, showing proof that it was legally registered, that there was a dealer's licence, and return with them next day. In Freetown, they again leased a small aircraft, for another $1,500, and returned to Kenema. They had, at his point, on this first venture, paid out $3,000 but neither the diamonds they bought nor their bag of money. True to their word, they reported to the police and they got their money back, but not the diamonds, because the police had an agenda. And Fred would have no part in it.

> When they asked me, do you own these diamonds? I said, 'No, keep them, just keep them. Do you think that we spent $3,000 on aircraft, going and coming back with all the money and then that we'll pay you $5,000 to get them back? Just keep them.'

The bag of money was returned to them, they were released and left for Freetown.

In Freetown they had time to reflect on their position, and over a drink at the golf club they mulled things over. Fred was rueful.

> We had money and if we had given them a million leone, half that, half a million leone, they would have been more than happy. But I said, 'No, we're not paying anything; we live in a civilized world.' That is OK, but in a world full of corruption! We can laugh now, but it annoyed me so much. We had all the documentation. And there was me saying, 'No, no we're not going to.' And that was more or less forcing them to turn round and say – We are the authority. And that was it finished.
>
> But Pete was right in what he said, and I was stupid. I didn't see that far because I was taking this stand.

There was anger too because they felt that they had been double-crossed. Their partner with the licence had stayed away from the scene.

> He could probably buy from the guy who stole them or dug them up; and he could sell them to the Lebanese, and he'd maybe make $10,000 or $5,000 or whatever, quite a lot of money, relatively speaking, whereas with us he wasn't getting that. We paid him; well we gave him some money; we looked after him very well, but it wasn't enough.[18]

And so, with a bag of money and another of diamonds, and no dealer's licence, they had walked into the waiting arms of the avaricious lawmen. As they sipped their drinks in the clubhouse, the full import of their position became clearer to them.

> Pete said, 'I think I'm flying out tomorrow.' And I said, 'Pete, it's a very good idea.' Because Pete was the one carrying the diamonds, they would arrest Pete for money.

So the next day, Saturday 4 May, Pete flew out of Sierra Leone, one step ahead of an arrest warrant from the guardians of law and order.

The project came to grief, and they lost out. But the loss extended beyond money:

> It was just a belief, our belief, that if we succeeded we would help the Chief to fight the war and we'd assist him in his administration and logistics. We would make money to support and expand the company and develop it into a much bigger one.

However, on the political front events were moving at such a pace that it began to appear as if there might be no need to train militias to fight the RUF.

Chapter Four

Democratic Vista

Away with themes of War, away with War itself!

Walt Whitman, 'Song of the Exposition'

After years of authoritarian rule, the people of Sierra Leone approached the prospect of a restored democracy with enthusiasm, maturity and determination. Elections were held in two stages during the spring of 1996. However, some people who exercised their right to vote were to suffer for it grievously. Although the RUF had been defeated in combat every time they were engaged by Executive Outcomes, rebel units still existed in the bush and their high command was in contact with them by radio. The advent of a democratically elected government was particularly galling to the RUF only nine months after they had been on the outskirts of Freetown and control of the whole country within their grasp. Outclassed militarily, the rebels adopted a barbaric revenge on individuals. A system that is common at election time in less developed countries is that of marking with indelible ink the back of the hand of a person who has voted . And in Sierra Leone at these elections, when rebels came across individuals with the tell-tale signs of having voted, they seized them and hacked off a finger or a hand as punishment.

Truly, the future was in their hands; and such wanton cruelty did not prevent the people from expressing their wishes: Ahmad Tejan Kabbah of the SLPP (Sierra Leone People's Party) emerged from the elections as President. Kabbah had campaigned on a ticket of bringing peace to the country. Chief Hinga Norman was also a prominent member of the SLPP and one of the front runners for a cabinet post. Such was his trust in Fred that Hinga Norman could air ideas with him, knowing that his confidence would not be betrayed, for Fred was a soldier through and through, and Hinga Norman had trained as an officer in the British army. On one occasion Hinga Norman told Fred that he had been sounded out for the post of Vice President.

I advised him against it. I said, 'Chief, the problem is with the army, why don't you go for the position of Deputy Minister of Defence?' He said to me, 'Fred I cannot do that; I've got to go back to my people and explain to them. I cannot just do it by myself. It was my people's will that I would follow.' So I said, 'You could be the Vice President but how much influence would you have in the army. The President is the Defence Minister, what power would you have as Vice President? But if you got involved with the army you would have direct dealings with them.'

Hinga Norman must have mulled this over. He would have known it was sound; a civilian politician would have deduced that after years of military rule, the army must inevitably be heavily politicized. Indeed, Brigadier Julius Maada Bio, who took over as the head of government when Valentine Strasser was ousted in February, later confided that some army officers had come to him the day he handed over the reins of power to a civilian government, 'to express their disappointment, and warned me that we would hear from them in the future.'[1]

At any rate, Chief Hinga Norman returned to Bo, and in discussions opened up an alternative scenario. When he came back, he told Fred that after explaining the reason for his change of direction, his people had agreed with him; they all agreed. After that, Hinga Norman would have relayed his response for the President's consideration.

> One day I came back from work; I had an arrangement that the Chief could come and stay with me. I was on the verandah cleaning out my weapon – I was still with Executive Outcomes – and I said, 'Chief how are things?' And he said, 'Fred my appointment is going to be announced on the 6pm news this evening.'

So they went indoors, had a cup of tea and tuned into the news broadcast, waiting for the announcement. The announcer read the news bulletin but there was no mention of the position of Deputy Minister of Defence. After the broadcast, Fred suggested that they go for a drive.

> And as we came off the hill, the Chief said, 'Fred let's go to the house of the Adviser to the President.' So we went, and, as we were approaching the house, we saw a lot of cars parked outside. We stopped and the Chief went into the house. Next thing he came back out and he said, 'Fred whatever you do, don't move; if you move and they think I'm not interested there's going to be a riot up and down the country.' And he went back into the house.

Whatever politicking took place, it happened behind closed doors. The President may have already offered cabinet posts to members of other parties for their support, or he may have been holding out such a prospect to them. But from what Hinga Norman told Fred, one group of the Adviser's entourage wanted Hinga Norman to make a call to the President; another group protested that it was the Adviser to the President who should call His Excellency and tell him that a special announcement should be made on the radio at 8pm, that there was an expectation that Chief Hinga

Norman would be named as Deputy Minister of Defence; and that, if he was not, there might be demonstrations.

They waited, and at 8pm a special announcement was made naming Sam Hinga Norman as Deputy Minister of Defence. 'And I said to the Chief, "Chief, come let's go." So we went down to Lagunda and had a meal and a bottle of red wine.'

After the new government was formed and Hinga Norman took up his portfolio, contact between him and Fred had to be on a more formal basis.

> We had an arrangement that I could make an appointment and go and see him; but he was a Minister and I was just a friend. And we worked on a system that if he wanted to tell me something he would tell me. And that was how we did it.

Early on in Hinga Norman's new role a conflict arose between the dictates of diplomatic protocol and his sense of loyalty to the private military company that had made his country secure enough to take the democratic path. The way he resolved it was a mark of his calibre. One part his remit as Deputy Minister of Defence was to pursue international arms control measures. In September he attended a United Nations conference in South Africa; the venue was in Pretoria; and he wanted Col Roelf van Heerden of Executive Outcomes to accompany him.

> Hinga Norman and I were very good friends. I chaperoned him in South Africa one time, just after he became Deputy Minister of Defence: a meeting with the United Nations, on arms control – stopping the use of small arms. So I chaperoned him in South Africa and I knew the man very, very well. I know his family, his wife his children – I know them very well.[2]

However, Hinga Norman's request to be received by Executive Outcomes' personnel in the Republic of South Africa turned out to be an issue for the South African government, but he insisted, showing his gratitude to the company that had done so much for his country. He and Roelf van Heerden travelled separately to South Africa, Hinga Norman by way of Abidjan. According to protocol, South African Foreign Affairs officials should receive and accompany a visiting government minister, and when Hinga Norman's flight arrived at Pretoria, Foreign Affairs officials were waiting at the airport. He told them, though, that he would rather go with the EO chaps, as they were his good friends. It could not have been easy for Chief Hinga Norman to take this stand against the apparatus of the host state, because protocol and precedent dictated that he be in the hands of South African government officials. And what happened next is known from what Hinga Norman later told Fred. As Hinga Norman was going through Immigration, he handed over his passport. The official, instead of stamping the passport, stamped a piece of paper and inserted it inside the passport. At this, Hinga Norman remarked that on his return to Sierra Leone he would inform his President that this was how a visiting minister of state from a friendly country was received in South Africa. Immediately the official asked for the passport back, removed the piece of paper, and stamped the passport.

Eventually, Hinga Norman got through the processing; Roelf van Heerden was waiting for him; they drove to the hotel in which Roelf had reserved a room for him, and then Roelf took him on a tour of the city. Roelf had been away from his home, on active service in Sierra Leone, continuously for some months, and so he brought his wife and daughter over from Namibia to Pretoria. One evening, as Roelf recalls, his family and Hinga Norman went out for dinner together.

> I can remember my wife over dinner really crying, pleading with him, saying, 'Ah it's time for my husband to come home.' And he said, 'No, no he can't come home; the war is not over and we need the man.' So he knew my wife, he knew my daughter and he was always very interested to know how it was going at home, and what was my situation there. And so we were very, very great friends, really great friends.[3]

Throughout the conference, Hinga Norman had been suffering from symptoms of a neck injury, and so with approval of Lafras Luitingh, EO's Second in Command, Roelf booked him into the Olive Dale clinic after the final seminar. Hinga Norman spent a few days in the clinic. Responsibility for him was shouldered by Executive Outcomes; the clinic staff were very co-operative, agreeing to the special arrangements that Roelf requested: no one should see Hinga Norman without the approval of EO management. When he was discharged from the clinic, Hinga Norman spent a day shopping in the city centre for some good clothing. Although he expressed a wish to see President Nelson Mandela, no meeting took place, and Roelf is pretty sure that Hinga Norman did not have a session with any other South African government minister or official. Such, it seems, was the official cold-shouldering of a visiting minister, determined to be his own man. Then it was time to depart, and Roelf and Hinga Norman set out on the trip back to Sierra Leone .

In Sierra Leone, as the war against the rebels continued deeper into the bush, Fred's role changed: instead of taking part in their combat operations, he became the link-man between Executive Outcomes and the Sierra Leone government through Chief Hinga Norman, Deputy Minister of Defence. Fred's role was to arrange visits and meetings up-country between Hinga Norman and EO commanders, as the company's operations continued against rebel bases. On some occasions, Hinga Norman wanted the advice of the Brigadier in charge of EO and Fred was the facilitator for these meetings. At all levels relationships were cordial and relaxed. There were times, though, when Hinga Norman wanted advice from EO on intelligence matters; Fred arranged these meetings, but did not attend them. He took the initiative in absenting himself on such occasions: he felt that he should not stretch the bounds of friendship with a government minister into matters of state importance; and Chief Hinga Norman respected him for it.

At the same time as he was carrying out the link role between the Deputy Minister of Defence and Executive Outcomes, Fred formed a security company, Cape International, along with Murdo Macleod and Paddy McKay. They received the Registration Documents for Cape International on 19 September 1996. Fred had first met Murdo Macleod when he was with the SAS in the Falklands campaign of 1982 and Murdo was in the RAF, flying Harrier jets. They met up again in Sierra Leone when Murdo was running Ibis Air Wing. It was when he was with EO that Fred first met Paddy. Thanks to the improved security situation in the country, mining operations were getting under way again; and Cape International, won the contract to provide security to Nick Worrell's company, Golden Prospect Mining, which had mining concessions in the north, in the Diang Chiefdom. The operations site was based up-country in Yara and head office was in Freetown. The three founders of Cape International gave it a structure of three directors: Murdo was Managing Director, Paddy was Financial Director and Fred was Operations Director, responsible for running the up-country operations and carrying out liaison with police and other agencies.

Recruitment of expatriates and locals was followed by training on site. Fred took a very systematic approach to training: testing and sifting for training took place first, then there followed training on basic aspects of security work after which there was further testing. Those who passed went on shift for a six-week probationary period. Further training then took place on basic first aid; and ex-firefighters carried out fire-fighting training; ex-police did the same in principles of law. A basic test was set and those who passed earned an increase in salary. Once recruits were allocated to their shifts, Fred or one of the ex-pats and the shift commander took them to the location at which they were to be employed and explained to them the details of what they must do.

Fred adopted a five-shift system at the operational site. There had to be three ex-pats up-country at any one time, leaving one or two in the Freetown office. The work pattern for locals was three weeks on duty followed by one week's paid leave; that for ex-pats was three months on duty and one month's paid leave. Air fares and in-country expenses were paid by the company.

The main site of the sampling operations was about 3 kilometres south of Yara village on the west side of Lake Sonfon. And from the initial sampling area, the company cleared a road round the lake for more test sites. The lake was thought to be rich in gold and diamonds; it was certainly rich in wild life – habitat of buffalo, crocodile and pigmy hippopotamus.

In the months that followed, thanks to Fred's links with Chief Hinga Norman, Cape International was exceptionally granted approval to carry weapons. One afternoon, Fred presented the approval document from the Ministry of Defence authorizing Cape International to carry weapons in the execution of their duties to the Chief of Defence Staff, Brigadier General Conteh. Such approval meant that the army could provide certain types of weapons to company personnel: shotguns for locals and pistols and AK–47s for expatriates, on condition that expatriates were responsible for supervision of training and testing and the security of weapons. When Fred met Conteh he was with his intelligence officer in the map room that EO had set up; his only response was to tell Fred to leave the document on the table. However, weapons were duly provided. And so now, recruits had to be given weapons training with shotguns. Some of the shotguns, Fred discovered, were antiquated and some were amateurishly adapted and too dangerous to be allowed on the shooting range. Most of Fred's local security staff were ex–Tamaboros, a local militia of hunters that had been disbanded. He found that they were very good men, who proved their worth during the critical days that lay ahead.

Part of the function of a responsible company exploring the resources of an area, as Fred saw it, was to put something in to the welfare of the local community. And as Fred observed local customs, he became aware that lack of simple hygiene was resulting in a lot of cases of eye infection, so he suggested to one of the village elders of Yara that the company's medical orderly could give health talks to the people of the village. This idea had to be put to the local chairman, who agreed. The medical orderly gave his first talk to half of the village wives, who not only received it well but asked that the same input be made for the men of the village. So successful was the venture that it ended up being delivered to all the villages in the chiefdom of Diang.

Meanwhile, at state level, President Kabbah was intent on achieving his election pledge to bring the war to an end; and he decided he would do so by entering into negotiations with the rebels. On the face of it, he was in a strong position: the RUF could not now succeed militarily, thanks to the impact of Executive Outcomes. Fighting still continued, though, but the rebels had been pushed back and were being sought out by EO alongside units of the Sierra Leone army or the Kamajors. So this was the strong hand that President Kabbah held when, on neutral territory in the Ivory Coast, he sat down to negotiate with Foday Sankoh, head of the RUF.

The negotiations concluded on 30 November 1996 with the Abidjan Accord.

Article 11 of the Accord stipulated that a UN body, a Neutral Monitoring Group (NMG) would be set up and be responsible for monitoring breaches in the peace agreement. However, given the way the pendulum had swung over eighteen months from the point when the RUF were on the outskirts of Freetown to their being crushed in battle by an agency acting on behalf of the State, a key paragraph, Article 12, spelled out ignominious defeat – but not for the RUF.

ARTICLE 12

The Executive Outcomes shall be withdrawn five weeks after the deployment on the Neutral Monitoring Group (NMG). As from the date of the deployment of the Neutral Monitoring Group, the Executive Outcomes shall be confined to barracks under the supervision of the Joint Monitoring Group and the Neutral

Monitoring Group. Government shall use all its endeavours, consistent with its treaty obligations, to repatriate other foreign troops no later than three months after the deployment of the Neutral Monitoring Group or six months after the signing of the Peace Agreement, whichever is earlier.[4]

President Kabbah later admitted that it had been a mistake to terminate the contract in the face of popular demand for Executive Outcomes to remain in Sierra Leone, at least until all threat from the RUF was eliminated.

But because of the persistent demand of the RUF that they would sign the Abidjan Accord only if it contained a provision for the termination of the contract of the Executive Outcomes, I yielded to their demand in spite of the popular opposition and the heavy financial consequences that followed from the wrongful and premature termination of that contract. My Government is still paying the damages which followed from such termination.[5]

The cost in human life, damage to property and lost revenues to the country from that decision to withdraw Executive Outcomes turned out to be horrendous.

Yet the extent to which Foday Sankoh was deceiving President Kabbah became known to the Sierra Leone government within days of the promulgation of the Accord when government agencies intercepted a radio message from Sankoh to one of his field commanders, Sam Bockarie, explaining to him that he had no intention of abiding by the agreement and had only entered the peace talks to get the international community off his back.[6] And to pile insult on ignominy, Sankoh, the day of the signing of the Agreement, refused to sign the document that Kabbah had personally drawn up, authorizing the deployment of 90 UN peacekeepers to monitor the observance of the ceasefire. This document required both their signatures as a pre-condition to the group's being deployed.[7] As a result no peacekeepers came to Sierra Leone; yet, in terms of the Accord, it was subsequent to this body being deployed that Executive Outcomes were required to leave the country.

So at this juncture, when the good faith of Foday Sankoh was known to be lacking, President Kabbah tenaciously persisted in terminating the contract with Executive Outcomes, and so clawed defeat from the jaws of victory.

In terms of the contractual arrangement between the previous government and Executive Outcomes, provision for terminating the contract provided for specified notice to terminate following the conclusion of a subsequent full calendar month. And so, in December 1996, Sierra Leone's Attorney General, Solomon Berewa, issued the formal notice in writing, which, at 31 January 1997, resulted in EO departing the theatre.

Before that happened, though, EO recommended two options that they could deliver to the Sierra Leone government: the retention of an intelligence gathering capability and/or a helicopter-mobile QRF (Quick Reaction Force). Considering the perilous position the government was now in with a military riven by factions and an intelligence capacity that the President later acknowledged could not be trusted, these were two shrewd options, probably calculated to be politically acceptable to a government that had just signed a peace agreement. Neither option was taken up.

The final payment for the contract, like the earlier payments, came from funds provided to the Sierra Leone government by way of World Bank economic support. It was not a direct payment, of course, for EO's services, because the charter of the World Bank precluded the funding of military or religious activities, but it could come under the budget heading of security in the country's submission to the World Bank.

On 30 January, the day before they were due to leave, it was reported that Executive Outcomes had pulled out of Kono one month ahead of the expected deployment of the UN peacekeepers. [8] It would seem then, at this stage, it was not widely known that the peace-monitoring process was in a cleft stick since it lacked Sankoh's agreement, a vital prerequisite for the UN to send the monitoring group. Then on 3 February, it was reported that Executive Outcomes had left the country the previous Monday; and its Commander, Brig Bert Sachse , was quoted as saying, 'I believe the government is quite capable of handling its own internal security problem. We must now leave the country.'[9] However, the report went on to include a piece of misinformation that has often re-appeared in print about the reason why EO left the country: 'On January 31 the group's Sierra Leone contract officially ended and was not renewed.'[10] Whereas in truth, it had been terminated in writing by the government.

On 14 February, news sources quoted the UN Secretary-General, Kofi Annan, giving a nuanced slant on the fragility of the peace process, in which he said, 'We are still trying to get Sankoh's agreement to the deployment of the force without wanting to give him a veto power over deployment of the force.'[11] Yet, a veto was precisely the power Sankoh held since 30 November. But by 7 March, the tone at UN level was more realistic: a senior official, arriving in Abidjan with the intention of persuading Sankoh to accede to the deployment of the mission said, 'We hope he will consent and let the mission be deployed.'[12] It was a forlorn hope.

Deputy Minister of Defence, Sam Hinga Norman, seemed to have no illusions about Sankoh. After rebels carried out a series of ambushes in which twelve soldiers and twenty civilians were killed, the government authorized the army and the Kamajors to flush out RUF groups. According to the terms of the peace agreement, the rebels were supposed to report to demobilization camps; yet three months into the ceasefire, only about 30 RUF fighters had turned themselves in. Hinga Norman said, 'Sankoh is vicious and is betraying the peace process.'[13] Trouble was brewing in other quarters as well: about twenty people died in a shoot-out between soldiers and Kamajors over diamonds. It was reported, soldiers started digging for diamonds in a gravel pit, and, when they were challenged by the Kamajors as to their right to do so on their lands, firing ensued.[14]

That incident was but an indication of a more deep-seated tension between the army and Kamajor militias: elements in the army saw them as a rival force, nurtured at their expense; while civil groups, after years of bitter experience, often distrusted the Sierra Leone army and looked on militias as more loyal. The term Civil Defence Force (CDF) came into being; the problem became so serious that President Kabbah set up a committee under the chairmanship of Bishop Keilii to investigate and make recommendations. Then the unexpected happened, the RUF leader, Foday Sankoh, went on a private visit to Nigeria and was first detained, carrying a firearm; then he was arrested.

In March a man arrived in the country who would become so committed to supporting this fragile democracy that it would cost him his diplomatic career, but earn him the highest honour that Sierra Leone could confer: the new British High Commissioner, Peter Penfold. By the time he was appointed, Peter Penfold was already a very experienced member of Her Majesty's Diplomatic Service who had dealt with civil emergencies and humanitarian relief in third world countries; but something about the sacrifices that people made to restore democracy in Sierra Leone made a profound impression on him.

They showed how to remove an illegal military government peacefully and to usher in a democratic civilian government. People made great sacrifices. One story had a major impact on my thinking. As we know in Africa, it's not all that sophisticated, after a person has voted they usually have the back of their hand marked with indelible ink. If the rebels found anybody with that mark on the back of their hand they chopped the hand or their finger off. One person who had had his hand chopped off by the rebels because he had voted was asked how he now felt about democracy and about voting. And he waved the other hand and said, 'I have got his hand, I can use this one next time to vote.' When I heard that it had an incredible impact on me. It made me wonder just how many people back in Britain, for example, would bother to vote if they had to fear losing a hand. It therefore gave a sense of how important democracy was to these so-called illiterate, uneducated people. It embraced the fundamentals of what democracy is in a way I found staggering. I therefore was fully committed to the struggle to ensure that this fledgling democracy did not wither and perish.[15]

But it was a fragile democracy, with factions of discontent within the army; and the government was now bereft of the intelligence gathering capability and the stability that Executive Outcomes had provided. President Kabbah had to call on the help of Nigeria to provide specialists to investigate allegations of an incipient coup. As a result, an army major, Johnny Paul Koroma and one or two junior officers were arrested. However, this did not stop the rot.

On 16 May, Deputy Defence Minister Hinga Norman sought President Kabbah's permission to call a meeting, which would be attended by the President and to which would be summoned the Chief of the Defence Staff, the Chief of the Army Staff and the Inspector General of Police. At the meeting Hinga Norman accused the Chief of the Defence Staff and the Army Chief of having prior knowledge of an impending coup against the government and doing nothing to stop it. Here, he gives an account of the outcome.

> After I had finished talking, the President turned to the two officers and said, 'Gentlemen, did you hear what Chief Norman said?' They said, 'Yes sir.' Then His Excellency went on further to say, 'Do you have anything to say?' The officers said, 'No sir.' The President then turned to me and said, 'Chief Norman, they say they do not have anything to say.'
>
> I became lost for words for a while. After a few minutes, I said, 'Your Excellency, I did not invite these two officers to say something, but since it is conclusive you do not intend to do anything, I am therefore inviting your Excellency as the Minister of Defence, Commander in Chief of the Armed Forces of Sierra Leone and the President of the Republic to order these officers not to carry out the coup or to allow it, otherwise, if they do, I shall have no alternative but join the people of Sierra Leone to fight and reverse the coup. Thereafter, your Excellency will be constitutionally required to sign their death warrants after due process of law. As of now I shall pray that God will make you survive the coup and see the consequences of your not taking the appropriate action to protect the people and the state.[16]

It was later reported that Hinga Norman felt a sense of betrayal by the President's unwillingness to act. And rightly so, as later events would prove – and as Fred put it, 'The saddest thing was that the Chief was the most loyal servant that he, Kabbah, had ever had.'

Later in the week, the British High Commissioner, Peter Penfold, and the American Ambassador also picked up rumours of discontent in the army that could lead to a coup; it was not specific, but it was worrying, and so they, along with the UN special envoy, met with President Kabbah. Peter Penfold felt that the President was a bit dismissive of their information: saying that he would have a few of the soldiers round and talk to them. But chatting with a few high ranking officers would not solve the problem – because they were the problem.

Peter Penfold found himself well placed to observe the way that the consequences of corrupt practices in the military played out. Britain had agreed to provide a military training assistance programme for the Sierra Leone army; a two-man team led by a major was dispatched to the country to train two battalions of its army. Not long after their arrival, the major came to Peter Penfold with the news that the Chief of Defence Staff had just informed him that he could not find 600 men to take part in the training programme. Peter Penfold immediately went to see Brigadier Conteh, Chief of Defence Staff, and expressed his disbelief that in an army of about

15,000 it was impossible to muster 600 for training. And he exerted pressure: the situation would have to be known at the highest levels for if the training programme could not be delivered other aspects of British aid to the country might be called into question. After hemming and hawing, the Chief of Defence Staff admitted that a more accurate assessment for the strength of the country's army was a fighting force of 6,000 with about 2,000 administrative staff. Peter Penfold reported this to the Deputy Minister of Defence, Sam Hinga Norman, who blew his top that the army had withheld this information from him.[17]

A meeting was called with the President, at which the true figures of the army's complement were revealed. The mythical missing legions of soldiers sustained a gigantic corruption: rice was issued to the army on overall numbers and it was rationed out according to rank: a private soldier got one bag of rice a month, and by the time it got to senior rank, a full colonel got thirty-one bags of rice, 'so in effect the officers were rice traders.'[18] In the light of this corruption, as well as the fact that there was a rice shortage in the country, the President ordered that the rice allocation should be computed afresh, commensurate with the true figures of the army's complement. However, the Chief of Defence Staff, instead of issuing an order for a proportional cut in the ration for all ranks, ordered that the rice ration to the private soldiers should be cut to half a bag of rice a month.[19] In so doing, he laid a smoke screen, concealing corrupt practice at higher levels in the army, imputing blame for the cut in rations to other ranks slap-bang at the door of the civilian politicians.

Chapter Five

Fubar

Things fall apart; the centre cannot hold;
Mere anarchy is loosed upon the world

W. B. Yeats, 'The Second Coming'

Two years, to the very month, after Executive Outcomes stopped the RUF on the outskirts of Freetown, the rebels were handed the capital on a plate. A coup d'état was sprung less than a week after the discovery of the scam about army numbers and the rice ration. Early in the morning of Sunday 25 May 1997, the Chief of the Defence Staff, Brig Conteh, received a radio message from an officer in the Signals Squadron stationed at Wilberforce that armed soldiers had sped by in a Mercedes Benz, claiming that they were staging a coup, and taking over the country. While the CDS tried to establish more details, sporadic firing broke out over the city. President Kabbah, an early riser, was monitoring the radio broadcasts between the CDS and the signals officer, and he contacted the CDS to find out what efforts were being made to quell the coup. The situation was unclear, and the President made several calls to Conteh.

Even among the fleet of foot, President Kabbah, Minister of Defence and chief of Sierra Leone's armed forces, had few challengers when it came to his swiftness of flight; he was already on his mark, and when the radio went off the air, the President, deducing that the instigators of the coup had already succeeded, 'quickly accelerated his plans to leave the country.'[1] He was taken to Lungi International Airport by the Nigerian ECOMOG troops, and flown to neighbouring Guinea.

Fred had driven to Freetown on the Friday before the coup. He met Will Scully, another former member of the Regiment whom they had recently recruited, about midway, at Makeni, passed over to him the company's permit to carry weapons, wished him good luck, and drove on to the office in Freetown. There he found a note for him from fellow director of Cape International, Murdo, saying that he was flying out that evening to the UK, and that Fred was to pick up Conrad Bronson, a Canadian investor, and show him round the concession. Fred went round to the Mammy Yoko Hotel to liaise with Conrad Bronson, whom he had met once or twice before, and to be briefed on their trip to Kono. The plan was for them to fly from the Mammy Yoko helipad to Lungi, then board a fixed-wing flight to Kono, where they would be met by Conrad's people. They flew out on Saturday morning, and were taken to the mine site; they watched the operation for some time, and spent the night there.

On Sunday 25 May, Fred heard the radio broadcast announcing that the government had fallen. The initial leader of the mutineers turned out to be a Corporal Gborie, and it was he who made the broadcast. After that they broke into the prison where Maj Johnny Paul Koroma, who had been awaiting trial for allegedly planning a coup, was being held and released him. Corp Gborie then passed the baton to Koroma. But Koroma did not assume the title of President: he called himself Chairman of the Armed Forces Revolutionary Council (AFRC), as the junta styled itself, after the model of Jerry Rawlings in Ghana.

Later in the day, the disaster that had overtaken the country was compounded when the junta leaders went on the air again and invited the RUF to come and join them, and become the People's Army . Any semblance of military discipline on the part of the AFRC would break down as it absorbed the barbaric RUF. Few rebels had handed in their weapons, as they were required to under the terms of the Abidjan agreement, and they were now being urged to come out of the bush and join the AFRC. With no guiding rationale to follow other than spreading mayhem and death, rebels moving towards centres of population would find the mining site a prime target. As he moved around with Conrad Bronson, Fred spoke to Yara station very briefly and for security reasons did not tell them where they were.

The ex-professional soldiers working for Cape International knew that they would never be able to make a stand at Yara; they would be overrun. Some of them had their own priorities: Will Scully, who had already indicated that he was leaving the company, desperately required his passport, which was in the company's office in Freetown, and so he left on his own; Duke MacKenzie, a New Zealander, who was suffering from malaria, wanted to get out of the country and into Guinea. Simbu, who was acknowledged locally to be the best hunter, led him by bush paths to the Guinean border. Simbu, Fred thought, was a true native of the land, 'very attuned to his surroundings, people and animals, and life in general.'

When Fred returned to the station, the expats collectively decided that their best course was to join up with the private military security company, Lifeguard, at Kono. Lifeguard was a company of significant force; its personnel had served with Executive Outcomes in Sierra Leone; and its role was to protect Branch Energy's mining interests at Kono.

Systematically the expats went about preparations for their withdrawal. Local employees, many of them Tamaboro hunters, would stay and blend back in with their own way of life. But first they stripped vehicles of their starter motors, so that the rebels would find them unserviceable, and they removed the radios from them as well. (Months later, after the coup had been crushed, these components were all returned.)

The expats gave careful thought to the way they loaded their small Mitsubishi pick-up truck, because the drive to Kono could be dangerous, and they were bound to come across checkpoints – the overthrow of an elected government, and the invitation to the RUF would breed petty warlords, armed with AK-47s. So the company's expats concealed all their weapons, ammunition and webbing under mattresses in the back, packed in their personal possessions, and piled in on top, and set off. The trip was not without incident, and they had very close calls with AFRC at some checkpoints.

From Fred's point of view there was no question of trying to surprise the nearest armed men at a checkpoint by kicking open the doors and attempting to accelerate through – the tactic that he had briefed his driver on two years earlier when the only enemy was the RUF –: too many of the team were vulnerable in the back, and even if the surprise move worked for them once, there could be army personnel at the checkpoints, and they had a communication system between military posts. So when the pick-up truck was waved down by a rabble, some wearing uniform and some in jeans, but all armed with AK-47s, Cape International personnel showed no belligerence. Fred took the initiative with a disarmingly friendly greeting, calling them brother, offering cigarettes. It worked. At one checkpoint they even ended up giving some AFRC men a lift to the outskirts of the town.

One of the unhappy consequences of a hazardous way of life, away from home for long periods, is that it can lead to the breakdown of family life. That had happened in Fred's case, and he now had a second family. His partner Hawah and their four-months old baby were in Freetown. All contact with the capital was cut off, even HF radio. Anarchy was being unleashed there; arson, killing, looting and raping would be rife. But for the drive to Kono, he had to play the affable expat.

In that fashion they arrived at Kono, and settled in with Lifeguard Security. Sleeping accommodation was arranged for them. There were several foreign nationals in the town, including Russians who worked in the mines, Lebanese who dealt in the diamond business and Canadians. Lifeguard was led by Jan Joubert; his second in command was Dino Coutinho, and they took on responsibility for securing not just the property of Branch Energy but the town as a whole. Lifeguard welcomed the presence of the Cape Internationals; they knew Fred from the days of Executive Outcomes, and Jan asked him if he would like to join them, but until he knew that his partner was safe, Fred could not commit himself.

That remained so until the evening of 29 May. He had already been in touch with Murdo in the UK, and that evening – it seemed just by chance – he phoned his friend Rab Wood in the UK to be told that Hawah and Maliaka had landed at Stansted. Hawah had called Rab, and told him that they were going to London to be put up by Sam Norman Jr, son of Chief Sam Hinga Norman. Hawah had been lucky: the British High Commission arranged for the charter of a Boeing 747 that took 395 passengers from Lungi to Stansted. Before that, though, she had been even more fortunate: she joined the queue of people at the British High Commission in Freetown, all of whom hoped to be evacuated. Fred was to learn the details later; they made a lasting impact on him. Hawah, when her turn came, was interviewed by an official.

I will owe, for the rest of my life, the wonderful and true gentleman, Dai Harris of Peter Penfold's staff, who issued my daughter Maliaka with a British Passport to get her out of Sierra Leone. I was out in the bush and he exercised true humanity and mercy to get Hawah and Maliaka out. A lot of people would have used the official line to do nothing, but this gentleman stepped up to the blade and did what he thought was right! I will be forever grateful to him till my dying day.

Elated by the news that they were safe, Fred went to Jan Joubert and said, 'If you still need an extra gun, I'm available.' Jan's response was, 'You're working for Branch Energy, and you'll be well rewarded.' But there was no discussion about rates of pay: Fred simply saw it as a job that had to be done, and he was well able to do it. Jan also oversaw the sites in Kono of the SSD (Special Security Division) who were a military arm of the police. Fred found that this branch of the nation's security was generally very reliable. But it was the professionalism of Lifeguard that maintained law and order in Kono. There were rebels on the fringes of the town, some high on drugs, and indisciplined soldiers who would have joined them in what would have become escalating violence; but Lifeguard organized security patrols at night in support of the SSD to prevent the looting of shops and banks.

I admired the calm dedication, professionalism and bravery of the men of the Lifeguard. A truly remarkable group of men that I was very proud to know and serve with. It was like the old days back again. Jan and his command group at the mine site, Tshisukka Tukayula De Abreu and his group guarding the workshop, fuel dump and all the heavy plant, and at night, doing two hours patrolling all over the town, doing stags at the four locations that we held. The fourth location on the hill was where the Lebanese community slept at night until they were evacuated to Guinea – except three old couples who chose to stay behind.

It was like the old days too in the way that comradeship, in some cases, developed into long-lasting friendship. So it became with Fred and Tshisukka Tukayula De Abreu – TT for short. Fred discovered that TT was an ardent fan of Liverpool football club. When he was young, TT had been a very good footballer, and he was offered what would have been a boy's dream – to leave his own country, Angola, and play professional football in Portugal. It got to the stage where he was on his way to the airport, but his grandmother sabotaged his chances, by phoning the authorities and requesting that he be stopped. Whatever she told them, she succeeded in having them prevent her grandson from boarding the flight. Back home, when he asked her why she did it, his grandmother said that if he had gone to Portugal, she might never have seen him again. Shaking his head, TT said to Fred, 'Braa [Brother], I missed an opportunity of a life time!'

Anecdotes like that emerged casually among men who were relaxed in their professional role, even although they were in a stressful environment. The calibre and military competence of Lifeguard's personnel had an effect far in excess of the company's numerical strength, and ensured that Kono, centre of the country's diamond area, was spared what could have been a bloodbath.

Jan Joubert and his 2 i/c did a brilliant job in organizing and maintaining a very 'dignified operation under great pressure'. Every day you were just like a show piece, being looked at by these AFRC and RUF scruffy gangs, whereas the Lifeguard personnel were in smart turn-out with pressed uniforms, discipline of old. I suppose that old habits die hard.

However, it was a very different story in Freetown.

The sudden breakdown in political and military structures had terrifying results for the populace. Within hours, soldiers took over the officers' mess. The Chief of the Defence Staff, Brig Conteh and several officers took to their heels and went into hiding. As the High Commissioner, Peter Penfold put it:

Then once the shooting started, the senior officers went to ground because they realized they had provoked this revolt, and the rest of the army joined in. There was nobody to stop them other than Sam Norman, the one minister who tried to stand up to them.[2]

But as heavy firing continued throughout the day, and soldiers went on a looting spree, Peter Penfold saw what he felt to be his moral duty, and he prepared himself to take an extraordinary initiative.

Peter Penfold rightly judged that there was still residual regard in Sierra Leone for the benign face of colonialism — represented by the office of British High Commissioner. And so the following day, Monday 26 May, he invited the coup leaders to the British High Commission.

The remarkable thing is they came. And what this demonstrated was that in Sierra Leone the role of the British High Commissioner was by far the most important international position there was, far more than, say, the American ambassador or the UN ambassador or whatever. It is just the way it was.[3]

He invited them into his dining room, with its highly polished table, but asked them to leave their automatic weapons outside in case they scratched the table. This they did. He produced a tray of sandwiches, which they wolfed down, having fed on nothing more than their revolutionary fervour for the previous twenty-four hours. Then he began the meeting. His topic was the wellbeing and safety of foreign nationals, but he also had a deeper agenda; one he was to sustain over a few days with consummate skill.

First he hectored them: if they did not grant access to the airport, he would broadcast on the BBC World Service, announcing 'a total evacuation of all the international community from Sierra Leone.'[4] The leaders went into a huddle, and agreed to his request. Then he changed the approach to sweet reasonableness, asking the junta leaders why they had staged the coup. Grievances with Kabbah's government, he was told. Listening closely to them, he realized that the AFRC had no plans or policies of their own worked out. He told them that they had put back the case for democracy by several years; and he slipped in the idea that it did not require a change to the country's constitution to have grievances addressed: their grievances could be put to Kabbah as the country's president and be resolved within the democratic framework. In the policy vacuum that the junta leaders found themselves in this was something to mull over. The meeting concluded with their agreeing to continue meeting to review the situation for evacuating foreign nationals.

That night in a surprise move, contingents of Nigerian and Guinean troops from ECOMOG landed at Lungi and Hastings airports and established control. All the while, conditions in Freetown were deteriorating. Electricity had been out since the morning of the coup; some areas were running low on water. Buildings were gutted by fire; looting was widespread, including the offices of the international relief agencies and the warehouse of the World Food Programme. Hundreds of prisoners were released from Pademba Road prison and issued with military uniforms. Koroma announced that the AFRC intended to disband the Kamajors. It was reported that soldiers arrested five government ministers.[5] And people were being killed.

The initial impact of the coup shocked the populace; but then a spontaneous reaction was set off – mass, passive resistance to the usurpers of the democratic government. Internationally, the coup leaders received no backing from any country. Britain laid its plans to evacuated its nationals; the United States sent a warship, the *Kearsarge*, which was equipped with helicopters.

Each day that week, the junta leaders met the British High Commissioner; and as he drove to those meetings, people lined the streets, hoping that a solution would restore order to their lives, for the word had got around that he was trying to negotiate a settlement. Psychologically there was pressure on the AFRC, because they had failed to win the support of the people. By his skilful handling of these daily meetings, Peter Penfold was on the point of achieving a breakthrough.

So they had a face-saver that all that they had done had not been in vain. So they agreed to stand down and say that Kabbah could come back. We even drafted the statement that would be issued on the radio announcing their decision.[6]

But nothing happened. Higher echelons of the RUF arrived, and, finding the AFRC about to hand power back to Kabbah's government, and give up what their five years of terrorist warfare had failed to achieve, they prevailed against them, and had the decision overturned.

Every morning that first week, talks with Peter Penfold and the junta leaders continued; he kept the pressure on them, to the extent that, on an occasion, his own safety was in danger – a tight corner he got out of with amazing sang-froid. It happened towards the end of a fraught week in which he had tried every tactic. Koroma was ill at ease dealing with officials, and he delegated the task to a senior officer among the junta hierarchy, Colonel Anderson. By the end of the week, Peter Penfold could see they were getting nowhere with the idea of bringing back Kabbah and standing down. Across the table, he told Col Anderson that if the AFRC did not go ahead with the declaration on radio, he would no longer come to the residence.

At that Anderson, fingered the gun he had on his belt, looked at me and said, 'Well, perhaps we had better not let you leave the residence.' It was a tense moment but I broke the ice by saying, 'You'll have to let me go because they are waiting lunch on me back at the office. They can't eat their lunch until the High Commissioner gets back.' And that broke the tension.[7]

It did not, however, achieve a breakthrough in the talks, and Peter Penfold continued with his contingency plans for evacuating foreign nationals and some Sierra Leoneans.

He advised foreign nationals that if they did not feel safe in their homes, they should make their way to the Mammy Yoko Hotel. Already based at the Mammy Yoko, and assuming more and more responsibility for the security of the building and its residents, were Major Lincoln Jopp, a British military adviser to Sierra Leone and Will Scully, who had recently left Cape International, and who had expected to be out of Freetown by now. Increasing numbers of people were moving into the hotel, in the expectation of being air-lifted out of the country – the figure reached about eight hundred, both foreign nationals and Sierra Leoneans. The USS *Kearsarge* arrived, and positioned itself about twenty miles off-shore. Then the evacuation got under way; and on 30 May, among those taken aboard by one of its helicopters was Hinga Norman.[8]

Whether or not the air-lifting of so many people in efficient fashion piled frustration on the mindless AFRC/RUF rabble confronting the Nigerian soldiers guarding the perimeter of the hotel, they opened fire. It quickly became an all-out assault. The Nigerians at times were in some disarray, and showed their lack of experience, and Will Scully and Maj Lincoln Jopp took charge of the defence of the Mammy Yoko Hotel. Both of them were subsequently decorated for their actions: in Will Scully's case, he was awarded Queen's Gallantry Medal for saving lives during a coup. The siege of the Mammy Yoko is graphically described in his book, *Once a Pilgrim*.

In the early days after the coup, Peter Penfold had asked around to find out if there was any resistance being organized.

Yes Sam Norman is trying to organize some resistance here and there – I picked that up second hand. Then I heard through the Americans that they'd helped Sam go into hiding in the Mammy Yoko. And then I sent messages to him through Lincoln Jopp, and then the Americans, John Hirsch [American Ambassador], who was not in the country at the time, had got Sam on board the ship; he'd arranged to get him on to the *Kearsarge*. And he was out. So Sam got out, and Sam actually left the country before I did.

I got to Conakry a couple of days later, and Sam came and saw me at my hotel, the Camayenne, I said, 'Have you seen Kabbah yet?' and he said no. Then I saw Kabbah and I said, 'Have you seen Sam Norman?' I said, 'You know he's here in Conakry.' Kabbah said no. And I thought this is funny, I mean these are the two key people and they're not even talking to one another. And I'm still learning, feeling my way about those relationships; it would be years later I realized the people who were anti-Sam and dripping it into Kabbah. But I said to both of them, 'Look, whatever your personal differences are you two have got to be talking.' I said, 'These are crucial times,you must talk to one another.'

And Sam made the first move and went and saw Kabbah. It was one of those things he always said to me in later years, he said, 'That was one of the best pieces of advice you ever gave me. You were right. I shouldn't have carried on like that,' vis-à-vis, you know what Kabbah's like and so on. I had a hand in pushing them together; and I would keep in touch with was going on. He would send one or two of his people to keep me informed about what was going on in Liberia. But there was not a lot of contact, but in our one–to–one discussions, I think we established a relationship. I think we trusted one another; we had an admiration for one another, for what we were both doing.[9]

In contrast to Freetown, Kono remained calm, thanks to Lifeguard and the SSD. But for how long? Unexpectedly, Fred was hit by a mild bout of malaria. The security company needed to be resupplied, and this could only be done by air. A resupply helicopter flight was due on the afternoon of the 14 June, and Jan told him he should accept being invalided out on it, along with some of the foreign nationals; otherwise, he would have to be evacuated to Guinea by road, and the roads could be closed. The rest of Lifeguard, however, would remain in Sierra Leone for the time being. So on 14 June, Fred and eight others, including Russians and Sierra Leoneans, were air-lifted from Kono to Guinea.

They landed at Conakry around 7pm, disembarked and went to arrivals. And that was as far as they got. Out of the blue, Guinean Immigration decided that they had no permission to enter the country, and informed them they had to return to the helicopter that brought them. There was no alternative but to comply. They were sitting in the helicopter, discussing possible options, when one of the Russians asked if anyone had a contact number for their country's consul in Guinea. By a stroke of luck Fred had kept the Honorary British Consul to Guinea's business card –

her daughter had given it to him two years earlier when her mother was out of the country and Fred required assistance to receive hostages at the country's border −, and he now fished it out from the back of his ID card folder.

The pilot called up the airport's control tower and asked for a landline connection to the helicopter. A call was put through to Honorary Consul, Val Treitlein, who not only responded but came to the airport. She asked Fred if the nine were all British, and he said they were. The Consul then informed the Guinean Immigration officials that these people had the right of access to the country; and the officials did not contest it. Fred warmly thanked Val Treitlein, and then took a taxi to a hotel, because as far as he was concerned, he would not be presenting himself at a hospital for treatment: he would use self-medication.

When Sam Hinga Norman was evacuated by helicopter to the USS *Kearsarge* on 30 May, he knew very clearly what had to be done to bring about the restoration of the democratic government of President Kabbah: it had to be achieved through armed conflict, led by, or reinforced with, militias such as the Kamajors. It was the same idea that he and Fred had endeavoured to introduce to fight the RUF, using two different models in both 1995 and 1996. Each time, the problem that defeated them was the project's funding. Now, on 30 May 1997, on board the *Kearsarge*, Hinga Norman approached another evacuee, an Israeli businessman, Yair Galklein, who was involved in the diamond trade, and told him that he was seeking assistance from companies in the diamond industry to bring about the restoration of the government of Tejan Kabbah.[10] To that end, funding was needed to train, arm, feed and provide crucial logistical support for Sierra Leonean militias. In subsequent discussions on board ship, Yair Galklein and some of his associates in the industry told Hinga Norman that they would be staying in Guinea at the Mamado Hotel.

The USS *Kearsarge* weighed anchor and sailed north, and its passengers were air-lifted to Conakry. Already in the country's capital was President Kabbah, who had been accommodated in the government Guest House by the Guinean President Lansana Conté. Although Peter Penfold had encouraged both of them to get together, fundamental differences surfaced right away between Deputy Minister of Defence, Hinga Norman, and President Kabbah on the strategy for restoring democracy to their country. The President put his faith in diplomacy; Hinga Norman argued for armed intervention,

> driven by a Sierra Leonean fighting force. The Kamajor militia of the Southern and South Eastern Districts would form the bulk of the force, under his direction and command. Hinga Norman invited great risks to his life and his credibility to put his vision into practice.[11]

As far as Hinga Norman was concerned, sitting in Conakry was the equivalent of Nero fiddling while Rome burned. He had to move to Liberia, where ECOMOG troops were based, infiltrate into Sierra Leone, and organize the Kamajors into a fighting force. First there was business to attend to in Conakry. He went to the Mamado Hotel and met Yair Galklein and some of his business colleagues. Their response to his request for their help in restoring democracy was the promise of the supply of food to him in Liberia to feed the Kamajors.[12] Then there was a need to find professional trainers to train a fighting force. So, for a short time, Hinga Norman moved back and forth between Liberia and Guinea, building a support network.

It seemed as though an alternating current flowed through Fred's experiences in Guinea: negative to positive at the airport; and that oscillation continued throughout his stay there. Among those who had arrived in Conakry was Fred's business partner, at Cape International, Murdo Macleod, who had flown there directly from the UK. The two partners were no longer in a strong position: funds had all but dried up in the company's account since the mining operations at Yara were suspended. Fred, in the interim, had been employed by Lifeguard, and on the payroll of Branch Energy, but in reality had not yet received any money. In Guinea, he was accommodated in a hotel on a room-only basis, and he had to eat at a food stall in the street. All the while, feeling rough and weakened, he was recovering from malaria. It was a low period for him. And this was how he was when Sam Hinga Norman was told Fred was in Conakry.

Hinga Norman was on one of the fleeting visits he made to Guinea at this time; he came to the hotel to meet Fred, and told him what he was trying to achieve, from a base in Liberia. Fred asked if he could be part of it. Hinga Norman's response was positive: 'Fred, you do not have to ask me. I would be delighted to have you with us.' But when Fred revealed that he could not even pay his fare to Liberia, Hinga Norman told him that life was very basic for him and his followers, and there was no excess of funds, and he suggested that Fred should phone Tim Spicer in London. Tim Spicer was Director of the private military company, Sandline International, which itself was part of the group of companies associated with Branch Energy. Hinga Norma had already been in touch with Tim and made soundings for external support, probably in the form of weapons, but also likely in the form of personnel. After this brief meeting, they parted, and that was the last Fred saw of him until they were to meet up in Liberia.

Fred's bout of malaria went through its stages, aided by the oral medication he was taking. When he felt he had recovered, he contacted Tim Spicer, who seemed to already know about Hinga Norman's overall strategy. Tim Spicer's response to Fred was immediate and precise. He agreed to employ him, but he was to work with Hinga Norman, but not for him: he was to work for Tim Spicer, and report to him what Hinga Norman planned to do before he did it, for Tim did not want surprises. Fred accepted the terms as Tim laid them out. His next step was to meet with a representative of Branch Energy in Guinea (Brig Sachse, formerly of EO)draw an advance and get himself to Liberia. However, the handwritten note he received authorized him to draw only $700 as an advance on his salary. He argued that it was not enough: he had no network of contacts in Liberia. The advance was increased to $1,700; Fred organized himself a visa for Liberia, and bought his air ticket.

In Liberia, as early as 18 June, Hinga Norman had given a signal to his countrymen, broadcasting from a clandestine radio, urging armed resistance to oust the AFRC, arguing that negotiations with the coup leaders had proven futile.[13] The junta had swung from one policy of proclaiming it would disband the Kamajors to the other extreme of inviting them into the government. A Kamajor spokesman rejected this idea, and shortly afterwards, from a base in Kenema, another spokesman claimed that the Kamajors would march on Bo. Skirmishes took place in early July, and it was reported that Hinga Norman was seen on Sierra Leonean soil in the area of the Mano river bridge which was being fought over by Kamajors and AFRC. This brought the response from the AFRC that President Kabbah, with the assistance of the Nigerian Foreign Minister, was arming the Kamajors to wage war against them.

Hinga Norman was clearly emerging as the prime mover in resisting the coup: he raised funding; he formed some structure for the Sierra Leonean militias; and he infiltrated into Sierra Leone to establish advance bases for military strikes. At an international level he formed influential partnerships. He was friendly with a Sierra Leone clergyman, the Reverend Alfred SamForay, who, though based in the USA, had a wide range of international contacts. The result was that the Rev SamForay became Secretary-General of a group known as the Sierra Leone Action Movement for the Civil Defence Force (SLAM-CDF). SamForay also linked with President Kabbah in Guinea, and confirmed later that Kabbah, 'greatly welcomed any assistance we would give to Chief Norman and the CDF.'[14]

Fred's destination when he arrived in Monrovia, capital of Liberia, was the Sierra Leone embassy. A surly uniformed officer told him that former Deputy Defence Minister, Sam Norman was staying at a house belonging to the Nigerian Ambassador. Driving through the streets of Monrovia during the final days before the country's presidential election, Fred came across the most bizarre partisan electioneering he had ever seen. Charles Taylor, the revolutionary leader who had waged the civil war which brought about the intervention of the ECOMOG force, and who allegedly sponsored and bankrolled the RUF in Sierra Leone, was a candidate for the presidency, and groups of his supporters were moving through the streets wearing white T-shirts emblazoned with the slogan, 'You killed my mother, and you killed my father, but I'll vote for you'. That really got to Fred; he thought it was a perversion of a basic sense of justice: 'If you killed my mother and you killed my father, I'll kill you.'

When Fred found Hinga Norman, he was in the process of moving out of the ambassador's house, because he had to be where his people had access to him. He moved into a small house in the campus of the Ricks Institute, a distinguished college about 16 miles out of Monrovia that had been badly damaged and plundered during the country's civil war. The Institute was taken over by Nigerian troops of

ECOMOG who were stationed in Liberia. Hinga Norman's base was modest by any standard: a two-bedroom house; he and his wife and daughter had one room with mattresses on the floor; four women shared the other room, some men slept in an outer building.

At their first meeting together, Fred told Hinga Norman about his briefing from Tim Spicer: he was to work with the Chief, but for Sandline, and he was to advise Tim of Chief Norman's major plans in advance. The Chief was perfectly equable with that, and said that Tim Spicer had been of great service to his cause. Indeed, in the course of time, Sandline gave the Chief $25,000, of which $20,000 was spent on communications, and $5,000 on medicine and food.

The road ahead, however, for Hinga Norman was far from smooth. A new factor emerged which made life dangerous for him in Liberia: on 19 July Charles Taylor was elected the country's president. And true to his trade, it did not take him long to put out an assassination order on Hinga Norman.[15] However, so long as Hinga Norman was escorted by ECOMOG soldiers, he was safe. Working more openly, at head of state level, Charles Taylor also wrote to President Kabbah, objecting to the active presence of the former Deputy Minister of Defence of Sierra Leone in his country.

President Kabbah, still based in the government Guest House in Guinea, along with several of his ministers, formed a War Council in Exile. Its status was advisory, and its remit was to discuss ways and means of ending the war through dialogue with the AFRC . The British High Commissioner to Sierra Leone, Peter Penfold, was also now based there, demonstrating Britain's support for Kabbah. In addition, Britain provided funding of £150,000 to acquire and maintain an office in Conakry for the Sierra Leone government, and Peter Penfold arranged for equipment to be bought so that a radio station could operate for the government in exile.

> Dr Julius Spencer, a Sierra Leonean academic, flew from the States and he and two others set up this radio station in a tent at Lungi airport which we called Radio Democracy 98.1, and through that radio station broadcast to the people of Freetown, just to keep democracy alive.[16]

High Commissioner Penfold and others broadcast on that wave length, encouraging people to anticipate the return of democracy to their country. The international community had refused to recognize the AFRC junta; Kabbah was therefore still accorded some of the symbols associated with his status as a head of state.

What Kabbah was not, however, was a charismatic leader, who showed by actions and words that he was determined to remove the AFRC junta. He put his emphasis on negotiation with the AFRC/RUF junta, even although his earlier dialogue with the RUF at Abidjan turned out to be appeasement that produced disastrous results. Nor was Kabbah a leader who gave the impression of being in touch with his countrymen and women's plight: thousands of Sierra Leoneans had fled to Guinea;

they gathered and queued for help outside their country's embassy in Conakry, which was just across the way from the government Guest House where Kabbah was staying; not once in the ten months the junta were in power did Kabbah walk across the way to greet them or identify with them.[17]

In such a situation, where the Deputy Minister of Defence clearly demonstrated qualities that Kabbah lacked, power politics inevitably came into play among members and officials of the Sierra Leone government in exile. President Kabbah's advisers were concerned that the power base for dislodging the AFRC lay with his Deputy Minister of Defence and not with the President. Hinga Norman had quickly emerged as the man of action, the leader defending the restoration of democracy in his country through military action. And he had a lot of support. The Nigerian Chief of Staff of the ECOMOG forces in Liberia agreed with Hinga Norma: a united front of Nigerian ECOMOG troops plus the stiffening of Kamajors could defeat the AFRC/RUF.[18] But in a real sense, Kabbah's advisers' concerns were groundless, because Hinga Norman's aims were to reinstate President Kabbah; he was not positioning stepping stones towards that post for himself.

Nonetheless, Kabbah wanted to replace Norman as the head of the CDF, or at least limit his power by bringing in another co-ordinator for the CDF in the north of the country. So on 17 August, Kabbah summoned Chief Norman to Conakry. Kabbah gave his Deputy Minister of Defence an ultimatum, either to stay in Guinea and contribute to the War Council in Exile, or return to Sierra Leone, basing himself at ECOMOG-held Lungi airport along with Vice President Joe Demby. To Hinga Norman such a choice was unrealistic as a means of helping achieve the restoration of Kabbah's government: staying in Conakry as part of the War Council in Exile was futile – it was an advisory body that met to discuss ways of ending the war through dialogue with the AFRC, and he looked on it as a talking shop;[19] whereas moving into the Nigerian enclave at Lungi would simply mean an impotent presence on Sierra Leonean soil, unable to move out into the heartlands of the militias.

Hinga Norman, however, had to be seen to comply with his President's wishes, and after mulling it over he made a quick decision. Ever since he had established himself in Liberia, his trips to Conakry were infrequent and of short duration, and he rarely stayed in the same location more than once. He told Fred that it was rumored there were influential individuals in Guinea supportive in principle of the AFRC; he might find an unexpected problem at a road block, for example. So he varied where he stayed on these visits; on this occasion, he was hosted by Murdo Macleod, Fred's business partner. They discussed a way round the problem, and hatched a plan, which Hinga Norman later recounted to Fred.

Although there was a shortage of funds in Cape International's account, the ploy that Murdo came up with required some cash. Hinga Norman would agree to go Sierra Leone, and fly to Lungi on an ECOMOG flight; Murdo, a former RAF fighter pilot, would accompany him on the trip, chat to the pilot before they took off, establishing their shared professionalism; and then, after take off, when the pilot was setting his course for Lungi, Murdo would go up to the cockpit and bribe him to divert to Monrovia in Liberia. And for the bribe, he had a limit of $5,000. Everything worked as anticipated, but Murdo was shrewd enough not to lead with the figure of $5,000: he offered $3,000, and this was sufficient to satisfy the pilot. He diverted to Monrovia and they landed at Spriggs airfield. Chief Norman was back on Liberian soil, ready to carry on preparations for removing the AFRC in the only way that he thought would bring results.

He made several incursions with trusted followers across the border into Sierra Leone to meet militia representatives. He got the agreement of the heads of hunter groups to fight back to restore democracy and re-establish Kabbah in power. He set up an intelligence network, recruited men, established bases and set out recce patrols to various areas that were selected as the first targets, moving westwards from the Liberian border. Then there came a point when the hunter groups like the Kamajors could be brought together at an eastern base. On that occasion, Hinga Norman took Fred with him on a cross-border mission to a pre-arranged meeting.

I went with the Chief to the Sierra Leone border, crossed the Mano bridge, and that was when he introduced me to all the head men of the CDF: Tamaboros, Donsos, Kapras, Kamajors. And his words to them that day were, 'This is Fred, he is an ex-British army soldier. Fred is not a friend, Fred is a brother.' I was very well received, and after shaking hands with everyone present, sat down next to the Chief, and straight away, the meeting started.

Their plan was to build a Civil Defence Forces base in Sierra Leone, close to the Liberian border. They chose their spot, and over the course of a few days, they cleared the area and occupied it. They took over a house and made it into an office and a medical room. Next stage was the base for the men, but out of view from the Liberian side. Group locations were sited and sentry posts were prepared. Slightly deeper into the country, they cleared an area where a helicopter could land, without it being seen from the Liberian side. There they cached their heavy weapons and mortars. These were weapons that the Kamajors had captured from the RUF in the past, for as yet they had received no weapons from Sandline. The light weapons totalled about a hundred old, poor-quality to start with AK-47s. These they cannibalized into 87 working weapons. Fred loaded them, but he felt that in any professional army they would have been drilled and discarded as useless.

Based as they were in the east of the country, hunter militias could attack military posts in the area, control the Mano river bridge until the AFRC counterattacked, or they could set up roadblocks; but they lacked the logistics to carry a war against the bulk of the AFRC/RUF in Freetown: they had to have a large base situated to the west. Their first step in that direction came thanks to the intelligence network that Hinga Norman initiated. Further reconnaissance confirmed a site for what was to become know as Base Zero. It was in the swamp area of the wetlands, but high enough to establish accommodation for a large number of fighters. All approaches to it were recced, and security was sited out of view. Cut-offs were planned and personnel to man them were selected.

Hinga Norman knew what he wanted to achieve and he went about it with drive, energy and insight. His turning a deaf ear to his President's injunctions on where to base himself went unchallenged. Kabbah may have been accused of being naïve about irregular warfare, or ingenuous in his trust of rebels or mutineers, but he had the political nous to realize that he needed a man like Hinga Norman in his government to do what one else seemed capable of taking on. So he set up a method of keeping in touch with his Deputy Minister of Defence through a three-way telephone conference on set occasions, at 6am US Eastern Standard time, with the Rev Alfred SamForay, Secretary-General of SLAM-CDF, Hinga Norman and the President.[20]

These sessions were of mixed benefit to Hinga Norman: on the one hand he had his President's backing; on the other, Kabbah's lack of understanding of what could be achieved and within what timescale, produced tension. For example, the President advocated a Kamajor assault on Freetown within months of the coup, whereas, Hinga Norman believed that it required both a Sierra Leone militia and ECOMOG forces to oust the AFRC. He had discussions with ECOMOG's Chief of Staff in Liberia, General Aziz Mohamed, who agreed with him. For that to happen, there had to be the agreement of ECOWAS, and there also had to be the logistical support to achieve it.

The coup had taken place in May, and by October, Sandline had no personnel on the ground apart from Fred; and he was starting to find that there was a limit to his usefulness in the situation. Then, overnight, all that changed dramatically when he met a pilot friend from EO days.

Part III

Chapter Six

Bokkie

O, for a horse with wings!

William Shakespeare, *Cymbeline*

Enter, flared up at fast speed, tail just off the ground, a warhorse of an Mi-17 called Bokkie. In the annals of warfare, when man's dependence on animal or machine has later been eulogized in verse or on film (from the gallant steed Roland, carrying good news for Aix, to the WWII bomber Memphis Belle) the helicopter Bokkie deserves to be ranked. Bokkie, the sole aircraft ferrying food, matériel and personnel to Sierra Leone's battle zone, responded to all that was asked of it, and performed far beyond its design specifications.

Bokkie was flown to Sierra Leone in 1995 by Executive Outcomes; it got its name – the affectionate diminutive of springbok – from EO pilot, Christoffel (Chris) Louw, who painted it on the fuselage. The helicopter remained at Lungi airport after Executive Outcomes departed the country, was guarded by ECOMOG after the coup, and was taken over by Sandline and leased to Roger Crooks (manager of the Mammy Yoko hotel and entrepreneur with several business interests) for a while until it was flown to Monrovia, Liberia by an outstanding South African pilot who had served in EO, Johann (Juba) Joubert. And here, from October onwards it was to provide a vital air bridge from the ECOMOG base at Monrovia to the force's main base at Lungi, its subsidiary enclaves and Base Zero of the CDF.

Successful though ECOMOG's military intervention had been in Liberia, it required western countries to provide the necessary logistics. Although the constituent countries that comprised the force provided their own arms, ammunition and transport, it was the US State Department that contracted the private company, Pacific Architects and Engineers (PAE), to provide air logistical support for the force's operations in Liberia.[1] Some of PAE's personnel were ex-US Special Forces.

ECOMOG's presence in Sierra Leone had originally been as support and a bulwark for the country's military against the possibility of a resurgent RUF, so its presence had been that of a friendly ally. But now, of course, all that had changed with the military coup: to the AFRC it was a hostile, foreign force. Yet to the Sierra Leone government in exile it was essential to sustain the force in the country; to

Nigeria it was crucial that these bases remain so they could become possible launch pads for military action against the junta. Therefore, the ECOMOG battalion and the bases of its CDF allies had to be kept maintained, resupplied and reinforced; and Juba Incorporated was contracted to do it.

Thus Bokkie came back into service with a private military company, and turned out to be not only a springbok but a true warhorse. Its new international crew of three had all served with Executive Outcomes: a South African pilot, Juba Joubert , an Ethiopian engineer, Sendaba Meri and a Fijian ex SAS loadmaster and gunner. As far as Fred was concerned, his change of role from ground warfare to aerial support was made effortlessly; he had been in a unit that was, after all, called the Special Air Service, whose capabilities since the Second World War included, 'infiltration ... by land, sea or air according to circumstances and training in all methods will be carried out.'[2]

Juba had joined the South African Air Force in 1979 for 10 years and in that time he mainly flew helicopters operationally during the conflicts in and around South Africa and then during the South West Africa/Angolan war. For the last part of his time in the SAAF he did an instructor course and gave instruction on fixed winged aircraft. After that he joined the Bophuthatswana Air Force and was an instructor on helicopters and fixed wing aircraft before joining Executive Outcomes in 1993. So by the time he was with the Air Wing of Executive Outcomes he was a very experienced pilot. After he left Sierra Leone in December 1996, he gained more experience, flying in some conflict countries across the world until just after the 25 May coup in Sierra Leone, when he was flown in by a private consortium to help with the evacuation of mining and security personnel. However, for political reasons it fell through. He then was asked by Rodger Crooks to fly Bokkie from Lungi to Monrovia to carry out contract work for the UN in connection with the presidential elections. This too failed to materialize.

Fred had first met him in Freetown when he joined EO. They got on well from the outset, and Juba made him feel at home with the group. When Fred had some free time between EO operations, Juba used to take him on flights to Kono, or wherever, tree-hopping and rolling as they flew over or near any villages – a practice that was developed fighting wars in southern Africa. The engineer, Sendaba, was very well qualified: he had been an officer in the Ethiopian Air Force, and had been trained in Russia and was a fluent Russian speaker. He joined EO as an engineer after Fred began with the company. All three bonded together, and over time they all developed great affection for Bokkie.

As Bokkie had been on the ground at Lungi since about February, Juba and Sendaba had to get it serviceable for contract work; and this was at a time when ECOMOG had urgent need of a helicopter to support them in the Sierra Leone conflict. None of the other operators in Monrovia was prepared to take on the job due to its dangerous nature. So Juba Inc was accepted, and contracted with ECOMOG on the 8th October 1997.

If there was any lingering question mark at ECOMOG HQ in Monrovia about the degree of commitment that might be expected of the three 'civilian' contractors, it was obliterated at a stroke with their first important mission. On the afternoon of 11 October, the HQ operations officer came rushing into the building which housed stores for transportation and asked Juba if they could fly an emergency resupply of ammunition to an ECOMOG Company at Kenema, which, logistically, had been cut off for three months, and evacuate three wounded soldiers. There had been a sustained attack on the post that had gone on for two days. If the troops were not resupplied with ammunition, the position could possibly fall that very evening when the enemy attacked again. The attackers probably knew from the defenders' response that ammunition must be short all round, so they would press home their assault. Juba asked the Ops officer to leave them to discuss the mission first and he would come back to him shortly with a yes or no.

After the Ops officer had gone, Juba asked Sendaba what he thought. Sendaba smiled, and said that it was up to Juba, the pilot, to make the decision. Juba put the question to Fred, who said, 'Juba, you're the pilot. If you're happy with it, let us do it, for those guys need our help.' Juba looked at them, paused, reflected a moment, and said that if they were to carry out the operation successfully, they would have written their names, and Bokkie's, into the history of the conflict, and gained the thanks of the ECOMOG headshed (headquarters). There was no demur. So he asked Sendaba to get Bokkie ready, and Fred to supervise the loading of the ammunition, while he went for his brief.

He was not away long. And when he, in turn, — was briefing them, all three felt the excitement and the apprehension of flying into the unknown. The ECOMOG troops were surrounded; to make matters worse, their base, a Lebanese school (for children of the Lebanese community working in the diamond industry) was overlooked by high ground. It would be very risky, especially if the enemy had heavy weapons on the hillside, so it was up to Fred to try and locate enemy positions and make them keep their heads down while they made their run in. Fred, of course, needed more than his AK-47 for helicopter duties, and he had been issued with a General Purpose Machine Gun (GPMG), a weapon he was familiar with from SAS days. Juba explained that they would make only one pass over the site to select the best spot on which to put down. He used a telling image to describe the awareness of being under small arms fire: 'You'll know you're being shot at when you hear the typewriter keys starting to tap outside.'

They got airborne from Roberts International airport, Monrovia. It was still during the rainy season, but the weather did not look like a real problem initially and the routing to target was 55 minutes, which gave them an estimated time of arrival over target of 16.00 hours local time — as arranged with the base at Kenema. Bokkie got airborne at maximum, all-up weight, due to the heavy load, and after about 20 minutes dark clouds became visible en route, pushing in from the west. This forced them to go further north to see if they could fly around it, but at 40 minutes into their flight, Juba realized it was a serious squall reaching into Guinea. He therefore decided to return to ECOMOG HQ, Monrovia and wait to see if they could get through the next day. After landing, when Juba went to Operations to debrief on the mission, he was informed that the Kenema base had been attacked by junta forces at exactly 16.00 hours. So it was clear that there had been an information leak. What was not clear, however, was where and how it was done, but Juba decided that the time over target the following day would only be revealed just prior to take-off, to cut the time for enemy reaction, if the message were intercepted.

Next day the weather was fine, and their flight overland was uneventful. The count down to the target was calmly and meticulously done, and they made their sweep over the location. Fred was keyed up, scanning the hillside for enemy positions; but in the interim, the junta forces seem to have lain back, relaxing, biding their time before their next assault, and so were taken by surprise. But the aircrew could also see no sign of the ECOMOG troops. From the air the site looked like a scene out of a Western: a smoking canvas shelter, burnt out buildings and no sign of life. However, when Juba wheeled Bokkie round at the back of the school, Fred saw figures in green waving, and Juba saw them at the same time. Swiftly Juba selected where he would bring Bokkie down, and in they went, landing facing down hill, rotor blades barely clearing the ground. Touch down was expertly judged. The next moment all hell broke loose. Small arms fire started, followed by a big bang that was probably a 105mm canon. It was not clear who was shooting, where they were shooting from, and what they were shooting at. But Juba decided he was not going to get airborne before the cargo had been offloaded.

Fred jumped down, opened the clam-like back door, climbed back in and started dragging the boxes of their 3.5 ton load of ammunition, food and medical supplies to the door. At first there was confusion with a lot of shooting and some troops jumped onboard, thinking they were getting evacuated. Then, though, soldiers were detailed to unload and ferry the ammunition from the helicopter; they were tense and excited when they ran up. Fred jumped down, heaving the ammunition boxes on to the earth. Next he climbed back inside and received the three casualties; then he sprang down again and closed the back door, only to find that the Nigerians had unloaded his GPMG. He had to leap down once more, pick up his weapon, then back into the helicopter, and they took off. The enemy gunners – and it was now clear who was firing – were having a golden opportunity and took full advantage of it. As Bokkie rose into the air, Fred raked their firing points with his GPMG; Juba flew Bokkie out of the battle zone, skilfully and tactically, since he was familiar with the area from his EO days.

Back at ECOMOG HQ Monrovia, news had already been radioed to them that the mission was successful; and when Bokkie landed, senior officers came out to congratulate the aircrew. By that afternoon's work, they had proved themselves to the ECOMOG hierarchy, just as Juba had anticipated. However, there had been one tragic element to the operation that the crew only then learned about. On the sloping ground where Juba put Bokkie down, during the scramble of unloading and ferrying, one of the soldiers carrying a box of ammunition, tense because they were in the enemy's field of fire, lost concentration on his immediate environment and had walked into the rear tail rotor and died instantly. The aircrew were not aware of it when they were under fire. But when Sendaba inspected the rear rotor, he confirmed that the tail rotor blade tips were damaged. Juba tried to get some tips from the CIS (a Russian company) crews but they were not suitable for Bokkie's blades. ECOMOG engineers, however, quite swiftly, managed to provide alternative rotor blade tips out of ammunition boxes; the crew fitted them, and test-flew the helicopter. Bokkie was back in service.

The net result of that operation was that senior officers knew that this crew could be relied on to fly anywhere, whenever they were needed. And so on 17 October, Lt Col S A Folorunsho, at HQ Monrovia, signed Fred's authorization, certifying that he was working with ECOMOG as helicopter crew, and requested all relevant individuals to co-operate with him.[3]

Requests and requirements multiplied as the conflict on the ground continued: conflict between the AFRC junta and ECOMOG troops, and between junta forces and Kamajors. The Juba Incorporated team operated out of Monrovia along with the other private company, PAE, which provided air logistics for ECOMOG – but not into Sierra Leone. Having already been there for a year, PAE with two Mi-8 MTVs and an Mi-26, had a more favourable site. Bokkie was parked in an open space adjacent to the ECOMOG HQ. This was where all the stores for transportation were loaded. About 500 metres away was the Monrovia Power station; power lines radiated out from it; and the open space where Bokkie stood was, in fact, within the compound of the power station. Fifty metres away in one direction the compound's perimeter wall faced them; about sixty metres in the other direction a power line cut across their flight path. The problem for Juba, in this confined location, was to get enough lift, by using the helicopter's in-ground effect, to clear these obstacles.

Finding the optimum method and maximum payload was a case of trial and near error. Once or twice they were close to writing off Bokkie, but Juba's experience and skill came into play. The pattern they developed was: ensure they had as little of the helicopter's fuel in the tank as possible; load up with the maximum payload they could carry to clear the obstacles; fly the 2 kilometres to Spriggs airfield; fill up with fuel, and take on more of a cargo load; and then, using the runway to gain transition while still on the ground, they took off like a fixed wing aircraft. They learned that 13 drums of fuel were the maximum they could load at the ECOMOG store and get clear of the compound. On a few occasions, the helicopter's payload was so heavy, and beyond the aircraft's limits, that Juba had to back up as far as possible, select emergency power on the augmentation levers and fly the aircraft forward using maximum power, building up as much airspeed as possible just above the ground. Take off was a risky venture. As Bokkie would hit transition speed and lose height, Juba would level her platform, then use the struts of the helicopter to bounce the aircraft off all 3 wheels, increasing the pressure on the ground cushion, and spring-boarding up at the last moment to get as much upward force as possible to gain height and clear the power line that stretched across their flight path.

During the initial phase, Bokkie's air compressor for the brakes seized and the other two replacement compressors only lasted one mission and also failed; so Juba, therefore, decided to fly without wheel brakes and only use aerodynamic braking on the ground. Another time, with a load for ECOMOG as well as ammunition, medicine and rice for the CDF, they found that they had taken on too much at Spriggs airfield, and were unable to fly normally at low speed. Experience taught the pilot what to do: he turned back, and flared up, coming in low and fast, pulling the nose up at the last minute, using the rotor disc as a wind-milling airbrake to slow the aircraft, and slammed it onto the ground before they fell out of the sky – a very skilled manoeuvre. Juba really did know what he was doing. After offloading a few bags of rice they were airborne again.

Juba's reason for flying so heavily loaded was as a result of the limitation of routes into Sierra Leone and the fact that Charles Taylor's troops as well as the RUF and AFRC were all intent on shooting down Bokkie. They had to change routes all the time in order not to set a pattern and be trapped. When anti-aircraft guns were moved into place between Liberia and Sierra Leone by the Liberian forces, Juba again changed routes and flew over the ocean, not closer than 10 kilometres and no higher than 15 metres above the water.

> At first I was flying at 5 metres above the water, but two dolphin jumped out of the sea next to the helicopter, almost as high as the rotor head; and when these two hit the water, another two jumped out close to the cockpit but missing the main rotors. I told the others I would fly a bit higher because it would be difficult for search and rescue to find us if we had a dolphin strike. After this incident a marlin sailfish jumped out of the water, and a whale and her calf surfaced just to see what was the strange noise they heard.[4]

The air waves too became important as a source of hope and encouragement for people in Sierra Leone. Working from his hotel room in Conakry, Peter Penfold managed to get the British government's approval to receive funds from the Department for International Development (DFID) to buy a radio transmitter. Bokkie was used to transport it to a masthead at Lungi.

> We flew the equipment, Juba and myself and set it in position. Juba said to me to lie out and look down and tell him left, right, forward or back. There were two guys waiting on the top of this tower. And it was put there, spot on.

Radio Democracy, 98.1, as it was called, became a symbol of hope for a lot of people. Its purpose was, said Peter Penfold, 'Just to keep democracy alive.'

From my hotel room in Conakry, I would phone Julius Spencer, who was in this tent with his radio set and one of these great mobiles; and I would talk to him from my mobile and he would put it to the microphone, and I would talk to the people of Sierra Leone, or mainly Freetown, from Conakry. And yeah, I'd be saying, 'Don't lose hope. We are still committed to getting rid of these terrible people. Don't worry, we know things are terrible for you.' And I'd talk to them in the early hours of the morning or whenever. The people in Freetown put their radios under their pillows, because if anybody was found listening to radio 98.1, they were killed. So they would go to bed with the radio under their pillows.[5]

While the ferrying of food and fuel to the troops and militia was going on, the international community took supportive measures to back Kabbah's democratically elected government. President Kabbah went to New York and addressed the United Nations General Assembly. And on 8 October, the UN Security Council voted unanimously to adopt a British–sponsored resolution imposing sanctions against Sierra Leone's military government; the sanctions included a ban on the sale of arms and military equipment to the junta.[6] This indeed is how UN Resolution 1132 was subsequently modified: an embargo on 'the sale and supply of arms and related matériel of all types to Sierra Leone other than to the government of Sierra Leone through named points of entry.'[7]

In the West African theatre, the Economic Council of West African States (ECOWAS) began negotiations in Conakry with representatives of the AFRC in an endeavour to restore the democratic government to Sierra Leone. That government was not a party to the negotiations, but it had observer status. The talks took place in the absence of President Kabbah who was attending the Commonwealth Conference in Edinburgh. The bargaining at Conakry produced a formula which promised the return of Kabbah to power, and an expectation that the RUF leader, Foday Sankoh, would be released from house arrest in Nigeria and 'return to his country to make his contribution to the peace process.'[8] But whether the AFRC/RUF were serious about restoring a democratic government, or whether it was a charade to gain immunity for the coup leaders and reinstate the RUF as a power in the land was in question. Within days, fighting was taking place in the country, and a spokesman for Kabbah's government claimed that President Charles Taylor of Liberia was trying to undermine the agreement, and that the AFRC was importing truck loads of arms from that country. Certainly Kabbah, on his return home, expressed some reservations about elements of the agreement, which suggests that he had learned something from his experience of negotiating with the RUF a year earlier. Thus far at least though, he seemed to pin his hopes on a negotiated settlement.

By contrast, the road that Hinga Norman took, as the only way to restore Kabbah's government, was hard and dangerous. In this brief note he wrote to Fred, requesting items to be air-lifted to him, Hinga Norman gives a vignette of the range of responsibilities he took on himself: a resistance leader in the bush with day to day concerns for cooking utensils; requirements for fuel; and specifications of weapons and ammunition. But he was also a figurehead with a secretary, channelling information to him from a communications network. It is simply addressed, 'To Mr Fred Marafono, with kind appreciation.'

November 8, 1997

Dear Fred

Kindly collect from Maj Del Yakuku few items including the ones we left behind the day of our departure:

1 drum of engine oil and 5 cartons of cartridges. In addition we have requested for AK grenades and 8 drums of petrol and diesel (4 each).

We mistakenly dropped a bag of mine at Gendema on our way on Wednesday. I will appreciate were you to kindly pick up that bag along with 2 sets of cooking pots from Gendema (SL – Lib) border whenever you have a chance to fly this way again. Please liaise with my secretary, Mr Zorokon, who will contact Mr Harding at the border to have the items ready whenever you fly them.

Also contact Mrs Norman through Mr Zorokon for messages and dispatches.

Kind regards
(signed) Sam H Norman
Hon. Sam Norman[9]

Base Zero was the destination for Hinga Norma's requests. It was situated in a wooded area surrounded by swamplands not far from the sea, in the Chiefdom of Bonthe, about forty-five minutes flying time from the Liberian border. The build-up of CDF militiamen there had been concentrated into a two-day slot in Bokkie's schedule. Of course, the CDF had not been airlifted from Spriggs, but from the clearing in the bush on the Sierra Leone side of the border that they had established as their eastern base in September. The area that had been made into a landing strip for a helicopter had a road leading into it. And that road helped the helicopter gain transition to normal flight when it was heavily loaded. Optimum capacity for personnel with packs that the Mi-17 can comfortably cope with is said to be about thirty-two. Fred organized the embarking of the militiamen for Base Zero.

Putting up the fingers of my hands, that's the number of men; and I lined them up, 20, 25 or 30, and I would say to whatever number. 'You come with me.' And I lined them up with their loads, light loads. So when we came to the sixth flight – the last flight – when they found out that it was the last flight to the war front, and that Chief Norman was at the war front! I nearly hit the Sierra Leoneans: I plucked them off from here, I plucked them off from there; they were even hanging on from the portholes. They wanted to go to the front; it was quite an incredible sight. When we took off we went up with 73 initially and Juba kept Bokkie in the hover for 5 seconds, then he landed back and told me to offload 5 passengers as we were too heavy. The second time we got airborne with 68 people on board! 68 people on board, 65 of them and 3 of us. I said to Juba, 'That was heavy.' He said, 'Like fuck, it was heavy.' I said, 'Juba why didn't you land?' He said, 'It's out of a confined area and once you start to move up and forward, I know when Bokkie is willing or not to carry the weight. If I was to try to land back, we would have fallen from the sky, we haven't got the power to overcome the momentum, so I would rather use it to our advantage.'

The landing at base Zero was going to be interesting, due to their brakes not working; and it was also a confined space with high trees upwind. Juba planned to break the speed in the turn from downwind to final approach, and then clear the trees with forward speed above transition speed to get into ground effect with the extra lift still available to help stop their rate of descent in the confined area. Once into the in-ground effect, his idea was to get Bokkie on the ground and pull the nose up to maximum without putting the tail rotor into the ground. There was a tail rotor skid that stopped the pilot from doing that on hard surfaces, but over the rainy period the soil was soft and the skid could plough the surface. With all the landings already done that day into the same landing zone, dust also became a consideration.

I told Fred that when we touched the ground with the main wheels, he must jump out and put the wheel chock in to help us stop such a heavy load. Fred jumped out as planned, but because of the dust he did not realize that the nose was so high above the ground and that the speed was still quite high. His feet and body almost simultaneously hit the ground, and he realized survival was now important, because there was a big wheel on its way and 13 tons of helicopter above it. He rolled to the side out of the wheel's way when it passed in the dust, and he hoped it would stop before it hit the trees. I kept the nose high, hoping to stop in time; because I realized the chock did not do what it was supposed to do, and so now the aerodynamic breaking was the only option.[10]

Once the helicopter stopped, Juba dropped the nose, and when the dust settled, Bokkie's blades were about 2 metres away from a massive tree's trunk and in its shade. After shutting down, there was a clear mark on the ground where the tail rotor skid dragged on the ground and broke in places.

Hinga Norman anticipated a large consignment of arms from Sandline; the weapons and ammunition that the CDF had, thus far, were either captured from the RUF or a token distribution from ECOMOG. But until they received a weapon supply, Hinga Norman saw to it that that training continued intensively. Bokkie's schedule for a CDF delivery of food and medicine often called for an early drop off at Base Zero before going on to Lungi. Fred recalls a frequent sight.

In the morning, it might be 7am or 7.30 am, we'd be landing with food; and the Chief was in PT shorts, and training with the guys coming up. And there he was – the leader of this group. And the training was quite incredible; and later on they were to prove it. Weapons were to be given to them to fight and take over all the AFRC positions, and kick them out from up-country. But unfortunately the weapons never reached them.

The AFRC and the RUF, on the other hand, despite the UN arms embargo on them, seemed to be getting supplied overland from Liberia, as well as from the sea – as Fred and Juba once saw for themselves.

On one of their supply flights, they spotted a vessel close to shore off Sulima bay. And on the beach about ten metres from the water's edge they saw, what they knew from their years of combat experience to be, shallow, green ammunition boxes of varying sizes in the process of being taken inland by a number of men, who, when the helicopter flew overhead, made a sprint for the cover of the vegetation about twenty to thirty metres away. On their return to Monrovia, Juba contacted the ECOMOG Chief Air Officer (CAO), Group Captain Tijjani Easterbrook, and reported the landing. The CAO ordered an Alpha Jet to be scrambled; the ship was intercepted and strafed.

In the sequel, the CAE called Juba and Fred to his office to meet the daughter of the ship's owner, who was a Ghanaian businesswoman.[11] The daughter remonstrated that they had had ECOMOG authorization for the ship to be in those waters, that her mother nearly had a heart attack when she heard it had been fired on, and she claimed that it had been unloading fish for the local people. Which perhaps goes to show that entrepreneurial flair, often said to be inspired by thinking outside the box, was on this occasion thinking inside the box, utilizing ammunition boxes instead of fish crates as a novel method of bringing a catch ashore. But what about the men on the beach running for cover? Perhaps just simple people's superstition about a hovering helicopter. And as for the unorthodox landing of fish on the sands instead of at Sulima harbour, well an entrepreneur might admit to the fiscal peccadillo of avoiding paying harbour dues. However, Gp Capt Easterbrook pointed out to the daughter that there was an embargo on shipping activities in the area, and directed her to the Chief Naval Officer (CNO) to sort things out.[12] A few days later he got a note from the CNO saying that the owner of the vessel – not the daughter – was in his office. Gp Capt Easterbrook slipped into his colleague's office as the meeting was in progress, without introducing himself, and listened in. The drift of the owner's complaint was that she knew nothing of an embargo, and had now lost so much money she would never recover her investment. Subsequent events went from bad to worse for her investment; so much so that the owner might even have concluded that ECOMOG was intent on thwarting honest business endeavour, for on 8 December, 'A Nigerian warship seized two fishing vessels owned by a Ghanaian businesswoman operating in Freetown. "The vessels were escorted to the ECOMOG headquarters in Monrovia."'[13]

But arming the legitimate government of Sierra Leone was also underway. It was now December, and in Conakry, at one of his regular meetings with Peter Penfold, President Kabbah told him that he had been approached by Sandline who were prepared to train and equip a number of his still loyal forces that were at Lungi. What would the British High Commissioner advise? Peter Penfold looked over the draft contract, and told Kabbah that the decision was his to make: on the one hand, Sandline seemed to be an off-shoot of Executive Outcomes, the company that had a very high reputation in Sierra Leone; but on the other hand, he told Kabbah that he had picked up in diplomatic circles that President Mandela of South Africa had adopted a hostile attitude to the company – this was a factor to bear in mind if Kabbah wished to keep good relations with other African leaders.[14]

Shortly afterwards, Peter Penfold went on leave to the UK, where he was contacted by Tim Spicer of Sandline who explained that Kabbah had phoned him and requested that he brief the British High Commissioner. The two met for lunch and Tim Spicer outlined more of his proposal. This led to another meeting among a series that Tim Spicer was having with Foreign Office officials ; and one advantage of these meetings for Peter Penfold was that he could find out what the ECOMOG forces were planning, since Sandline was flying into Lungi airport.[15] Nigeria was the key player in ECOMOG, yet the irony of Nigeria's strong support for restoring Kabbah's government to power was that Nigeria itself was not a democracy; there was a coolness at official level – perhaps even a ban – in the UK about its military talking to the Nigerian military. So, thanks to Tim Spicer's knowledge from his people on the ground, Peter Penfold was getting some insight into the security situation in Sierra Leone, and what Nigeria, in particular, was intending.

In the sub-region, that intention was pointing to the military option. Certainly it was not Nigeria's decision alone, but Nigeria held the chairmanship of ECOWAS and was the prime mover. The Task Force Commander in Sierra Leone was the Nigerian, Colonel Maxwell Khobe. He announced that a build up of troops would be flown in from Liberia. This was said to be in response to increased attacks on the force by the junta. On the ground, the Kamajors were increasingly harassing the junta in the south and south east of the country. A co-ordinating committee of ECOMOG and CDF oversaw the Kamajor activities. In December, Hinga Norman, in a BBC interview, referred to a set of actions, authorized by the Government in exile, code named Black December, where Kamajors made concerted attacks on the junta's supply lines. And in a symbolic gesture that took place on Sierra Leone soil, on 21 December President Kabbah flew to Lungi airport and met Hinga Norman and Vice President Joe Demby. News of the meeting was broadcast to the Sierra Leone people on the government's radio station, Radio Democracy 98.1 at Lungi, a reassurance that the time would come when the junta would no longer be in power.

Meanwhile, the entire burden of keeping the Task Force and Base Zero supplied was carried by Bokkie. Men and machine were stretched to the limit each day. And each long day began about 5am, the helicopter having been loaded the night before;

they took off around 6am, and flew to Sierra Leone, offloaded, distributed, loaded up – sometimes they took personnel going on rotation, sometimes, acting as medivac, they had a steady trickle of wounded from continuing skirmishes with junta forces – then took off and flew back to Monrovia. They went through this sequence three times in the long day. Fred noted the details of each flight in his diary, and at the end of the day Juba used these notes to write up his flying log book.

Most of their route was over water, but as the whole project was being done on a shoestring they did not even have life jackets. As they approached the Sierra Leone coastline, the adrenaline really started to flow: they could be subject to ground and air attack. The junta had one Mi-17 helicopter and one Mi-24 gunship; Fred's concern was that his GPMG was no match for the Mi-24. The gunship's four-barrelled Gatling guns could fire 12.7 mm shells at the rate of 5,000 rounds per minute, and it was also equipped with four rocket pods. On the ground, the junta had access to the Sierra Leonean army's arsenal of weaponry, and the RUF component of the People's Army was rumoured to have a Surface to Air Missile (SAM) but apparently they had not been trained in its use. Juba's final approach to Lungi was made at high speed and at a very low level so as not to give the army gunners a chance. He called the technique, 'mowing the lawn.'

On a fuel run Bokkie became a potential flying bomb. They loaded up with 13 drums of fuel at the ECOMOG store – the maximum they could take to clear the compound –, refuelled at Spriggs airfield, then took on board another two drums of fuel as cargo.

One of the most dangerous things was the drums splitting and the fuel leaking. And when we loaded the fuel, I put the petrol in the centre and then the oil and diesel on the outside, in case they shot at me! But if it was a shot from underneath! And one time, one of these petrol drums, filled to the top, split because of the vibration; and the smell was very strong and there was a pool of petrol on the floor behind the cockpit. And there's the door and there's me sitting with my gun and the engineer and there's nobody else. I thought to myself, suppose there's a bare electric wire and a spark. Puff! But then you wouldn't feel it.

This was a possibility they accepted and had lived with since a flight in the early days, when after leaving Roberts International for Lungi airport with a full load of fuel, they crossed the Mano river into Sierra Leone, and Juba saw a open clearing on the Sierra Leone side of the river into which a man came running out of the bush firing an AK-47 at them. While Juba was taking evasive action, he could see the whites of the gunman's eyes – the man was that close. Initially everyone who had something to shoot with, friend or foe, shot at the helicopter until the word was put out to own forces not to shoot at their own helicopter.[16]

During the last part of the final flight back to Monrovia at the end of the day, with the fuel gauge reading low, Juba would say, 'Sendaba, turn off the fuel gauge.' The craft would fly a little while, and then Juba would give the thumbs up to Sendaba who would turn the fuel gauge on again for Juba to recalculate fuel for distance left. Nursing Bokkie in this fashion, triggered off the warning message recorded in a woman's voice in Russian. They called the voice Natasha; and over the headset she warned the crew they were running low in fuel. First the voice came on intermittently, but then Natasha's nagging became constant in the earphones, as they strained their eyes looking for the spot at Mamba Point that would come up as Monrovia, wondering if they had enough fuel to make it. When they landed, Sendaba would check over the helicopter a last time while Juba wrote up his flying log book and Fred opened the inefficient cool box, and they would crack a couple of beers.

Sendaba was a dedicated professional. He treated Bokkie with infinite care and patience. Once, on a flight to Base Zero, as they were touching down, an engine warning light alerted him to a partially blocked filter. He reckoned that he could effect some remedial work to get them back to Monrovia. So for three hours, beneath a blazing sun at Base Zero, Sendaba laboured under great difficulty because he was suffering from malaria. Fred and Juba helped him; they sat with pieces of fine wire painstakingly clearing out blades of grass and debris from the filter, but the bulk of the work was Sendaba's; and they could see he was weak and that he was struggling. But he succeeded with the repair, and they took off for Monrovia.

For this arduous, dangerous work that no other aircrew was undertaking they were certainly not receiving a king's ransom: Juba was paid by the hour, while Sendaba and Fred earned $1,500 per month. Killing them became a priority for the junta leaders, because they were obviously the supply line for the Task Force. For their part, ECOMOG officers were fulsome in their praise of the trio, 'They're unbelievable, unkillable,' said a Nigerian major.[17]

Not that they themselves thought so – quite the opposite. Daily exposure to the risk of death heightened the kind of awareness that humdrum work might not have inspired: a sense of the mystery behind creation.

In the silent moments we were in the air, as the sun rises from the horizon – each to his own God. Juba can vouch for this because we often discussed it.

Juba put it this way,

I'm not a churchman, but the spirit world in WAWA was revealed to me. There is only one Creator and that is the way we are still alive.[18]

The term that Juba used, WAWA, means West Africa Wins Again, and it has many facets to it. Some of them played a part in the groups that made up the CDF. Fred observed the CDF training at Base Zero, and he suggested to Hinga Norman that it might be an idea to invite the ECOMOG Task Force Commander to see the CDF for himself.

I said to the Chief, 'Chief why don't you invite Col Khobe to see the training?' And he asked Col Khobe and he came down – we picked him up and brought him to the camp. All the CDF were out there, and the colonel with his entourage. And after the Chief introduced Col Khobe and his entourage, all the men of the CDF, welcomed him. Then they did a demonstration. And the demonstration was to get Khobe's bodyguard to shoot at a chicken that was hanging on a piece of wood about fifteen metres away. And the bodyguard, when he was told to shoot the chicken, thought it was a joke. But the Chief said to him, 'You can use your weapon.' And he took aim and fired and missed the chicken. He couldn't believe it, and then he took aim and fired again and didn't hit it. Then he knelt down fired, and never hit it. He emptied the whole magazine and never hit the chicken. And then they brought the chicken and gave it to him, and they said you can take it as a souvenir. The chief Kamajor, the chief initiator, stepped in front and he said, 'Do you want to shoot at me?' Khobe would have none of it. At the time we didn't realize why, because from that moment on it was the turning point, I believe, because if weapons were to get to these people – they have this belief that they are invincible. Their belief was that they would take over Freetown without anything.

Whatever the reason for the bodyguard consistently missing the target with his own weapon (there were stories later about initiates to the Kamajors being fired at with doctored ammunition and having survived, convinced it was by some miraculous power, they believed themselves to be invulnerable) this demonstration begs questions. Juba's take on this sort of thing is interesting.

They have many different beliefs, and especially when you look at all the Ju–Ju activities in these countries. It is mind boggling to see what they are capable of, by tapping into the spirit world. Power and survival are important to them at any cost.[19]

And what also needs to be brought into the equation is the contrast – among fellow countrymen – between, on the one hand, the fiercely loyal militiamen, whose efforts were focused on restoring democratic government to a centre of power that would probably always be remote from them, and on the other, the mindless killers and rapists who, in large part, comprised the AFRC/RUF People's Army. Well, it appears that the leadership brilliance of Hinga Norman lay partly in his tapping into the societies of pre-existing warrior/hunter cults with their rituals of rights of passage, testing, oaths and initiation, and imbuing them with a common aim to fight and restore the democratic government.

However potently belief fuelled their determination to bring that government back into power, the CDF needed the military muscle of the sub-region; and maintaining and building up the fibres of the ECOWAS arm meant unremitting toil for Bokkie's aircrew. They worked all Christmas Day and Boxing Day, but 27 December was completely free. On 30 December, they made their last flight of the year, taking fuel to Lungi and Kossoh, and then they flew on to Base Zero. In his diary, in case he was compromised or it fell into other hands, Fred used a code to write up certain names and places: 'the junction' was Base Zero; 'friend' or 'the old man' stood for Hinga Norman; and 'presents' was the code for AK-47 shorts (rounds of ammunition). So having off-loaded ammunition, they picked up 'friend' from Base Zero and flew him to Monrovia to have discussions with ECOMOG commanders.

On the evening of the following day, Juba, Fred and Sendaba went to the Ricks Institute, where Hinga Norman's family had been staying, and had a glass of beer with him and his wife and daughter. On 1 January, Fred lazed on the beach in the morning then joined Chief Norman, and they toasted the New Year. And well they might, for this was the lull before the storm.

Word had been put about, probably at clerical support level in ECOMOG HQ, that Hinga Norman, Sierra Leone's Deputy Defence Minister in exile — branded persona non grata by President Charles Taylor – was in Monrovia. After these two days, secure in the Ricks Institute, on 2 January, Hinga Norman was driven to the ECOMOG HQ where he and four of his headshed boarded Bokkie and were flown first to Spriggs airfield for refuelling. The airfield was guarded by the ECOMOG forces, but the Liberian authorities had a locus there for civil traffic. As Bokkie was being refuelled, a number of Charles Taylor's security men appeared, and one of them approached the helicopter. In his brief diary note later, Fred referred to them as 'goons who tried to become big guys but lost nerve and failed miserably.' What happened was the head goon stepped forward and tried to board the craft, saying he wanted to inspect it. Fred told him that he had no business with their flight; but he tried to call Fred's bluff. At this, Fred called to an ECOMOG soldier and told him to escort the goon out, and shoot him if he refused. There was no resistance. In his diary Fred simply recorded that when he got back into the helicopter, 'the old man smiled.' But the Liberian security service's attempt to get close to Hinga Norman did not come about by chance, and the likeliest source for tipping them off was local support staff.

Fred's alertness to danger for Hinga Norman from Charles Taylor's security service was activated earlier by related incidents. Playing power politics, and having failed to stymie Hinga Norman by confining him to Guinea or Lungi, President Kabbah tried to neutralize him by looking for another national CDF co-ordinator, but this came to nothing, so he tried to install a co-ordinator of the CDF for the north of the country, and thereby limit Hinga Norman's influence. The man the president chose for northern co-ordinator was S Dumbuya. Shortly after, Dumbuya turned up in Liberia at a time when Hinga Norman was making a stop-over at the Ricks Institute. The hotel that Dumbuya booked into in Monrovia was the Palm Hotel, where both Juba and Sendaba were staying. By chance he was booked into a room on the third floor, next to Juba's room. And it was in the hotel that Fred first met him.

On one of my visits to Juba, I saw this guy dressed in fine traditional African dress and he introduced himself as Col. Dumbuya. He came as an envoy from President Kabbah. He told me that he trained some of the Liberian Army when Siaka Steven was in power. But the curious thing was that in Monrovia, he was a guest of Taylor's deputy minister of tourism, a young woman. He wanted to see the Chief who was at Ricks with the ECOMOG battalion securing the area. Yet Charles Taylor had declared the Chief a persona non grata in Liberia. Juba said to me that this guy is up to no good. I told Juba that I totally agreed with him; it was very obvious what he was busy with. Dumbuya asked us about the Chief and we told him that we had not seen him for a while.

I went and told the Chief about Dumbuya as an envoy of the President here in Monrovia, and he just smiled and said, 'Fred, you know why he is here.' The following day Hassan [Fred's driver] and myself went to visit the Chief and update him on what we were doing regarding our flights to Lungi. On our way back we saw Dumbuya and that woman in a car going towards Ricks. So we called and warned the Chief off. They went to the Chief's place but people there told them that the Chief had gone up-country. We believed that the aim was to eyeball him and confirm that the Chief was there. ECOMOG tightened the movement of people visiting the Chief afterwards. Dumbuya went twice but did not see the Chief. The last attempt was a meeting to be held in Dumbuya's hotel room with the Chief. The Chief came with his escort but I went in first, and as I was going up I saw Taylors' security men on the second floor. I quickly came down and told the Chief that it was a trap and he must leave immediately. Which he did, with his two-man escort.

Thus, on 2 January 1998, when Fred took the initiative with the security man at Spriggs, it was because he had learned from experience that Hinga Norman had to walk circumspectly in Liberia, and so he took it on himself to watch out for him. There was no follow-up by Taylor's men, and when Bokkie was refuelled, they took off for Base Zero

Two days later, on 4 January, Kamajors launched an operation against junta forces in the town of Bo. International aid workers there reported that the Kamajors were fighting with AK–47s, machetes and spears. The following day the junta radio put out that Kamajors had been airlifted to ECOMOG bases at Lungi and Jui. It was to be a month of intense fighting by the CDF, and it would tie up considerable junta forces and prevent them reinforcing their western command. All the signs were there for mobilization in preparation for an offensive. The Nigerian Defence HQ announced that a new overall commander of the ECOMOG force in Liberia, Major General Timothy Shelpidi, would take over from Major General Malu, who indicated that the force's presence in Sierra Leone would be increased to about 15,000 troops.[20] The change-over happened swiftly, and on Friday 9 January, Juba, Fred and Sendaba took Gen Malu in Bokkie to Lungi to bid farewell to his troops and commanders in Sierra Leone. A formal ceremony was held, and Bokkie took part with a lone fly past in front of the general and his command.

On Friday 16 January, Bokkie flew a special consignment to 'the junction': personnel, food and fuel; the load also contained a package of money, amounting to $25,000 from Sandline, supplied via Lifeguard. The money was allocated as follows: $20,000 on communications – to buy radios and repeaters; and $5,000 for food, fuel and medicine. Fred was involved in organizing the radios from Lebanese contacts; Hinga Norman's nephew, Samuel Margai, and Michael Josiah, who later became a doctor, bought a range of medicines following Hinga Norman's directions. That day a series of co-ordinated attacks were made by Kamajors in the south and east of the country. A fierce fight developed for control of Tongo. On 19 January, Hinga Norman said on the BBC World Service that 'Tongo is going to be a tug of war.'[21]

At the end of January the Task Force drew up its final battle options. Phase one would concentrate on the liberation of Freetown, and Col Khobe wanted to know what CDF strength he could count on for this part of the operation as well as the next phases up-country. Hinga Norman was flown to Lungi in Bokkie. On the evening of 28 January, a meeting was held at Lungi, in the house used by the company Lifeguard, who still operated in the mines at Koidu (since the AFRC tried to sustain a veneer of normalcy to encourage external investment). Brig Bert Sachse, formerly of Executive Outcomes, and now of Lifeguard, was in attendance; and during the meeting Hinga Norman asked Fred to take notes. Khobe wanted to know how many men of the CDF he could count on to back up his force. Hinga Norman read out figures from twenty-one chiefdoms, chiefdom by chiefdom; and Fred's notebook contains the numbers: Bumpe could muster 2,500; Gerihun's figure amounted to 800; Tongo produced one of the largest numbers at 7,000. The total came to 37,050 men. In the circumstances of wartime, this figure would have been inflated, but it was still an impressive backup that chiefs could muster. Then Fred noted down the logistical problems: transport, which ranged from on foot, by bicycle, by air; medivac would be mancarry; feeding could meet with local resistance from already deprived and suffering communities; but the biggest problem in an operation of this kind was communication.

That date of Col Khobe's meeting to ascertain CDF support is a noteworthy anniversary: it marked one year since the Sierra Leone government terminated Executive Outcomes' contract; a contract, by means of which the country had paid for fewer than two hundred men to bring about a level of stability that to re-attain now required about 15,000 ECOMOG troops and an indeterminate number of militiamen.

Airlifting contingents of CDF to support the taking of Freetown, Bokkie ferried them from Moyamba, Bonthe and Bambatok to back up the ECOMOG battalion stationed at Kossoh.

They were so happy, as if they were going on a picnic. Quite an incredible sight to see men dressed in their fighting gear, mostly without weapons except their traditional fighting knife.

The final build up of the attacking force took place on 5 February. A Hercules C-130 made three flights from Liberia to Lungi airfield, ferrying a battalion of ECOMOG troops and their equipment. They were then airlifted in Bokkie to Kossoh, six loads for each C-130 flight; and each round trip took about thirty minutes plus. At the end of the eighteenth flight, they made one more trip this time taking a cow for the battalion feast before the coming offensive.

A total of 275 troops and 37 tons of freight and equipment were moved in one day with one helicopter. Some loads went up to 5.5 tons due to the fuel being low, but still, with 1.5 tons over maximum all-up weight, Bokkie was setting new world records.[22]

Bokkie's crew were about to round off a long day with their usual evening beer, when an urgent call came through that an ECOMOG soldier on a recce foot patrol had stepped on an Anti Personnel Mine (APM) the junta had planted; the man lost both legs. The crew immediately took to the air and got the soldier back to Lungi, where they had a good medical set-up with a small team of doctors who were able to stabilize cases before having them moved to Monrovia and then on to Nigeria.

At 04.00 hours on 6 February, the assault on Freetown began with an ECOMOG bombardment from Lungi using heavy weapons, followed by a break out from Kossoh to the west towards Freetown. Initial progress was satisfactory: Fred noted in his diary that the Task Force, 'took over Waterloo and Wellington. Casualties were light, 5 dead and 42 wounded.' Timed to coincide with the ECOMOG offensive, Kamajors launched an all-out attack on Kono. And a few days later Kamajors took on the junta's forces at Koribunda. Throughout the fighting to retake Freetown, Bokkie was flying long hours most days, resupplying and extracting casualties or whatever was required. At the end of a flight between Kossoh and Lungi, when the crew reported in, Col Maxwell Khobe informed Juba of reports that the enemy were firing at the ECOMOG force from a gunboat in Freetown harbour. Juba took note and followed their previous route back to see where the firing was coming from.

The next moment waterspouts as high as the main rotor shot up into the air. The high explosive projectiles landed about 100metres short of Bokkie, and I eased away from where they were shooting for tactical reasons. They kept on shooting till we disappeared over the trees. On our route back we saw massive clouds of dust and water going up into the air as ECOMOG opened up with their artillery on the gunboat. ECOMOG knew the value of Bokkie and its crew. If they had to lose it, the outcome of the war might be the opposite from the way it was going at the time.[23]

The junta knew they had to eliminate Bokkie, and they ordered their Mi–24 gunship into the air on two occasions to do it. The first time was on 5 February, when Juba and team were ferrying the Nigerian battalion to Kossoh. Juba had flown that Mi–24 in his EO days; it was old then, and he knew that it had not the speed of Bokkie. But the danger was increased because Kossoh is only 1.8 kilometres from Hastings airport, which was in rebel hands. Mountains surround Hastings airport, and Juba had narrow corridors in which to operate: at one point his route took them to about 800 metres from Hastings, and he had to fly very low and fast. His tactic was to spend as little time on the ground, because that was when Bokkie was vulnerable. On their last trip, carrying a cow for the Nigerian battalion feast, they were on the ground no more than three minutes. Unknown to them, the gunship was waiting behind a mountain to hit them on the ground, but its crew misjudged the length of time Bokkie's crew needed for a turn–about. Nigerian officers later told Juba that a few minutes after they had left, the gunship came over the mountain; its pilot saw that they had gone and pulled out and went back to the other side.

On 12 February, ECOMOG Task Force attacked State House, the symbolic centre of power. Both sides were at a critical stage. The junta had prepared itself for a defence of the capital with a huge arsenal of weaponry at its disposal. Perhaps for the first time in urban warfare, a powerful component came into play in the assault on Freetown: the British government-financed radio that Peter Penfold had arranged to be installed at Lungi kept people informed about the battle, as its presenter, Julius Spencer, accompanied the Task Force, mobile in hand, linked to the radio transmitter.

> Julius walked alongside Khobe with his mobile and was broadcasting to the people live on how the fight was going. 'We are now coming up to Siaka Stevens street, so all civilians remain off the road now. Anybody seen on the road we will know is an enemy, and ECOMOG will shoot them.' And also by being told where the Task Force was, people could get round the back and into safe places. The result of that ... if you look at how we took Freetown, with such few lives lost, it's remarkable. An urban war, but in terms of deaths, the deaths were minimal. I think it was about 100 at most. One major reason for that was that people listened to the radio.[24]

Fred noted in his diary, 'Col Maxwell Khobe led the assault to State House and was slightly wounded in the process.' The wound was caused by a fragment of an RPG; and Bokkie's crew evacuated him along with other wounded.

Then sod's law kicked in for Bokkie. Returning on the last flight of the day to Lungi, it suddenly became very vulnerable. Due to fatigue at the end of the long day, the helicopter sustained damage to one of its main rotors. And later that evening the junta sent their Mi-24 again, this time to Lungi, in preparation for the second attempt to ambush Bokkie, but this time it was flying very high. All the while it was in the air, the ECOMOG anti-aircraft guns simply monitored its movements. But Juba stressed to Nigerian officers that this was a reconnaissance flight to see where Bokkie was parked. He told them the gunship would be back and they should get all their systems on full alert to prevent it getting within striking range. Sure enough, next morning, 13 February, at 03.00 hours the junta's Mi-24 returned to bomb Lungi airport. To the surprise of the gunship's crew, the ECOMOG anti-aircraft guns' radar was fully operational and had already tracked them at 10 kilometres out. The gun crews let them get to 8 kilometres from the airport before they opened up on the Mi-24. This seemed to unnerve its crew, and they decided to 'drop their 250 kg bombs in the ocean and run back to Freetown.'[25]

On the streets, forced out of one position after another, the junta/RUF went into full retreat. But Col Khobe had decided not to seal off Waterloo completely, and this allowed the enemy an escape channel from Freetown to the country. His reasoning for this at the time was that sealing it up would put too much pressure on his battalion at Kossoh. As a soldier, Fred thought this was flimsy; he was in a position to know, having been involved in the troop build up at Kossoh: the battalion had been reinforced and was equipped with heavy and medium mortars. But an alternative explanation for the decision was adduced later: it was done deliberately so as not to bottle up the junta in Freetown and thus avoid a fight to the finish in the capital, causing greater damage and more loss of life. Whether or not this was later rationalization, militarily the decision was a serious error of judgment; the channel became an inverted funnel that spewed out into the country the spawn of a new guerrilla war that ECOMOG could not hope to win. For ECOMOG was no Executive Outcomes; it was a cumbersome machine designed to fight other armies; it could have destroyed the junta forces contained in the peninsula; but it was unable to move swiftly into the bush after a guerrilla enemy and follow through with overwhelming momentum.

Fortune's wheel then turned again, and this time to the advantage of ECOMOG's air capability. The air wing of the junta was under the command of Major Victor King, who was also a member of the AFRC government, and he and some colleagues tried a different escape route that would take them by air to Liberia to Roberts Field airport, which was not controlled by ECOMOG, and from thence into the welcoming arms of Liberia's president, Charles Taylor. At around 04.30 hours, after refueling and packing both their Mi-24 and the Mi-17, they were airborne, but they were spotted by a Nigerian Air Force officer at Spriggs airfield, and he alerted the Alpha jet commander that they were on their way to Roberts International. At that very moment, two Alpha jets had just taken off for a mission to Sierra Leone, and they were ordered to intercept and escort the helicopters to Spriggs airfield, which ECOMOG controlled. There the junta airmen were arrested and taken into custody. President Charles Taylor retaliated by threatening to attack the airfield. The ECOMOG response was to buzz his state mansion with an Alpha jet every half hour.

Although Bokkie was slightly damaged, ECOMOG now had in its control at Spriggs airfield one Mi–24 and one Mi–17; its airmen were unfamiliar with the Soviet-built machines; however, Juba was an acknowledged ace pilot of both aircraft. And at Lungi airport there was a Cessna 337 that had been used for reconnaissance by Executive Outcomes when they were in Sierra Leone; it had been handed over to Sandline and was available to be flown to Monrovia by their operator, Bernie McCabe, who was ex–Delta Force. Bernie McCabe took Juba, Fred and Sendaba on what was the start of a shuttle, flying them in the Cessna to Spriggs from Lungi. When they arrived at Spriggs, they found that tension was high between ECOMOG and Charles Taylor's forces. Taylor presented ECOMOG with an ultimatum, giving them 3 hours to release the helicopters and crew to him; if not his men would attack. Senior ECOMOG officers were not cowed by the threat, and they put on a maximum show of force.

Juba inspected the Mi–24 and realized its battery was no good. He told Sendaba to bring the Mi–17's and connect it, so that they could get both helicopters as quickly as possible to ECOMOG HQ. Then Juba climbed into the cockpit of the Mi–24 and started her up; 3 minutes later they were airborne with Alpha Jets giving top-cover in case they were fired on by Liberian anti-aircraft guns. After landing at ECOMOG HQ they were driven back to Spriggs, through the streets of Monrovia in a Nigerian armoured car. Next, with Fred carrying his GMPG, they boarded the Mi–17, and flew it to ECOMOG HQ, where Juba was briefed and planned his routes. Once airborne with the Mi–17, they flew it to Roberts International to refuel and then on to Lungi, with the intention of having a replacement helicopter for the damaged Bokkie. For the final shuttle, Bernie McCabe flew them again to Monrovia in the Cessna, and they took the Mi–24 gunship back to Lungi. This shuttling, which they were aware of but were powerless to stop, goaded Charles Taylor's forces: there had to be revenge for the loss of both aircraft, and so the bounty on Juba's head increased.[26]

Good luck continued with them a bit longer: they did not have to replace Bokkie with their newly acquired Mi–17. At Hastings Airport was a set of blades that were slightly damaged by an airstrike and suitable to get Bokkie serviceable again. Its crew carried out the replacement: they used a forklift truck, did a blade track, using chalk marks and a pole, carried out a test – and so Bokkie flew again.

In the final retreat from Freetown, elements of the junta set a wave of barbarism into motion, and went on a killing spree. In defeat their level of cruelty was even worse than when they were in the ascendant. To cite one case alone is sickening enough: retreating rebels found a Nigerian civilian, tied him one arm and leg to one vehicle, the other arm and leg to a second vehicle, and so pulled him apart alive.[27] But there was also a spate of revenge killings – the same pattern that frequently occurred in European wars of the twentieth century after a country was liberated from an occupying force. For an occupying force is what people considered the junta to be. A gauge of the depth of public feeling after the coup may be taken with one example: all schools in Sierra Leone had remained closed since May when the main teachers' union called a strike; this was acceded to by families who were prepared to accept this interruption of their children's education. As recently as January, AFRC soldiers had beaten up teachers at Collegiate College School on Wilkinson Road in Freetown for refusing to hold classes. So antipathy to the junta was very strong. Of course, there were collaborators, and when they were found, there were reprisals. On 15 February, Col Khobe ordered that anyone caught looting or taking part in revenge killing would be shot on sight.

That same day, the BBC reported that over 10,000 Kamajors captured Bo, entering it from three points, singing war songs and looking for junta soldiers; they found around eight of them and handed them over to local youths for execution. This act on the part of the local youths may have been less a surge of blood lust than calculated eye-for-an-eye retribution, for shortly afterwards, when the necessary health safeguards were able to be put in place, the decomposing bodies of 102 men and boys, slaughtered by junta soldiers and rebels, were exhumed from a shallow mass grave.[28]

Although no longer in meaningful control, having been dislodged from the capital city, the AFRC/RUF were still strong in number in certain areas. One of those areas was Kono. It was eight months since Fred had been airlifted out of Kono, suffering from malaria, leaving his comrades of Lifeguard guarding the mining works. The company was still there because the junta not only tolerated its presence, but wanted to encourage an impression abroad of business as usual. Now that the junta forces were the rump of a movement without a head, the RUF component in its mix rose in the ascendancy; as diamonds were a means of acquiring arms, in Kono they forced Lifeguard to work for them. This uneasy coexistence lasted a short time until the rebels were informed through their own contacts that Lifeguard's executives at Lungi were working hand in glove with ECOMOG.

After the coup, a small number of the Sierra Leone military remained loyal to the democratic government and attached themselves to the ECOMOG force. However, the species known as *sobel* could turn up in any number of places. And in this case, one of the apparently loyal troops, a junior officer, was sympathetic to the junta and was spying for them; he reported to the Kono contingent of rebels that he had seen Bert Sachse, a senior executive of Lifeguard, working alongside ECOMOG officers at Lungi. The rebels retaliated by putting the South African nationals under house arrest, but not Fred's buddy, TT De Abrea: they used him as a radio operator on Lifeguard's HF communication system for their own needs, calling friends and family abroad, in Ghana, the USA and the UK. However, TT felt that it would only be a question of time until he and his comrades were executed. And so from the 14 to 18 February,[29] he planned a method for Lifeguard's escape, and did the ground work for it.

A well-disciplined, experienced soldier, he decided to capitalize on the rebels' sloppiness, indiscipline and lack of systematic routine, and exploit these weaknesses. While not operating the HF radio for their whimsical calls abroad, TT offered to drive a bulldozer for them, whenever they wanted to use it for their illegal mining. But while he did this he recced every checkpoint, and, as he drove around, he gave himself a high profile, smiling, waving and talking to them at every opportunity. At night, back at base, he bought them drinks and drank with them. When he was an aspiring young footballer in Angola, he had to be abstemious, but over his years as a soldier he had developed a phenomenal capacity for alcohol tolerance, and he now used it like a weapon for a few nights running: many of their captors were already high on drugs, and he made sure they were topped up with booze until they were well and truly sozzled, while he stayed clear-headed. Then, on 18 February, when he judged the time was right, he told his Lifeguard comrades that this was the night they would try and break out; he went over the details with them; and he used the HF communication system to contact Lifeguard in South Africa to arrange for the final element: to be airlifted out of Kono.

That night, like the preceding two, he supervised the heavy drinking session while his comrades loaded two Land Rovers, and then boarded them – the white South Africans out of sight, lying down in the back, their black comrades sitting up in front. TT left the rebel carousers in their drunken stupor and joined his comrades. At 02.30 hours, the two vehicles moved forward at a sedate pace, one behind the other, with TT sitting in the front of the leading Land Rover. They drove to the checkpoint he had selected, through which they would have to pass, where, of course, the guard on duty waved them down, before he saw it was TT. With a friendly wave, TT simply called to him to open the gate. Immediately, and without any questions, the man obeyed. The first vehicle moved through, the second at its bumper.

The rendezvous where Bokkie's crew had been tasked to land and extract the Lifeguard team was the playground of a village school in the hills. All went well for the Lifeguard operatives until one of their vehicles got bogged down. They abandoned both, camouflaged them, and continued on foot for the RV. Meanwhile, as arranged, Bokkie was on stand-by for the operation.

We got the signal and Juba and myself flew to pick the guys up. At the RV point we did not see them at first, so Juba called TT on the radio. And they asked Juba to go on the same heading just a bit further. Juba asked me on the intercom to keep a sharp look out because the lads were in the area. Trees made detection very difficult, but as we passed an opening, I saw a figure running out of the trees, waving his hands and I told Juba to orbit, which he did, and immediately we saw the rest of the group coming out into the open. Relief was an understatement of our feelings, because we knew for sure that they were OK. The pick-up was very quick indeed, and when I saw TT and the rest of the group, we were overwhelmed with joy. Arriving safely at Lungi Airport and meeting the headshed of Lifeguard was a true scene of joy and relief.

Later, at Lungi, through a chance encounter that Fred had with him, the suspected spy was unmasked. Because the rebels at the mining site at Kono, wanted to show private military company operatives that they too had an intelligence network, they ingenuously told them that the Lifeguard executive's activities had been betrayed by one of their own men working alongside ECOMOG at Lungi. As a result of the increased military action, Sandline operatives quite often mixed with the Nigerian troops and Sierra Leone contingent at Lungi, and on one occasion Fred was very surprised to bump into a young Sierra Leonean officer, who, before the coup, was involved in underhand dealings and had used Hinga Norman's name as a shibboleth to get some advantage. As a result he had been banned from access to Hinga Norman's office and prohibited from using his name. When Fred saw him at Lungi with a friend, he expressed surprise at his being there.

They quickly disappeared after our chance meeting. I saw one of our senior Nigerian officers and told him about those two guys, and they were shortly arrested. And what happened to them, I don't know. But whatever they got, they deserved it in my view.

By the end of the month, the situation in Freetown was stable, and the government in exile prepared to resume its rightful role. Apart from imposing sanctions on the junta, the UN had adopted a supine position with regard to restoring the democratic government to Sierra Leone; even at the height of the fighting to retake Freetown, some members of the Security Council were pointing out that ECOWAS had no UN authority to carry out military action. That was true, but it was also an implicit self-criticism of the international body.

Peter Penfold returned to the capital as the British High Commissioner. With Britain giving a lead, several countries began giving humanitarian aid. The British warship, *HMS Cornwall*, docked at Freetown. Within days its aviators and engineers were looking over the Mi-17 that had supplied the ECOMOG force and the CDF. Juba offered to land Bokkie on the flight deck, an idea that was taken up with alacrity by the ship's officers. Shortly after, the crew flew the Mi-24 gunship on to the ship so that the crew could see it at close range. In the three weeks that the ship was docked at Freetown there were times when Juba and his crew flew the Mi-24 up-country; on their way back they were always picked up by the ship's radar and its weapons locked on to the helicopter. The gunship's intercom registered this contact and Fred imagined, 'It must be a horrible feeling, knowing that weapon systems are locked on to you and you could be vaporized within seconds.' Interestingly, a few months later, a newspaper in the UK published photographs of Bokkie on Freetown dock with its crew pointing out some of the helicopter's features to Royal Navy engineers, purporting them as proof that Britain was aiding mercenaries.[30]

However, at the time of these events in February and March, sensationalism in a story about mercenaries had not been created. On 11 March, in an interview on BBC, High Commissioner Peter Penfold said that Britain had made no demands on President Kabbah in exchange for British assistance in restoring the civilian government.[31] In response to a question, he denied that he had put Kabbah in touch with mercenaries or had helped in the recruiting of mercenaries. It was a question that would recur.

Deputy Minister of Defence Sam Hinga Norman had been a Hercules with a clear vision of what had to be done to oust the junta through a co-ordinated effort of the external military force of the sub-region supported by local militia. Some months after the restoration of the government, he was asked in an interview. 'Shortly after the AFRC coup, many people ran away. But you, rather than do that, put your life on the line. Where did you get that inspiration from?' Hinga Norman's reply in essence is the timeless motive of the patriot, who takes up arms to defend the homeland.

> Ah ... I got the inspiration from the simple fact that this is the only country that I have. If I lose it, my very belonging – I will be ... be dispossessed of belonging to a nation. Even the bird perching on the tree would be better than me.[32]

He too was asked about mercenaries, and the question was put to him citing Executive Outcomes as an example. Hinga Norman's reply is thought-provoking: he said that Executive Outcomes were not mercenaries. He argued that if the definition of a mercenary is a foreign national being paid for what he does, what is the essential difference between paying a professional doctor or teacher to come and work in the country, and paying professional soldiers – provided they are requested by the constitutional government.[33]

Individuals no doubt had their own reasons for working with private military companies – Bokkie's crew were single-minded, and they kept a sense of self-respect for what they did. Reflecting on it later to Fred, Juba wrote:

> The two of us did what we did in Sierra Leone and Liberia because we felt for the people that suffered, and there were only us from the air side, that were involved, that truly believed in what we did.[34]

On 10 March, President Kabbah made a triumphant return to Freetown. Thousands of people assembled at the national stadium. Bokkie ferried the VIPs there and remained in the stadium throughout the ceremony. Its crew were proud of the moment when their craft was photographed and filmed by the world's media. Juba later had reason to remind high officials.

Often the statement has been made by senior Government and ECOMOG officers that the helicopter played a major role in the February 1998 offensive against the rebels, and without the helicopter support, the offensive would not have been the success it was.[35]

It might be thought that in their sense of commitment, Bokkie's crew, in their enthusiasm and fondness for the helicopter, became influenced by the animism that lies not far below the surface of monotheistic faiths in West Africa. But that belief holds that spirit resides in all things in the natural world; so it surely could not apply to a machine? Oh, but this was a machine with personality, this was Bokkie.

Chapter Seven

Carrying the Can

For the manner in which men live is so different from the way in which they ought to live, that he who leaves the common course for that which he ought to follow will find that it leads him to ruin rather than to safety. For a man who, in all respects, will carry out only his professions of good, will be apt to be ruined amongst so many who are evil.

Niccolò Machiavelli, *The Prince*

A random sample of those with long service in a hierarchy like a bureaucracy or the military would settle for the proposition that when it comes to the crunch in subordinate-superordinate relationships a proper bastard is to be preferred to a proper shit. The former is readily identified, and patterns of behaviour anticipated − not that the type is by definition unable to respect fairness. The latter, on the other hand, may not be instantly discernible, but invariably comes to light when a crisis grips the organization, during the resolution of which some strive desperately to gain praise or, even more vitally, avoid censure − and unlike the former, this type is consistently contemptible.

Such considerations were a world away from West Africa in March 1998; so not long after President Kabbah's triumphal return to Freetown, when Bokkie was a focal point in the large stadium, and the loudest chant going round the huge crowd was, 'Khobe; Khobe; Khobe' (in tribute to the ECOMOG Task Force Commander), and the second loudest chant was, 'ninety-eight point one; ninety-eight point one'[1] (the wave length of Radio Democracy, funded by the British government at the urging of its pro-active High Commissioner), the last thought that could have been on Peter Penfold's mind, when he received a summons to return to the UK, was that he was heading into a maelstrom which was engulfing the Foreign Office, in danger of dragging political careers below the surface, and would test the moral fibre of ministers and officials.

Quite the opposite: it would have been reasonable to expect a discussion and decisions on follow-up to bolster Kabbah's restoration. But then, on the day before his departure, the High Commissioner was told to bring with him any papers he had on Sandline; more ominously, when he arrived in the UK, he was phoned at home and told that he must not go into the office, he must have no contact with anybody in the African Department, and he would be required to give a statement under caution to HM Customs and Excise.[2] It got worse: he was advised to get a lawyer (the Foreign Office were prepared to pay the cost), and he learned that if things went wrong, he could face a prison sentence of seven years.[3] But why?

Straddling the moral high ground, which he had scaled and claimed (in his public life) stood Foreign Secretary, Robin Cook, pronouncing that Britain would pursue an ethical foreign policy. In so doing, he made himself hostage to his own rhetoric; his political opponents knew it, and they knew too that there was now only one direction in which he could go; and they saw a chance to topple him.

Claims had already appeared in the press that the British company, Sandline, had breached the terms of the UN resolution 1132, banning the supply of arms to Sierra Leone during the period of the junta. These were officially denied, until Tim Spicer's lawyer sent an open letter to the Foreign Secretary refuting allegations of sanction-breaking and claiming that officials in the Foreign Office and High Commissioner, Penfold, knew about his company's contract with President Kabbah. And, of course, Peter Penfold did know about the contract.

> As far as I, President Kabbah, and many others were concerned, the Sandline contract did not breach UN sanctions. None of my discussion with colleagues in the FCO [Foreign and Commonwealth Office] led me to believe otherwise, and indeed the Legal Department of the UN were later to confirm that this was their understanding. However, to put a UN sanction legislation order into UK legislation, an Order in Council had to be made, and it had to be written into the UK administration procedure. And in transposing the UN sanctions order into the UK Order, mistakes were made, in my view. The legal draftsmen in the FCO tried to use an 'off the shelf' sanction order, e.g. Angola – just cross out Angola and put in Sierra Leone. They then, supposedly being helpful, tried to define what was meant by 'Sierra Leone'. They prepared a list of definitions of Sierra Leone relevant to whom the sanctions order applied. In the list, the first category was 'the government of Sierra Leone', believing it to be the illegal junta. Now our whole diplomatic stance had been that the government of Sierra Leone was in fact President Kabbah's government. The AFRC junta was not even mentioned by name.[4]

Indeed, the British government had got itself into a strange position. Prime Minister, Tony Blair, had personally invited the exiled President Kabbah to the Commonwealth Prime Ministers' Conference in Edinburgh the previous October, an act symbolizing the recognition of Kabbah.

The notion that the AFRC junta could have been talked into giving up power or compelled through sanctions was wrong-headed. The junta were in a very strong position, and they were being supplied with arms. When ECOMOG planners came to the decision that force would be necessary to liberate Freetown, their problem was that the Task Force was vulnerable if its logistical support was cut off: the battalion at Kossoh could not be supplied by road along the peninsula, nor by sea because of the junta's gunboat; the air corridor was all important for it. Hence Juba, as the pilot of the only helicopter keeping the air corridor open, was often consulted on matters of strategy by Gen Khobe. And at a briefing meeting Khobe told him that,

> the junta never planned to leave Freetown, and they made sure they got themselves well dug in with lots of arms and ammunition. The first arms deal was for about US $60 million, of which the $10 million was in cash and the balance in diamonds.[5]

Juba thought that Khobe's source came from Sierra Leone informers, embedded inside the junta, who managed to pass out information that was useful for ECOMOG's planning. But, as we shall see later, ECOMOG was also receiving information from a different source. At any rate, the arms, as Juba understood it, were from the Ukraine or Belarus, and some of their citizens, according to whatever sources, came as part of the package. He certainly needed to have that information, for if the junta, as the result of an arms delivery, now had SAM-7 missiles and personnel trained to use them, Juba, who survived a missile attack on his helicopter in Angola, and amazingly walked away from the wreck,[6] had to take it into the reckoning when planning his flight paths. ECOMOG strategists were right that the only way to remove the junta was by armed force. Yet, the British government expressed satisfaction with the ends, but not the means through which the junta was brought down, and ministers denied collusion with private military companies in undertaking those means.

Then on 9 May, a picture appeared in the *Times* of Fred, aboard Bokkie, in a civilian shirt, his GPMG slung across his knees, the helicopter over water, a Nigerian soldier beside him. The caption underneath claimed that the civilian was a member of the South African company, Executive Outcomes.[7] On the facing page, there was also a photograph of Tim Spicer. The following day, the *Sunday Times*, had pictures on its front page of Juba talking to two Royal Marines at the dockside in Freetown and Fred with five Royal Navy mechanics carrying out some repairs to Bokkie.[8] The headline claimed these were proof of Britain's role in the coup. The wording at times made it difficult to know whether the paper was referring to the coup that brought the junta to power or the counter-coup that brought it down. The photos were taken when HMS *Cornwall* was docked at Freetown in early March. Juba explains the background to them.

> By the time HMS *Cornwall* arrived in Freetown port, their air contingent came to meet with us in Lungi and asked if we could assist them in certain aspects, seeing that we'd been involved in the operation from the beginning, and with our vast knowledge of the country. The British took a new stance with regards to the

operations and said it would be better for a soldier to talk to a soldier than to work through the political protocols. From the start we had good communication with each other, and the relation grew within a short time to where they were helping us with some maintenance on Bokkie. I also landed the Mi-24 next to the ship, and that is where the photographs were taken that featured in the international newspapers that caused major problems for the Foreign Office. Before the ship left after weeks in Freetown, I was awarded the full size Union Jack that their helicopter crew would have put down on the ground as a signal for us to come and rescue them if anything went wrong on their operation.[9]

Newspaper headlines kept Robin Cook turning on the spit. His response to the whole thing showed that although he claimed to have an ethical foreign policy, he seemed not to have much of an ethical management culture for the officials who served him. The ideal type bureaucracy (of which the British Civil Service might well have been thought an example) has the superior taking responsibility for lower levels. A predecessor Foreign Secretary, Lord Carrington, was in post in 1982 when the Argentine military junta invaded the Falkland Islands; he took full responsibility for the shortcomings in the Foreign Office that failed to pick up the warning signs of Argentina's intentions, and resigned. But Robin Cook took a different road, and he distanced himself from his officials, as Peter Penfold was to find out.

I can't understand why Robin Cook, when he heard that accusations were being made about one of his high commissioners, didn't first of all just call me back and ask me to explain what the hell was going on. That never happened. In fact, exactly the opposite. I was not allowed to actually talk to anybody. That is baffling, and in fact, to this day, I have never been debriefed on the Sandline issue by anybody in the Foreign Office.[10]

The distancing device brought in to play was a well-tried construct that has served governments in the past: an investigation whose terms of reference were closely defined by government itself into: what was know by officials and ministers about plans to supply arms to Sierra Leone. So it was not an inquiry into whether sanctions had indeed been breached, but to find out whether ministers had been informed. This sort of approach sends unpleasant shock waves through the organization, and in this case gave the message that the Foreign Secretary who, though not willing to be tainted by the shedding of blood to remove, what he himself later referred to as, 'a brutal and savage military regime',[11] wanted heads to roll to preserve his political reputation.

In this sort of witch-hunt, broad brush blame of work-overload is likely to surface, and a recommendation like tinkering with structures usually appears (and appeals) as a partial solution, but the essential element, from the political point of view, is that responsibility must be found to lie with one or two scapegoats – not too many, that would defeat the purpose. And when a tone like that is set at the top, it badly shakes the culture of the organization. Unaccountable things happened, it appears: letters went missing, for example; one of which was very important.

It was a hand-written letter, posted around Christmas 1997 when Peter Penfold was at home in the UK, incorporating two elements: the first was about his meeting Tim Spicer and being told that Kabbah had gone ahead and signed the contract with Sandline; the second was a carry-over from recommendations for awards that he had submitted as a result of the outstanding service of a number of people at the time of the May 1997 AFRC coup. He had recommended MBE for his deputy Colin Glass; OBE for another member of his staff, Dai Harris; the Queen's Gallantry Medal for Col Andrew Gale, his Defence Adviser; Military Cross for Maj Lincoln Jopp; and a Queen's Gallantry Medal for Will Scully. This was particularly notable as it was to be the first time that an ex–SAS man ever received an award. (He also nominated Solomon Lebby, the local Sierra Leonean, who was left in charge of the Mission, for an MBE, the following year after they returned from Conakry.) His recommendations had been accepted, and the individuals informed before the release of the New Year Honours list. They were all in touch by phone, and when they learned that he had not received recognition for his part in saving lives at the time of the coup, they were all indignant: they all considered that they had worked as part of a team at the time; there was talk of their refusing theirs. So in the circumstances, Peter Penfold thought that he ought to flag it up.

> I was about to go to Canada to stay with family for Christmas with my wife. My wife had had a rough time, and she had been in tears and so on. And I persuaded the office that I should be allowed to have at least two weeks break, for up till then I'd been staying in this hotel room in Conakry. So they agreed that. But equally, this is the time when I met up with Tim Spicer, and that's when Tim told me that the contract had been signed and they were going ahead. Now he told me this the day before I was flying out to Canada, and as I was going away for a couple of weeks, I thought I can't leave this for two weeks, so I wrote a letter to the head of the department, telling her I'd met Tim Spicer again and that he'd confirmed that the contract had been signed. And I also put in that letter, because I'd just spoken to the guys, 'You should be aware that Colin and Dai are a little concerned that I have not been nominated for a New Year's honour'. When I said concerned, they were livid, so I put it in. And fortunately, because I put that in, and I knew that it wasn't really their department, in a way – it was honours department – I thought I'd better keep a copy of this letter. And I had one of those fax machines with a copier, so I ran it through and made a copy of this letter and posted it.
>
> Now, of course, this is the famous letter that never arrived in the Foreign Office. The letter that was confirming that I'd met Tim Spicer. And what was interesting was that when I next went into the Foreign Office, two people in the department started explaining to me about the honours, and why I hadn't got an honour. Now

if the letter had never arrived, why were they talking about the honour? It's just unbelievable isn't it?[12]

This is the important letter of 30 December that, conveniently, never arrived.

30 December 1997

Dear Ann

    Thank you for your Christmas card. I trust you had a good Christmas.

    I have been in touch with Tim Spicer over the holiday. Kabbah has signed the deal with Blockstone for EO/Sandline to provide $10 million of equipment and training for the civil defence militia. This will begin to flow in Jan. At my suggestion they will station someone in Conakry to stay alongside Kabbah. I have asked them to keep Colin Glass fully briefed. As you know, it has always been my view that only a serious threat of force will persuade the junta to stand down, therefore I welcome this development not least because it means that Sierra Leoneans will be directly involved in getting their legitimate government back.

    I was also in touch with people in Freetown and Conakry: Christmas passed off quietly, but there was little celebration.

    I am sorry that we did not have more time to talk when I called in to the department. I told Richard Dales that I had some misgivings about our appointment of a Special S of S representative. I believe that it will undermine my position vis-à-vis Kabbah and others in Conakry and Freetown. The Americans have already appointed John Hirsch as their special representative, Francis Okelo is the UN's special envoy, and hitherto the three of us were seen as a team representing the international community. I fear that John Flynn's appointment will be seen as a sign of lack of confidence by HMG in me. This is further exacerbated by what will be seen as the very pointed omission of myself from amongst the other team members who have received awards in the recent military and New Year Honours List, for their efforts in Sierra Leone.

Happy New Year,
Yours ever

Peter (P. A. Penfold)[13]

It could be argued that a letter can get lost in the Christmas mail, but less convincingly that, separately, two individuals intuitively could assume that there was concern over the honours' awards. However, denial, when under stress, in order to cover one's back is one thing – and to some extent an understandable human failing –, but to spread disinformation into the public domain, clearly with the intention of discrediting someone, is sinister. And that is what subsequently appears to have been engineered.

Again it happened when Peter Penfold was in the UK and the inquiry was underway into what was known and by whom about Sandline.

> I was at home here, and a friend telephoned from London, and said, 'Have you seen the article in today's *Times*?' I said, 'What article?' He said, 'There's an article in today's *Times* attacking you; well the Foreign Office attacking you, talking about how when you were in Conakry all that time and you never kept the government and the Foreign Office informed about what was going on.' And I get the *Times* and I checked it and said to him, 'Are you sure?' He said, 'Yes, page so and so.' I looked again. It's not here. What had happened, I pieced it all together later, the Foreign Office fed this story in to the *Times*, and they printed it in the first edition. Clearly someone in Customs and Excise, who was investigating at the time, picked it up immediately and they must have telephoned them to say this looks rather strange because Peter Penfold has left on our desk all these reports that he sent to you daily from Conakry, which Customs and Excise had. So the news people realised that they'd gone too far and they withdrew the article before it got into the second edition.[14]

Who would have fed that disinformation to the *Times*? 'Somebody in their news department who was working with Robin Cook.'[15]

However, Peter Penfold's friend retained the article that appeared in the first edition, and only in the first edition, before it was pulled. And it is fascinating to look closely at the text and do an analysis of the technique and elements that were chosen to isolate and discredit their man in Sierra Leone. It appeared on page 15 under the Politics and Government section of the paper.

The 'missing' telegram that was never sent

By Michael Evans, Defence Correspondent

The mystery of the 'missing' telegram from Peter Penfold, the High Commissioner in Sierra Leone, was resolved yesterday when it emerged that he had not cabled London between May last year and April this year.

Recent reports had suggested that Mr Penfold sent a telegram to the Foreign Office last December giving warning that Sandline International, the security company at the centre of the arms-for-Africa affair, wanted to break the arms embargo, but that this cable had not been found. It was also reported that Mr Penfold had sent a second telegram in January pointing out that there had been no reply to his first one.

Senior Whitehall sources dismissed this version of events. They said that as soon as the military junta took over in Freetown, the capital of Sierra Leone, in

May last year, Mr Penfold became High Commissioner-in-exile in Conakry in neighbouring Guinea

In the 11 months he spent there Mr Penfold had no way of communicating confidential reports by telegram, the sources said. He had a fax machine in his hotel but it was an open system and therefore not suitable for sending classified material to the Foreign Office. Throughout his exile in Guinea, the High Commissioner, now in Britain to help with the Customs and Excise investigation, was able to communicate with London only by an open telephone line.

One Whitehall source said, 'There is very little in writing from Mr Penfold during the time he was stuck in Conakry. Far from there being one missing telegram, there weren't any telegrams at all from May 1997 to April.'

This belies the impression given that the Foreign Office is awash with telegrams from the High Commissioner.

However, Mr Penfold returned to London on at least one occasion. Sandline claimed in its letter to the Foreign Secretary on April 24 that the High Commissioner had visited its premises in January and had been briefed about its plans to send arms and personnel to Sierra Leone and its tactics on helping to overthrow the junta.[16]

The paper's defence correspondent was fed the details. The sequence of the material had been carefully crafted. It begins with the vague and imprecise 'recent reports had suggested' to introduce the fallacious claim that the communication was a telegram – thus creating a man of straw – which allows an authoritative source to knock it down with the true statement that no telegram had been sent. Peter Penfold never said he sent a telegram, but because the source can demolish the fabrication it set up in the first place, the reader is nudged into a position with regard to the High Commissioner's integrity. And the significance of inverted commas round the word 'missing' now becomes apparent. However, what was most damaging is the line, 'One Whitehall source said: "There is very little in writing from Mr Penfold during the time he was stuck in Conakry."'

The fact is that practically every day I had sent a hand written report, often graded Restricted, to the African department by fax from the hotel in Conakry keeping London fully up to date with what was going on. All these reports were on file in London and had been passed to Customs and Excise.[17]

Civil servants were traditionally the grey people in the background; they served their political masters who took the credit but also took the blame. So it was a new departure to have a civil servant named – and his reputation besmirched by his own department in the press – on what was insider disinformation, dutifully relayed by a lackey close to the horse's mouth (or some orifice of the horse). And it was a new experience for Peter Penfold to have the press milling outside his home.

We had to slip out through the garage to go shopping. Quite frankly, we had very little support for the Foreign Office. I had tremendous support from individual colleagues, but from the African Department and Personnel Department, two key departments, support was minimal.[18]

For the first time too the public became aware of the drama being played involving a civil servant and politicians. The public would become very much aware of this naming and shaming five years later when the government scientist Dr David Kelly, a weapons expert in the MoD, was traced by the press after information had been leaked by his department as a result of political pressure to discredit him because of his views that Iraq did not possess weapons of mass destruction. His family also felt he had no support from his department. Indeed, at the time that David Kelly was being hounded, Peter Penfold felt for him.

I said to my wife at the time, and to many friends, that I felt a great empathy with David Kelly. He had more publicity than I had, but I know exactly how he felt because I too had to go through the foreign affairs grilling. And apart from the Legg inquiry, I had to appear for four hours. And you're sitting there having all those questions fired at you, and you're saying to yourself, 'What am I doing here? This is not my job.' The way we run our country is that we're the civil servants, we get on and do what our political masters tell us to do. They set the agenda, the policy; they get all the kudos when it goes right, but equally they have to take the flak when it goes wrong. And we are the faceless people; we just get on with it. And equally, you're having questions fired by MPs, who a week previously had probably never known where Sierra Leone was, whose agenda purely is to score points against the other party, couldn't really give a toss about the actual situation. And there you are, you're being used as a punch-bag for this.

I really had a go back at them when they were going on and on at me, and I said to them, I said, 'Look, quite honestly the people in Sierra Leone do not understand what all this is about. As far as they're concerned, we, Britain, have helped bring back peace and democracy to their country.' I said, 'Out there we're regarded as heroes,' and I said, 'the essence is the restoration of democracy, because we, Britain, had told them a couple of years ago that this is the way to solve all your problems. They look to you and this parliament as the mother of democracy.' I said, 'It just doesn't make any sense to them that the mother of democracy is now saying it's a scandal now that democracy has been returned to their country.' And I said, 'And the point about all this is that it's the suffering of these people that is important', I said, 'I should not be having to spend all my time here answering questions to you, when there are people there trying to get back on their feet out there, and I'm supposed to be out in that country helping them.' And I said, 'They just don't understand it.'[19]

At one point, Robin Cook told the House of Commons that he had doubled the number of people working in Sierra Leone. 'What he didn't say was that all the extra people were working on the Sandline case; they weren't actually helping Sierra Leone.[20]

Out of the blue, Customs and Excise decided to drop the case. 'They said it was not in the public interest to pursue this.'[21]

> Both my solicitor and I were disappointed that we did not go to court so that I could clear my name, and I am sure that Tim Spicer felt the same, although I suppose that I should not speak for him.[22] The point is that we both maintained that we had not breached the UN Sanctions Order (a point subsequently corroborated by the Legal Department of the UN in a letter). Because HM Customs and Excise dropped the case against us, we never had the chance to prove this in court.[23]

Sir Thomas Legg's inquiry was the first to report. Foreign Secretary, Robin Cook, presented its findings to the House of Commons. He reiterated that 'Sandline International and its arms played little or no part in the removal of the junta from Sierra Leone.'[24] Within the limits of the inquiry's remit that may have been the case: the consignment of arms destined for the Kamajors/CDF as part of the contract signed by President Kabbah had been seized by ECOMOG at Lungi. But in the overall picture of what actually happened, the inquiry's findings on Sandline's role fall short.

However you view the contract arrangements with ECOMOG and Juba Incorporated, Bokkie was owned by Sandline. It was the only aircraft providing logistical support for ECOMOG − without which they could not have mounted a battlefield campaign − , and it ferried an entire battalion of soldiers and their arms to Kossoh, from where they launched the attack on the junta. Then the company itself had the capacity to operate at a sophisticated level; it was not a group limited to a gung-ho mentality. It had been in contact with Kabbah from July 1997, and it had involvement in the ECOMOG planning group at the highest level, up to and during the invasion of Freetown and the recapture of the main rural towns. This task was conducted on a daily basis. The 'Sandline Affair' made their task and influence much more difficult in terms of liaison, nevertheless, it continued out of operational necessity. In addition, it was able to provide discreet tactical intelligence to both UN and US agencies.

At political level, there was an implied difference in the attitude of the USA. It too, officially, took the line that the junta should be removed by peaceful means. However, its State Department, as we saw, contracted the US company PAE to provide logistical support to ECOMOG. Although (at this stage) PAE did not fly into Sierra Leone, when ECOMOG began its build up of troops and munitions for the attack on the junta, there would have been a grey area in which PAE, in Liberia ferrying Nigerian troops redeployed for battle, was providing the first leg of a relay of men and arms which would then be flown by Juba Incorporated in the Sandline helicopter from Monrovia to Lungi. The US lived with this ambivalence without any breast-beating in public. But then no US secretary of state had painted himself into a corner. Little wonder that Customs and Excise decided to drop the case on the grounds that to pursue it further was not in the public interest.

None of that, however, was central − or indeed of the least interest − to the political motivators who initiated and shaped the remit of the inquiry.

All that became superfluous to what it then became, a political thing in Britain, and essentially it was not a question of whether the sanctions had been busted or not, it was a question of saving Robin Cook's face. I remember Diane Abbott standing up in the House, when the Commission of Inquiry was set up; and she was absolutely right when she said, 'The Commission of Inquiry is a nonsense because they're already pre-set by what it is they are being asked to do.'[25]

From the standpoint of politicians, the main focus of interest was on personalities and the Foreign Office. Referring to Peter Penfold, Robin Cook paid tribute to his courage and commitment to staying at his post during the coup, and he recognized the high standing he had won for Britain in Sierra Leone. However, the Foreign Secretary found fault with him over Sandline.[26] The inquiry also noted flawed communication channels in the Foreign Office: information was not passed on; the African Department had not been aware of the precise wording of the Order in Council, which included Kabbah's government in the arms ban. It was evident too that both ministers and officials had played down the comprehensiveness of the ban in news lines; the junta was always referred to, but not the legitimate government of Sierra Leone. Hence Peter Penfold was not aware that the ban applied to Kabbah's government. But he was to bear the brunt of it. He received a written reprimand from the Permanent Under Secretary on the grounds that he should have been more judicious in his meetings with Tim Spicer, and he should have reported more fully. But there was no reprimand for the other officials in the Foreign Office, who had met Tim Spicer.[27]

The debate in the House of Commons gave some members the opportunity to express righteous indignation about the role of private military companies. Robin Cook assured the House that in future, 'contact with such firms occurs only with permission and with a full report on a written record.'[28] The Foreign Secretary was now off the hook, and Peter Penfold was allowed to return to his post in Sierra Leone. But on one of his return trips to Freetown from a session at the Foreign Office, quite by chance the first two people he met were Fred and Juba.

Peter Penfold came back to Sierra Leone with two BBC reporters, and Juba and myself happened to be there to meet one of our American friends, but he was not in the first flight. But when Peter Penfold got off the helicopter followed by the two BBC reporters, Juba and myself were the first people Peter met, and our meeting appeared to have been arranged! There we were shaking hands, hugging and smiling and welcoming each other, oblivious to all the rest of the people. We were genuinely so pleased and proud to see Peter on Freetown soil, and so was everyone there that evening.

The Foreign Office guidelines about no contact with private military companies without permission, which, of course, had only been introduced after the Sandline inquiries, were unworkable, given the situation in Sierra Leone. The UN was now entering the scene; the UK was emerging as the dominant provider of support and training; and ECOMOG, still reluctant to commit its helicopters, was urging Juba to make the Mi-24 gunship serviceable for combat. It was inevitable that there would be liaison and discussion among representatives of those three elements and the Sierra Leone government. On one occasion, Juba found himself standing next to Peter Penfold, who, trying to keep a straight face, turned to him and said, 'I'm not supposed to be speaking to you.'[29]

The political holier than thou stance in relation to dealings with private military companies did not last long. Two years later, with Britain committed to retraining the Sierra Leone army, the RAF would have a liaison officer attached to the private military company which comprised the Sierra Leone air wing, and during the spectacular British raid on a rebel base to free hostages, the same PMC would be called upon to give assistance.

Before that came about, however, there was yet more drama to be played out when the House of Commons Select Committee on Foreign Affairs – without the warm enthusiasm of the Foreign Secretary – opened its inquiry. The Select Committee's view was that 'it is important not to be mesmerised by the Legg report: theirs is not necessarily the last word in this affair.'[30] True, but neither would its report be the last word on Sandline; it could not be: the committee was refused access to intelligence reports, and it was not allowed to interview, or take evidence in private from the Head of the Secret Intelligence Service (SIS). However, it did focus on the machinery of government, and it had a forceful go at the Foreign and Commonwealth Office in London.

The committee found that 'senior officials who received both Mr Penfold's minute of 2 February and Sandline's Project Python document (Ms Grant and Mr Dales) made serious errors of judgement and failed in their duty to Ministers by not acting promptly and decisively on the information it contained.'[31] Officials who met Tim Spicer took inadequate notes of meeting, considering the import of the agenda. A senior official was referred to as, 'the dog who did not bark.'[32] Nor did the Permanent Under Secretary escape censure. In his statement to the committee, Sir John Kerr, said that Peter Penfold had a duty to understand thoroughly government policy, as it affects the country to which he is accredited ('he should have made it his business to find out'), though he did concede that 'it was also the responsibility of the Department to make sure he came across all [relevant] information.'[33]

Some concession – in bureaucracy it is a fundamental tenet that hierarchy has such responsibility. However, the committee's next sentence could have come from the script of the TV series *Yes Minister*.

We are amazed that Sir John did not disclose, when making these comments that the practice of the Government was not to disseminate Orders in Council or summaries of them.[34]

Indeed the committee itself, after concluding that the Permanent Under Secretary bore some responsibilities for lack of information to ministers, went on to allude to a *Yes Minister* flavour about practice in the Foreign Office.

The way in which no-one with a right to put papers up to Ministers – Ms Grant, Mr Dales or Sir John Kerr – did in fact do so reveals at best political naivete, and at worst a *Yes Minister*–like contempt for civil servants' duties towards their Ministers.[35]

In the larger scheme of things, this report, like its predecessor, would soon sink into the sands; they had served their purpose. But Sir Thomas Legg hoped that his would close the chapter for officials. Robin Cook agreed with that; he said, 'There will be no scapegoats, and this should be the end of the matter as far as individuals are concerned.'[36] And he may have meant it too – at the time.

But what if President Kabbah were to confer an honour on the British High Commissioner for his outstanding support to the country during the time of the coup, would the chapter still remain closed? For that is precisely what Kabbah informed Peter Penfold his government wished to do. Protocol, of course, demanded that he pass this proposal back to the Foreign Office for permission to accept; and given the recent background, with evidence of papers not being put up to ministers, it is reasonable to assume that this request was placed in a minister's in-tray, or, at the very least, discussed. Permission to accept the honour was refused. No doubt reasoning would have been adduced along the lines that they could hardly let the chap who had been their fall-guy now be made a hero of the state of Sierra Leone. But to an outsider, it seems unnecessarily vindictive.

However, justice was done and was seen to be done to Peter Penfold by a system that does not require bureaucratic assent: traditional authority – in this case the chieftaincy system with its own intricate arrangement of checks and balances, whose great strength is its closeness to the people. It happened as Peter Penfold returned from one of his visits to the UK. In those days, flights were from London to Conakry,

Guinea, and it was here that he was met by Desmond Luke, Chief Justicee, and one of the ministers who were there to escort him back to Sierra Leone.

I thought that's strange, it doesn't normally happen. Having said that, they said that they could only escort me back if I chartered a plane and I gave them seats on it. I said OK, and I was told that I had special permission to fly not to Lungi but into Hastings. So I said fine.

When I got to Hastings, I saw all these crowds and crowds of people there. I stepped off the plane and was escorted into the hut of the airport, and King Naimbana was there and some of the chiefs. And he said that I was going to be made a chief. And they had a suit there ready to put on me, and then I came out from that and was driven into Freetown from Hastings, and all the roads were lined with people. It was a hell of a lot of people.

Then I got into Freetown itself, and there was a whole convoy of about 30 vehicles, and the convoy stopped and I got out, and they put me in this hammock. It was a specially made hammock, an amazing thing. It had a big wooden awning – very heavy – with the Union Jack painted on the outside and the Sierra Leone flag on the inside and **His Excellency Komrabai, Peter Penfold**, and I was getting carried through the streets up Siaka Stevens Street. So I was carried about a mile. There were thousands of people. And one of the things that always endeared it to me, they were all waving Union Jacks. But the Union Jacks they were waving they had to make themselves. You couldn't go into a store and buy them, so the night before they'd all got their pieces of paper – thousands of them.

It was over thirty years after independence, and there's this white guy being carried through the streets of this African capital – thirty years after independence –, with more British flags being waved than when Queen Victoria was on the throne. It was just unbelievable. And even after that I had another coronation when my wife came back, we had a proper coronation in the old municipal building. Again with King Naimbana, and what was interesting about that was that it was King Naimbana's grandfather who had originally signed over the piece of land that Freetown was on to the colonial representative of Britain at the time which signalled the start of Freetown as a colony. And there's his grandson now crowning me, the successor to this other person.[37]

Honorary Paramount Chiefs are few and far between: in the twentieth century, the Queen and Prince Philip had the title conferred on them, and now Peter Penfold joined the ranks of a select number. At risk to his own life, he had responded to the country's need at the time of the coup, and he sustained strong support over the months its government was in exile, and he did so (as it turned out) at a cost to his professional career. But not to his standing as a man.

One final ceremony was arranged for him, this time in the east of the country, where the eastern chiefs were gathered along with a huge assembly of people. A key figure on this occasion was Regent Chief Sam Hinga Norman, and his concise summing up of Peter Penfold's contribution to his country was spoken – as no other assessment of it had been – in the name of the people of Sierra Leone. He said,

> something that really brought tears to my eyes, when he made this remark, in front of these thousands of people and local chiefs, 'In Sierra Leone's history, Britain has sent us two great Britons.' He said, 'In the last century they sent us Governor Clarkson, and Governor Clarkson gave us a prayer.' (And indeed that's right, it's famous, and they used to read out Governor Clarkson's prayer on the radio every morning, even when I was there – a beautiful prayer.) 'In this century they sent us High Commissioner Penfold, and he gave us hope.' And boy – was that powerful to me![38]

The Memorial to David Stirling at Ochtertyre, Perthshire. Fred flew especially from Sierra Leone to attend the SAS Regimental Association unveiling ceremony. (*Fred Marafono collection*)

Serving with Executive Outcomes, Fred, on the right, gathering his kit at Kono helipad, as he prepares to leave for Freetown with Col Karl Deats (centre) and Col Renier Hugo. (*Jim Hooper collection*)

Executive Outcomes personnel after one of their operations. Fred is second from the right, Cobus Claassens on his right. (*Cobus Claassens collection*)

Col Roelf van Heerden outside EO operations HQ at Koidu. (*Jim Hooper collection*)

Fred leaving Koidu with Sierra Leone troops on the first leg of the assault on Gandorhun. (*Jim Hooper collection*)

Col Renier Hugo leading the mortar team for the assault on Gandorhun. (*Jim Hooper collection*)

After two days and nights on a hill near Gandorhun, EO operators wait to be airlifted out on Bokkie. (*Jim Hooper collection*)

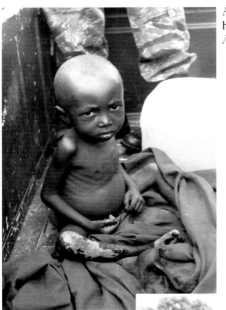

An injured little boy left to die by the rebels. Fred found him and handed him over to the Red Cross at Bo. (*Fred Marafono collection*)

During a joint EO/SL army operation, Fred briefing a helicopter protection party at Bo. (*Fred Marafono collection*)

Chief Hinga Norman and an EO officer inspect local militia. (*Fred Marafono collection*)

Pete Flynn, his case packed for a quick departure, Fred and Hawah at Freetown Golf Club shortly before Pete flew home. (*Fred Marafono collection*)

Fred and Chief Hinga Norman celebrate with a bottle of wine at Lagunda on the evening that Hinga Norman's appointment as Deputy Minister of Defence for Sierra Leone was announced. (*Fred Marafono collection*)

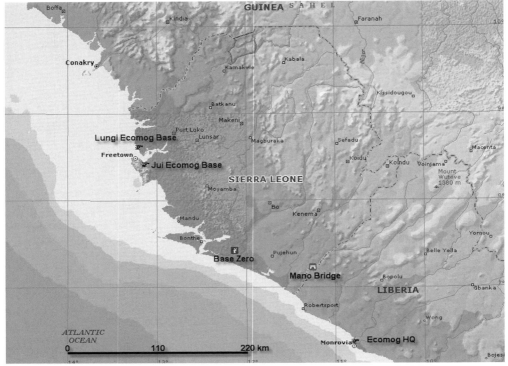

Positions of the Sierra Leone militia and ECOMOG bases that Juba Inc. linked, supplied and reinforced from Monrovia with Bokkie during the period of the AFRC junta. (*Juba Joubert collection*)

Bokkie bringing VIPs to the ceremony at Freetown marking the restoration of democratic government. (*Fred Marafono collection*)

British High Commissioner Peter Penfold with Kamajors in Bo, March 1998, after the restoration of Kabbah's government. (*Peter Penfold collection*)

Juba and Nigerian ECOMOG officers in Kono. (*Juba Joubert collection*)

Peter Penfold being carried through the streets of Freetown as Paramount Chief. (*Peter Penfold collection*)

With ECOMOG top brass: Gp Capt Tijjani Easterbrook, Chief Air Officer on the left with Juba and another Nigerian Air Force officer. Behind Tijjani's right shoulder, Gen Timothy Shelpidi, the Force Commander; framed between Tijjani and Juba, Gen Abdul One Mohammed. (*Juba Joubert collection*)

Fred, armed with a GPMG, on his way with Rick to bring out wounded from the besieged American embassy in Monrovia. (*Rick's collection*)

The killing fields of Freetown around Connaught Hospital when the rebels entered the capital in January 1999. (*Fred Marafono collection*)

Innocent civilians bear witness to the barbarism of the rebels. (*Fred Marafono collection*)

Inside an AN 124 transport plane, Juba's procurement in the Ukraine for the government of Sierra Leone, a partially disassembled Mi-24 gunship and freight. (*Juba Joubert collection*)

Rocket pods for the gunship in the AN 124 cargo. (*Juba Joubert collection*)

The AN 124 arrival at Lungi with the gunships and ammunition. (*Juba Joubert collection*)

Juba, Neall Ellis and team arriving in Bokkie to off-load the AN 124. (*Juba Joubert collection*)

Juba piloting with Fred as gunner, in one of the newly acquired Mi-24 gunships, taking off from DHQ on the first mission against rebel positions. (*Juba Joubert collection*)

Fred, Chief Hinga Norman and Ft Lt Wakili at the helipad at Cockerill HQ. (*Fred Marafono collection*)

Fred and Juba at Paddy's celebrate the rebels suing for peace. (*Fred Marafono collection*)

Chief Hinga Norman and Fred attending a pentecostal church service. (*Fred Marafono collection*)

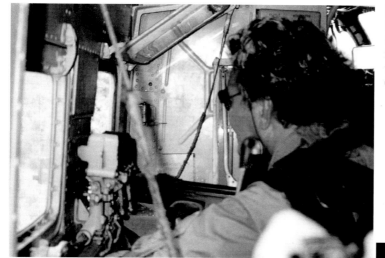

Post Operation Barras, Fred positioned with GPMG as the gunship flies over the Rokel Creek towards Gberi Bana. (*Fred Marafono collection*)

Gberi Bana, showing the devastating fire power the British raiders deployed during the hostage release operation. (*Fred Marafono collection*)

Alongside the gunship, wearing DPM, from left to right, four of the British soldiers who took part in the Gberi Bana raid, then Fred. On his left, pilot Neall Ellis and on his left Deputy Minister of Defence Chief Hinga Norman. (*Fred Marafono collection*)

Prime Minister Tony Blair greeting Chief Hinga Norman on a visit to Sierra Leone. President Kabbah is on the right. (*Fred Marafono collection*)

Centre of the group, Fred, Peter Penfold, having retired from Her Majesty's Diplomatic Service, and Juba. (*Fred Marafono collection*)

Fred, the actor Jeffrey Wright and pilot Cassie Nel. (*Fred Marafono collection*)

Jeffrey Wright, Daniel Craig and Fred at the premiere of Casino Royale. (*Fred Marafono collection*)

Left to right, Juba, Chief Hinga Norman, Peter Penfold, Hassan (Fred's driver) and Fred. (*Fred Marafono collection*)

The price he paid for fighting to restore democracy – Chief Hinga Norman, shackled, indicted by the Special Court for Sierra Leone. (*Fred Marafono collection*)

Hope for future generations. Fred and Juba with children, made homeless by rebels, now given a fresh start. In the background the Lebanese school at Kenema, about 75 metres behind which Juba landed Bokkie when they resupplied ECOMOG in October 1997. (*Fred Marafono collection*)

Chapter Eight

Air Wing

Their shoulders held the sky suspended;
They stood, and earth's foundations stay;
What God abandoned, these defended,
And saved the sum of things for pay.

A. E. Housman, 'Epitaph on an army of Mercenaries'

Hope having been fulfilled and the country's democratic government returned to power, the scope and scale of the air logistical support for ECOMOG increased, as the force took the battle to the rebels up-country. It became a new ball game for Juba Incorporated in terms of assets, intelligence, combat role and movement throughout the country; and they relocated their base from Lungi to Defence Headquarters at Cockerill Barracks in Freetown. A problem for the returning civilian government was that the rump of the loyal elements of the Sierra Leone military had to have leadership — its Chief of the Defence Staff was among those of the junta in prison awaiting trial for treason —, and so President Kabbah appointed Maxwell Khobe, the ECOMOG task force commander, and now Brigadier General, to be CDS for Sierra Leone, although he was a foreigner.

Juba's status with ECOMOG had been high, resupplying the force and acting as medicav during the period of the junta, and it rose higher. Throughout the period of the junta, Juba was the sole pilot keeping the air bridge open. This was known to the Liberian backers of insurgency in Sierra Leone, and Nigerian intelligence officers told him that that Charles Taylor had put a ransom of $80,000 on his head; they also warned the crew that there was a chance they could be ambushed in Liberia, travelling by road between Monrovia and Roberts International airfield; and they advised Juba, in particular, never to leave his glass unattended when he was drinking in any of the city's bars in his off-duty hours. In the light of the Liberian security people's attempts to entrap Chief Hinga Norman, Fred, Juba and Sendaba took these warnings to heart.

However, from the beginning of the company's contract, there should have been two pilots for the aircraft, and although, on his own, Juba had succeeded brilliantly, the company, Juba Incorporated, was now to take on the role of Air Wing of the Sierra Leone military. There was no Sierra Leonean fall-back they could rely on:

Victor King, the senior air officer and member of the junta, was among the military personnel awaiting trial. But Sandline, also with a presence in Freetown, stepped in, and in the third week of February, Neall Ellis, a South African pilot who had served in EO, 'for a short period due to bad performance',[1] was flown to Sierra Leone to be Juba's co-pilot.

ECOMOG senior officers learned lessons from Juba's tactics in flying Bokkie in ways not conceived of in the Nigerian military manual. The CAO, Tijjani Easterbrook, pointed out to his superiors that the Alpha jet was not suitable for counter insurgency/guerrilla warfare in forested areas due to its speed; and in May, he was able to convince the Force Commander to raise a letter with President Kabbah about the urgent need to repair and service the Mi-24 gunship.[2] Consequently, on 27 May, Juba received a letter from ECOMOG headquarters to reactivate the Mi-24 gunship. Juba, it will be recalled, flew the gunship from Liberia to Lungi after Victor King's foiled escape attempt in February, and he was not impressed by the level of maintenance it received at the hands of the junta, for it was flying on two different engines; so he ordered the Air Wing technicians to inspect it and draw up a list of spare parts that were required. When ECOMOG took control of the gunship, there was a document for the right engine, whose specification was TB3–117VM, but there was no document for the left engine, a TB3–117V, which had a lower power capacity. Therefore, on the list of spares to be acquired, the technicians added two according to the specification of the right engine. There was a lot of pressure to get the gunship airworthy; Neall was not qualified to fly it, and Sandline wanted Juba to give him the conversion to the Mi-24 as quickly as possible.

Juba first gave Neall his refresher on the Mi-17 that he hadn't flown since he left EO. 'It was not an easy task to get him up to the standard that was required to fly this helicopter single-pilot,'[3] as Juba had been doing for the last 8 months. It was necessary, however, because Juba had to be on the ground much more to co-ordinate the operations and requirements of ECOMOG and the Sierra Leone Government, as these were becoming more involved. After flying with Neall for a month during the dry season, Juba decided that he should fly single pilot in future, because planning on the ground was now imperative as the war progressed. A French fixed-wing pilot, Jean Jacques Fuentes, joined them. He was usually known among them as JJ, and Juba allocated him to fly the Sierra Leone government's Partenavia light aircraft to carry out reconnaissance.

Fate, however, seemed determined to wipe out the Air Wing on the evening of Saturday 15 August, and it was only Fred's sixth sense that saved Bokkie's crew and the aircraft. Neall was the pilot and they had been tasked to carry resupplies and ammunition to the group from Lifeguard, the PMC that Fred worked for in June 1997, who were based at Kono. It was a very heavy load, but all went well, and they left Kono at 19.00 hours. Which turned out to be a mistake. The harmattan was blowing, carrying minute particles of sand on its way south from the Sahara, making visibility very difficult. By the time they arrived at Lungi the pick-up was hazardous, and then they had the last lap to cover from Lungi across to HQ at Cockerill. It was difficult to gauge the horizon and they were flying very low so that the sea was always visible. Fred is not given to overstatement and his diary entry reads: 'en route to Cockerill nearly went into the sea – saved by my warning – not a second too soon. Very, very close call indeed.'

I put my gun down on my normal seat, my feet were hanging out of the doorway, I was straining my eyes to make sure that we did not go in. Everything was going well until I had this horrible feeling and when I looked down, we were heading into the water as we went. I shouted on the intercom to pull up, and we just made it in time. I had visions of the front tyres hitting the water at high speed and the helicopter somersaulting or doing a back flip into the water. Should that happen, we would stand no chance at all.

They celebrated their good luck that evening with two Russian pilots and some Americans from PAE, at a dinner paid for by Sandline.

Even two pilots, however, and two helicopters would not be able to cope with ECOMOG's logistical needs and at the same time provide a combat role, so the American company, PAE, that hitherto operated for the peace-keeping force only in Liberia, was assigned to work from Freetown. The company comprised three Americans, all former American Special Forces, and they flew two Mi-8 MTVs and an Mi-26, at times crewed by Russians. In charge was someone who, for this account, will simply be called Rick. Rick had served in the US Army Special Forces for 33 years and retired from active duty as Command Sergeant Major. He had extensive operational, medical, weapons and demolitions experience, and he served in a variety of combat zones. From now on, both Juba Incorporated and PAE assisted each other in combat missions, and socialized when off duty.

However, one of their most important joint operations came from an unexpected incident, not in Sierra Leone but in Liberia, when the US embassy was besieged by Liberian government forces. Controversy still exists about whether the country's ethnic Krahn leader, Roosevelt Johnson, and his followers were set up by Charles Taylor's security forces so that they could be attacked. Rick outlines what happened.

On 18 September, Liberian government forces fired on rebel Krahn leader Roosevelt Johnson and his entourage as they were talking to U.S. officials at the Embassy entrance. The attack wounded two U.S. personnel (one with a serious belly wound), a few local guards with minor wounds and killed four Krahn. The Americans returned fire, killing two policemen. The Americans and the Johnson party retreated into the embassy compound, setting the stage for an extended siege.

The only American Forces in Liberia were the US Marines guarding the US Embassy and they were very busy protecting the US Embassy and personnel from attacks by Charles Taylor's forces. PAE-Freetown received a message from PAE-Monrovia that the US Embassy in Monrovia was under siege and two Americans were wounded and a 100% evacuation required immediately.[4]

Rick contacted Fred who went to Juba and asked if they could assist. Juba immediately agreed. PAE had two helicopters, and Juba, because of his experience during the time of the coup, briefed the Russian pilots on the approach paths to the embassy at Mamba Point in Monrovia. He co-ordinated the whole operation from Freetown, with HF radio communication to the aircraft and telephone communication to different points. He held Bokkie in reserve as medivac at Kenema. If one of the PAE helicopters went down, it would go in. Rick picks up the narrative from there.

I only had the three other Americans working with me (all former Special Forces) and needed assistance. Some former Executive Outcomes South Africans and Fred volunteered. Our staging area was in Kenema, Sierra Leone. I divided the team between our two helicopters, Fred with me in the first helicopter and Neall Ellis and the Mi-17 (Bokkie) crew in reserve as a medivac.

We took off from Kenema with the intent to fly directly to the US Embassy but were diverted to the Nigerian ECOMOG Base in Monrovia. While we were at ECOMOG base, Fred and the other GPMG gunners set up an inner security for the helicopters. There were two outer security perimeters set up by the Nigerians. When Charles Taylor's SSS [Special Security Service] thugs breached the ECOMOG Base outer perimeter we loaded the helicopters and flew 10 km out to sea and out of range of anti-aircraft threats.

We flew a pattern for 30 minutes until the Embassy cleared us to land. Fred and I landed in the first aircraft and loaded the wounded American and 15 Embassy Personnel. That helicopter immediately flew off to Freetown where there was a medivac plane waiting for the wounded American and flew him to Europe for medical treatment. He made a full recovery.

Fred and I stayed on the ground with the Security Officer, who was also shot in the arm, and he told us that he and the remainder of the Embassy personnel were going to stay. We soon called in the second helicopter and Fred and I boarded and flew back to Kenema to pick up some ECOMOG personnel who were wounded in Sierra Leone and took them back to the ECOMOG hospital in Freetown.

This operation expanded when EUCOM [United States European Command] responded by directing SOCEUR [Special Operations Command Europe] to dispatch a 12-man survey and assessment team (ESAT) a couple of days later. Fred assisted with every mission inserting and re-supplying the US Embassy, the ESAT, US Navy Seals, and later the evacuation of Roosevelt Johnson and 22 Krahn from the US Embassy in Monrovia.

On every mission Fred carried a 7.62 GPMG with 200 round belt chambered and had an Alice backpack with another 2,000 rounds of 7.62 belt. He sat with me in the door of the aircraft and wherever we landed he hopped off the helicopter with me and pointed the GPMG at any direction that I looked at. Fred is so fucking strong; I've never seen anyone hold a weapon, let alone a GPMG, in a standing position and carrying that load on his back. We couldn't have supported the American Forces without Fred's assistance.[5]

What if the US had followed the UK government's song and dance about no contact with private military companies except through formal channels, would their embassy officials have been unable to summon the most effective means available to counter force with force and evacuate the wounded without first seeking permission from Washington? What if, indeed, the UK's quickly cobbled together guidelines had been in place a year earlier, at the time of the siege of the Mammy Yoko hotel in Freetown, would Peter Penfold have been prevented from including an operative of a private military company (who was decorated for this action) in the team that saved lives until he had gone through the palaver of obtaining permission from the Foreign Office?

ECOMOG commanders, of course, had no such hang-ups about private military companies either during the period of the coup in Sierra Leone or after the fall of the junta, and they wanted the Mi-24 in action as soon as possible. On 7 October, Juba test-flew it and found its weapons in good working order. Then three days later, he took off in the gunship on an armed reconnaissance because of an emergency that had arisen. He had JJ as one of the crew.

He was over a very hostile area, 120 kilometres from DHQ, an area that had not been known about during the EO days (Juba felt that it may have been because of strong political connections with the RUF). It only became apparent when he entered the area and realized how it was possible for the rebels to move from the south-east of the region to the north-west without any problems. The stronghold would not have become known had not the rebels given it away by attacking friendly forces so close it.

Juba had the target visual that JJ in the front cockpit directed him to. On this old Mi-24 there was mounted a 12.7mm Gatling gun in the nose with a firing rate of up to 5000 rounds per minute and 4 x mini-guns on the wings with 6000 rounds a minute firepower each.

He approached the target from the south and delivered effective fire on its eastern side, and then swiftly changed direction to direct fire to its western side and so create pandemonium among the rebels. He then flew north of the target to come in for the final attack, when he experienced engine vibration and oil pressure reduction on No. 2 engine, and at the same time the guns started giving problems. He recalled from EO days that, 'The rebels liked their human soup', and visualized himself and his crew ending up in the pot by dark the same day, if the other engine malfunctioned. Without alerting his crew, he very calmly requested the direction back to DHQ. By this time he had already turned on a south-westerly direction for the shortest route out of the area to cross the closest river to give them some headway in case the other engine failed.

He managed to return the helicopter to DHQ under extreme conditions. After landing, inspection showed that there was no oil left in the engine due to a leakage, and it was about to seize. The helicopter was then grounded until spare parts could be acquired. The Chief Operations Officer of ECOMOG apologized to Juba for putting him under pressure to fly the unserviceable Mi-24 that nearly did not make it back to base.

The order for two reconditioned engines and spare parts for the gunship was won by Chatelet Investment Ltd, a company with an office in Luxembourg and another in Freetown; the engines would be bought in a former Soviet bloc country. However, Gp Cpt Easterbrooke, ECOMOG Chief Air Officer, and Juba were refused entry visas for Russia to carry out advance inspection of the engines because the firm that invited them was not a recognized company.

Good news and bad news arrived together at the end of October in a communication from Sandline. The company gave Bokkie over into the ownership of its crew at no charge; it was theirs and all monies accruing. But Bokkie was long overdue complete refurbishment. Keeping the air bridge open between Monrovia and Lungi demanded much effort and commitment on the part of the crew, but it took a greater toll on the aircraft. Juba had nursed it along beyond the designers' limits, and now they were going to be responsible for maintaining it. The three who flew Bokkie since October the previous year plus Neall Ellis, the pilot Sandline sent in February, formed a company and called it JESA, taking the first letter of each name: Juba, Ellis, Sendaba and (an exotic variation of Fred's to provide a vowel) Alfredo. They would be contracted to the Sierra Leone government through ECOMOG.

On 7 November, the first consignment of spares for the gunship arrived at Lungi along with a military equipment contractor, who had had dealings with the Sierra Leone government for some years, and three Russian technicians to be met by a reception committee that included Gen Kbobe CDS, Abdulai Mustapha, an adviser to President Kabbah (or as Fred described him, 'Kabbah's Mr Fix It'), Chief Air Officer Grp Capt Easterbrooke, Juba and Sendaba. When the engine logbook was inspected, Sendaba noticed that on the cover, the engine specification and serial number was pasted over and sellotaped; and moreover, he checked and found that some of its pages were missing or not completed. As he explained later to a Board of Inquiry,

The details that are supposed to be contained in the missing pages are as follows:

1. Page 65 (missing) is supposed to be the 'acceptance certificate' containing the engine type, engine serial number, 3 signatures stamped to certify that the engine has been correctly overhauled.

2. Pages 35, 36 and 37 (not missing but not filled) are supposed to contain the engine parameter details.
3. Pages 382 and 383 (missing) are supposed to be filled with the bench test report after overhauling.
4. The graph showing the engine parameter reading is also not supplied with the log book.

It is based on all these reasons that we did not install the engines on the aircraft.[6]

The logbook, in Juba's view, was a legal document. He refused to accept the engines, and reported the matter to Gen Khobe. Over the next couple of days, while the contractor and the Russian technicians were still in the country, further meetings were held. The contractor's position was that he felt he had been treated in a hostile manner, that the Russian technicians had no doubts that the engines ordered were for the Mi-8 transporter, not the Mi-24, but that is what they were asked to provide and that was what they delivered.[7] But when the technicians were challenged about the missing and uncompleted pages, their position was that the engines were operated in different conditions, so it was not necessary to include the missing pages of the logbook. Then matters were compounded when the Russian technicians assessed that the Mi-24's airframe was due for a complete overhaul. CAO Tijjani Easterbrook summarized it thus,

> Some interest in Sierra Leone, hoping to make a profit decided to order for the required helicopter spares, engines and armaments. The engines delivered were expired, the arms and ammo were for the ground forces and could not be used from an airborne platform, while the spares were not the ones required. I raised an observation to the Force Commander and the President. The President set up a Board of Inquiry.[8]

The upshot was that the gunship remained grounded, and the Sierra Leone Defence Headquarters set up a Board of Inquiry. However, due to the worsening security situation with the AFRC/RUF rebels, it would be the following year before it was able to report.

Without a gunship, the Sierra Leone government forces had lost a valuable edge over the rebels. But Tijjani Easterbrook took an important initiative.

In November 1998 when the rebels' push towards Freetown became a real threat, a meeting was held between the President, Force Commander, Deputy Minister of Defence Mr Hinga Norman, and myself on how the Air Force could stop the rebel advance and raise the morale of ECOMOG troops. I used the opportunity to rekindle the helicopter issue and told the meeting that a helicopter gunship would be the only solution. The President agreed and the Deputy Minister of Defence was directed to handle the matter.[9]

Hinga Norman proposed to President Kabbah that Juba be mandated to procure a replacement helicopter from the former Soviet bloc, and should be accompanied by CAO Easterbrook as well as Sendaba, in the light of his knowledge of Russian. The president concurred, and he issued Juba with a diplomatic passport and the mandate for the procurement of helicopters: Juba's original idea was both an Mi-24 and an Mi-17 because 'Bokkie was on its last legs'.[10] He would also procure ammunition. The implications of that decision were then discussed with the CDS and one or two of President Kabbah's advisers.

It may have been before this time that Juba began to sense that the change in Brig Gen Khobe's role from ECOMOG Task Force commander to Chief of the Defence Staff for Sierra Leone had introduced a certain detachment on Khobe's part, and it dawned on Juba that there might be an agenda there.

In the first week of December, Chief Hinga Norman called a meeting to discuss the implications and finer points of the president's decision. The meeting was held in Gen Khobe's house. It began around 12 o'clock at night. Among those present were both Tijjani Easterbrook and Juba. Chief Hinga Norman outlined to the CDS and the others who were there, including one of President Kabbah's advisers, that the president had agreed to give Juba the mandate to procure an Mi-24 gunship. Counter suggestions were made: one of Kabbah's trusted advisers, perhaps even more than one should be involved in the procurement. But the Deputy Minister of Defence held firm.

> That's when the Chief said to Khobe, and everybody else who was sitting there, 'Juba will make a success of it.' And then he said that if I didn't succeed in doing the procurement of these machines for them, they could take his head. And what happened after the meeting was that they went out in full force and tried to get me to fail because that was the way to get the Chief out of the way.[11]

Juba felt that Chief Hinga Norman knew that others had their own agenda. The meeting ended at 3 am; it was sobering, in the still night, to realize that there were people at a high level whose undisclosed aims were to further their own interests. And he formed that impression not simply from that one meeting but over a host of others in what was to become a saga: he was supposed to be out of the country for ten days, but it was to be over three months before he was able to return. However, there were two great strengths on his side: he had the mandate from the president for the final decision; and the budget was underwritten by the UK as part of its £30 million package of support – most of which was for economic reconstruction – and, because of that, contracts would be monitored by Britain's Crown Agents.

So on 30 December, Juba and Tijjani Easterbrook left Sierra Leone, bound first for London before going on to Russia. As the plane touched down, alarm bells ought to have been ringing for some members of the House of Commons, who, a few months earlier had been intoning high-minded sentiments about the scourge of private military operators in Africa, for here was a South African former member of Executive Outcomes, travelling on a diplomatic passport (carrying a visitors' visa for entry to Russia), mandated by the President of Sierra Leone to procure war machines with a budget of $3.3 million of British taxpayers' money at a time when there was a UN embargo on importing military equipment to the country.

The country that they had left was badly in need of an Air Wing with a gunship. On 6 December, ECOMOG forces backed by CDF fought for control of Lunsar. Four days later rebels were fighting less than 40 miles from Freetown. On 18 December, Fred noted in his diary that they flew to Masiaka with food for the Guinean troops, then on to Kenema with the Old Lion (Chief Hinga Norman) on board with supplies of shotgun ammunition for the CDF, next to Daru with ammunition for the ECOMOG force there. They returned to Kenema where they refuelled and picked up Chief Hinga Norman again, then back to Masiaka to air-lift some casualties before returning to DHQ at Cockerill. Next day the BBC reported that Deputy Defence Minister Sam Hinga Norman had distributed weapons to the CDF in Kenema.

> The move followed the passing of enabling legislation on Tuesday and marks the first time the government has officially distributed arms to the militia. Norman said the move was to help deal with the remnants of fleeing junta forces, and that the CDF will now be allowed to accompany ECOMOG troops fighting AFRC/RUF rebels.[12]

Not before time too: the only indigenous force that could be relied on to fight the AFRC/RUF, ill organized though they were, the CDF needed ammunition. But the rebels kept up the pressure. ECOMOG removed its heavy artillery from up-country, and UN personnel were evacuated to Freetown. The rebels took Koidu on 20 December, and two days later thousands of civilians fled Waterloo as it came under attack. They were being supported, supplied and armed despite an international embargo. Britain sent two RAF Hercules planes to evacuate its nationals. A foreign ministers' conference was held in Abidjan with representatives of several African countries. Britain was represented by Peter Penfold. Meanwhile, UN personnel left the capital.

Bokkie flew daily with ammunition and food resupply to areas under severe pressure. From 24 December and in the days leading up to the fall of Makeni, they took ammunition for an ECOMOG force and shotguns and ammunition for the CDF. They were often under fire, and they had taken on – and Fred trained – two Nigerians to act as rear gunners, because their blind spot was at the rear. Both

newcomers were called Mohammed; so they were known as Mohammed and Old
Mohammed.

On our run in, we came in so low and fast that they did not have time to react,
even though Mohammed (right rear gunner) and myself were ready, for them.
But on our way out, all hell broke loose. I saw them running towards the path of
the flying helicopter and I let loose with my GMPG. It was really music to the
ears. One guy with his RPG tube was lining up to shoot us, but I beat him to it.
The last I saw of him was him flying into the air as we passed over.

Under such pressure, the discipline of some ECOMOG soldiers broke, and the
danger for the helicopter crew in medivac role was their being swamped with
deserters in a panic to get out. In the event of the helicopter being rushed by
deserters, Fred and Neall agreed that whenever Fred called 'lift off', Neall would
pull power immediately, even if the steps were still down. On this particular run in,
they landed with a heavy load of ammunition, and, as usual, no soldiers ran to assist
with the unloading. It was the CO himself, covered by six soldiers, who came across
as Fred unloaded and said, 'Sir, do you know you're under fire?' After they unloaded
the ammunition, they loaded the wounded and dead.

It was to be a memorable flight back, and one in which they had to call on PAE for
assistance. After the casualties were loaded on board, some soldiers, in desperation
to get away, started to pile on board.

I tapped Mohammed on his back and told him to get inside. He jumped out again
to close the doors. Unfortunately, at that very moment, thinking that we were
all in, I told Nellis [Neall Ellis was often called Nellis] to lift off. Mohammed
managed to unhook one of the bars but unfortunately, he was unable to close it
properly and it was still outside. Worst of all, the helicopter was pulling up, and
Mohammed told us later that he was hanging on to the tail, and realizing that
he was going out of the camp perimeter eventually let go of the helicopter, but
fortunately, still inside the camp safe area. On landing at Port Loko and realizing
that Mohammed was missing everyone was very sad but promised that we would
go back tomorrow come hell or high water to bring Mohammed back.

One of the funniest sights I will never forget was on our landing at Port Loko.
The door that Mohammed unhooked was still loose, and whilst in the air, the
speed of the slipstream forced the air around to the rear and this kept the door
closed. But on landing the sudden touchdown threw the door open and the
2 soldiers that were sitting on it flew past us as the door came off the wing! They
just flew past like surfers on an improvised surfboard. But miraculously, they
were not hurt.

But our troubles were not over because the uninjured refused to get off the
helicopter, and we had to get the rear door back with us to see what could be

done immediately if we were to be back in the air again. No one got off until the PAE helicopter arrived and took the wounded. We asked them not to take any of the useless soldiers who deserted their posts. Finally, we got off on our way home. On arriving in Freetown, Sendaba and his staff flew with Nellis to Lungi and took one of the rear doors from an old shell there and soon sorted out Bokkie.

On 6 January, the rebels entered Freetown in force moving from east to west leaving a trail of destruction and huge loss of life.

We got a call very early, at about 6am in the morning, and we took off. And when we came back we had 10 bullet holes in the aircraft. RPGs were fired and we moved to the eastern side of Freetown. When we came back and landed to refuel, I said to Neall, 'Neall you carry on and I'll go and see the Chief.' So we got one of our vehicles, it was a Toyoto and I drove to see the Chief. It was about 7 am that I came and he was in his house in Freetown with two of his people, no weapons, nothing. I said, 'Chief what are you doing? You cannot stay here, you've got to come with me.' He said, 'Fred I tried to call the President this morning and there was no answer. I tried to call Gen Khobe; there was no answer. And I said, 'Chief come, you've got to come with me.' So he came with me to the base at Cockerill, and when we arrived there was Dr Jonah, he was the Finance Minister. He said that he got a message from the President that they were to meet up, the Chief and him at Lungi, at the VIP lounge at Lungi, meet him, the President. But Kabbah was nowhere near Lungi, he was out at sea.

Where was the president? Deputy Defence Minister Sam Hinga Norman did not know the whereabouts of President Kabbah.

'I don't know where he is. I wish I knew,' Norman told journalists at Lungi International Airport. 'As a president, (Kabbah) should not go too far from his people. He should be in Sierra Leone,' Norman added. 'I'm not president, and I haven't left.' Norman said the Civil Defence Forces 'controlled certain points' in Freetown, but maintained he had no knowledge of rebel positions. 'Only their friends, their collaborators, know where they are,' he said.[13]

Not agonizing long over a lost leader, Hinga Norman linked up with the CDF and the remnants of government forces, and was in the thick of the fighting to turn the tide of the RUF advance from east to west. There was heavy destruction to the city, with the rebels torching what they could and Nigerian Alpha jets dropping bombs on rebel positions near Freetown. The RUF advance got as far as Congo Cross bridge. An expert eye-witness: Brig (now Gen Sir) David Richards (currently Chief of the General Staff of the UK) had been sent by the British government to make a military assessment of the situation. He discovered the importance of Chief Hinga Norman in the fight against the RUF:

> We had not picked up his role with the country as much as I then discovered it was. So I was more focused on ECOMOG and Brig Gen Khobe at that time on that first day.[14]

And on that first day in Sierra Leone, Gen Khobe took David Richards from a rudimentary command post to observe the fighting for a key crossing: Congo Cross bridge, from where the RUF, if they crossed it, could fan out and probably capture an armoury that contained arms and ammunition. With a pair of binoculars, behind some cover, David Richards observed the fighting.

> I observed the government forces successfully stopping the RUF advance and they got across the bridge – the government forces got across the bridge and took some prisoners. I had observed 10, 15 minutes before that, through my binoculars, the killing of some people on the far side of the bridge, the RUF side of the bridge, which everyone had seen from the safe side, if you like. It was clear that the government forces were very excited and angry when they captured the prisoners and I think I remember the atmosphere. It was very dynamic, a lot of shouting, excitement. There were still bodies on the road from the fighting. All this sort of thing. And I saw a group of people go across the bridge to where the prisoners were being held. And I said to Khobe, 'What are they doing?' and he said, 'That's Chief Norman.' And I remembered that I had been introduced to him on my first day here. And he remonstrated with the government forces, the group I'd say there were about 10 or 12 of them, who had captured the RUF or AFRC, I don't know which they were, … I mean, basically the RUF and the AFRC were on one side of the bridge and the government forces on the other. They [government forces] had attacked across the bridge and another group came down the line of the river or stream. And they had – it was a very neat little operation; and they had captured – there was a fight, and they had captured some of the RUF…
>
> And I saw Hinga Norman – well Gen Khobe said, 'That's Hinga Norman,' because I said, 'What's he doing?' and he went up to the group and, through my binoculars and from what I could hear …Hinga Norman went up to the group and remonstrated with them. And it was clear that he was, even from what I could see, telling them that they must behave and stop getting so excited. And they were threatening to shoot these prisoners… And from what I saw, the impression I gained was that Chief Norman prevented that abuse from happening… During the fighting I and everyone had seen at least one apparently innocent person killed by the RUF group on the far side of the bridge. They were firing their weapons indiscriminately. And so everyone was very angry. I was very angry. I couldn't believe what I was seeing… In my judgment, Chief Hinga Norman

calmed it down. Because if he hadn't gone across the bridge, what might have happened, I don't know.[15]

That operation turned out to be a turning point in the fight for Freetown. ECOMOG and CDF/government forces drove the rebels back. However, in the rest of the country there were large areas where insurgents were in control. Gunships were badly needed.

But in early January, when Juba and CAO Tijjani Easterbrook turned up at the Sierra Leone High Commission in London from where the contact with suppliers in Russia was to have been initiated, they found that there had been a complete breakdown in communication because the rebels were knocking at the gates of Freetown and government functionaries had abandoned their offices. It was only after the immediate threat to Freetown receded, and not until 26 January, that contact was re-established with the High Commission. Finally, on 29 January, the two flew to Moscow.

They made contact with the Sierra Leonean ambassador to Russia, Melrose Banja, and she informed them that she had already made arrangements for them to inspect two helicopters. Sendaba had been unable to get a visa until later, and when he did, he flew direct from Freetown to Moscow, where he joined the other two. When Juba saw the aircraft documentation, there was no way he would accept those aircraft, much to the displeasure of the ambassador. She was informed by Sierra Leone's CDS, Gen Khobe, that they should return to London, and on 9 February, they left Moscow. In London, Juba worked through arms dealers who were based in the UK and also in Latvia and found that they could procure two Mi-24s in the Ukraine. But pressure began to be exerted on them from what Tijjani Easterbrook called 'an interest group' of Sierra Leoneans who, through senior government staff were directed to join them unofficially. And the interest group tried to put a new deal together. As a result, Juba and the team found they were being offered two rejected helicopters from Algeria.

They tried to put a new deal together: they got a deal in Algeria where the machines were basically scrap already, you know. So they thought they still had $3.3 million and they would buy those two machines for $1 million, and then they would put two million in their pockets sort of thing. I said to the high commissioner in London, I said to him, 'There's one thing you must understand, it's I'm the guy who's flying those machines, so I'm not going to buy rubbish. We've got a job to do, if you buy rubbish, we're not going to do the job.'

If you look at it all over, basically, there were people there who didn't want us to succeed, it didn't matter which way it was going: whether it was the Nigerians who wanted to make money out of the deal, but mainly it was actually the Sierra Leoneans themselves. It was a nasty situation really. But the UK made sure the money didn't go into private pockets because that's why they appointed Crown Agents.[16]

So on 18 February, refusing to have anything to do with the Algerian aircraft, they left London for Kiev, but the sting in the tail was that a Sierra Leonean was sent with them. For what good reason? And there, in the Ukraine, two machines were procured that met the specifications Juba required. When the procurement was settled, the next stage was for the Ukrainian authorities to obtain UN authorisation to export the war machines and exempt them from the international embargo, and at that point, on 16 March, Tijjani Easterbrook left for London.

During the time it took to get clearances from the UN, Melrose Banja, Sierra Leonean ambassador to Russia flew into the Ukraine; she tried first of all to cancel the deal, but it was too far advanced for that; then she arranged through President Kabbah that she would sign off the deal. Crown Agents appointed the International Chamber of Commerce to act on their behalf for the procurement in the Ukraine, and the ICC official, Sergey Pilipenko, questioned the need for this. Finally, the ambassador got the president's approval to sign it off. And she also got the president's agreement to have $80,000 she said she needed, to arrange to pay the flight back to Sierra Leone with all the hardware. Juba had to take $80,000 out of his budget for ammunition and give it to her.

However, the saga of the helicopter purchase ended in success, and at an Independence Day ceremony on 27 April, President Kabbah announced the purchase of the gunships from the Ukraine. 'I am delighted that the helicopter gunships are now with us, to build up our defences and to combat the ongoing war.'[17] The two helicopters were delivered in a Russian AN 124, about the largest air transport in the former Soviet Union. They were partly disassembled, with the blades removed. Two Ukrainian technicians came with them, as Juba had to have work done on the aircraft: the blade tracking and some systems were not working properly.

> But I had to wait for these guys to get the aircraft serviceable, because they were so happy to get paid and they used that money to screw the locals and get pissed. It's Africa [laughing] nobody said it was going to be easy.[18]

Nor was it easy for him to get his own pay. On 6 May, two weeks after he got back, he wrote to Gen Khobe, Chief of the Defence Staff, requesting reimbursement. He had left Sierra Leone on 30 December with an advance of $3,000 to cover a ten-day absence at an approved allowance of $300 per day. He did not return until 23 April, a period of 115 days, and in that time he received a total of $9,850, which included $5,000 from Crown Agents London, so he had to use his own resources for visas, flights and hotel accommodation, and was owed $24,650 as the balance of Estacode payment.[19] Sendaba, who was out of the country for 33 days, was also in the red. But on top of all that, Bokkie's crew had not been paid since October 1998 and Juba Inc. had had to sustain the burden of payment and food allowances.

When the Ukrainian technicians could be prevailed upon to ease off on their venial pleasures and work on the two Mi-24s, the hand over programme went ahead each day, and was finalized on 2 May. The following day the Ukrainians departed, and Fred's diary for Tuesday 4 May reads, 'Dawn of a new day!' They fired the S8 rockets and the 12.7 Gatling gun. Compared to the GMPG, the thunder of the 12.7's four-barrel Gatling gun, followed by the ground-breaking landing of the rounds, was a devastating weapon. Both Mi-24 gunships were ready for action a week after they were handed over to the Sierra Leone Government. And so the first part of the mission to go and purchase them as arranged and agreed the previous December at 3 am was finally successfully achieved.

One of them was in action with ECOMOG forces right away, and CAO Tijjani Easterbrook described the results from the point when the rebels were in control of perhaps 85% of the country.

> The helicopters were deployed for operations and that changed the tide of the war and made the rebels have a rethink.[20]

Juba co-ordinated all the information available on the enemy's movements and did his planning accordingly to change the situation in favour of the Sierra Leone Government. He made use of the French fixed-wing pilot, JJ Fuentes, to do reconnaissance flights for him, and to report back the enemy positions and movements. He then decided what weapons were to be used on the gunship for the attacks; his idea was that the fixed-wing would also get airborne and obtain the latest information on rebel positions, and relay it to him by air in the gunship.

> At the time the rebels moved from the Port Loko area south-east, raping, killing and burning people alive in the villages, leaving the infrastructures completely destroyed with very few or no inhabitants alive. It was a trail of devastation with bodies and body parts piled up in the roads of the villages – innocent citizens living in the bush minding their own business, getting slaughtered by savages. Some of these rebels that caused these atrocities were as young as 8 years. It is not something that people in the western world would believe or understand unless they were there to see the full impact of brutality. Sad to say that these rebels had strong support from the western world, but no big noise was made about it.[21]

But he had the experience, and he now had the capability, to stop a rebel advance, with a force equivalent to a 1000 men moving at 300 kilometres an hour – the Mi-24. The first target he was given by JJ was a village where the rebels had already killed the villagers and were about to burn down the dwellings; when Juba got a visual on them they were between the houses, dashing for the dwellings to get cover. At 2 kilometres from target he stabilized the arms platform with the sight set just on floor level of the first houses and pressed the firing button, which in turn released 20 x S8 80mm rockets, and 'within a break of a second adjusted the sight slightly higher to the centre of the village and released the second 20 x S8 rockets.'[22] At this moment Juba had to break off from the attack to avoid flying over the village that was covered in black smoke with dust already rising up to 300 feet. As Juba returned to Freetown, JJ remained in the area to confirm the situation on the ground. His feedback, as well as that of the ground forces, was that that rebel group would not commit any more atrocities.

> Five similar attacks in the next 10 days throughout the country destroyed the entire killing force of the rebels and forced them to the Lomé accord, because their position of strength had all of a sudden disappeared like mist in front of the sun. The first and major agenda point was to get both Mi-24 grounded ASAP, but what they didn't realize at the time was that I had only used one of the Mi-24s for these attacks. After these successes the bounty on my head from Liberia was raised to $5 million USD.[23]

Juba by then, 'had given Nellis his long awaited Mi-24 conversion, realizing the full implication of the power struggle Nellis had with me' [an allusion to developing tension within the company], but was left with little choice to keep the momentum of the war against the rebels as the priority.

The UN Special Envoy to Sierra Leone, Francis Okelo, confirmed to government officials that the RUF was very unhappy about the recent purchase of the gunships.[24]

Forced to rethink by the government's devastating air power, the RUF went again to the negotiating table, this time in Lomé, Togo to negotiations brokered by the Rev Jesse Jackson, President Bill Clinton's special envoy. Foday Sankoh was released from prison in Freetown, after having been condemned to death for treason in October, and sat alongside President Kabbah, and was still able to convince – amid all evidence to the contrary – that the RUF really sought legitimate political recognition. The Lomé Agreement was signed by Kabbah and Sankoh in July, giving the RUF eight cabinet posts and Sankoh the position of Vice President, with responsibility for strategic resources. Given it was the lure of blood diamonds that fuelled rebel activity for ten years, Sankoh unbelievably gained what insurgency had failed to give, the sort of prize only associated with the board game, Monopoly – advance from the condemned cell in one move to State House, picking up all the diamonds you can gather.

By November, RUF breaches of the cease fire agreement were causing alarm for the UN, which, the previous month, had established UNAMSIL, the UN Mission in Sierra Leone; it would be headed by General Vijay Jetley of India. All the signs pointed to the Lomé Agreement turning out to be the same con as the Abidjan Agreement of 1996; only this time the forces of democracy, under US pressure, had caved in even further.

Juba recruited another pilot, Cassie Nel, who had been with him in 31 Squadron SAAF (South African Air Force) as he himself had other obligations to attend to, but all the flying he was doing was hampering him; and there was also the fact that Neall wanted some leave.

As the new millennium approached, it was not high politics but good company that saw out the old year. High Commissioner, Peter Penfold had recommended for the award of MBE in the New Year's honours (to some raised eyebrows back in the Foreign Office) Paddy Warren, owner of the popular bar, Paddy's. Fred and the crew gathered in Paddy's on 31 December, for the ceremony when Peter Penfold conferred the honour on this well-liked, former Merchant seaman who had stayed on when his ticket ended at Freetown. He had built up a popular bar and did a lot for his Sierra Leonean workers, making them partners in the enterprise; he was much respected, and in these stressful times, his establishment was a pleasant haven.

Chapter Nine

Operation Barras

Most of 'L' Detachment's work is night work and all of it demands courage, fitness and determination of the highest degree and also, and just as important, discipline, skill and intelligence and training.

David Stirling in, *Birth, Growth and Maturity of 1st SAS Regiment* (The Paddy Mayne Diary).

The template that David Stirling had in mind when he selected men for the unit he founded in the North African desert in 1941 would perhaps be just as appropriate for its future generations. Certainly, over the years, those same qualities and characteristics have been evident in its members. A worthy example – although he does not see it this way – is Fred Marafono, only three months short of his seventh decade, in action, supporting his old unit in one of its most successful lightning raids since the Second World War when, under the command of Blair 'Paddy' Mayne, at Capo Murro di Porco in Sicily, it captured three enemy gun batteries in rapid succession and destroyed a fourth with the loss of only one man. Its commanding general at the time said of that raid, 'That was a brilliant operation, brilliantly planned and brilliantly carried out.'[1] The same evaluation could equally well apply to Operation Barras in Sierra Leone in 2000.

However, there are significant differences between then and now. During the later stages of the Second World War, Paddy Mayne was making representation because the unit received no publicity; the public at large was unaware of its existence; he felt its achievements should be known.[2] Sixty years later the position is reversed: some newspaper headlines are written on the assumption that the public has an insatiable appetite for information about the SAS; yet the nature of present day conflicts and counter-insurgency means that the MoD insists that little is given away about the operational details of special units.

That is a reality (and one he subscribes to) within which the account of what Fred would call his very minor role in Operation Barras has to be placed.

The months leading up to the brilliant rescue operation of British army hostages were marked by drama, farce, in-fighting in UNAMSIL and more needless loss of life. Fred took the leading role in a brief dramatic happening with political implications, that took place, not in his favourite haunt, Paddy's, but in the bar of the Cape Sierra hotel. Air Wing personnel had not been paid for months; they were still awaiting payment of their money as promised by the President. It is not hard to see why they were aggrieved: they had committed their own resources to maintain Bokkie after they took it over and they needed the money. During the time they were being paid by ECOMOG there was no problem about their receiving their due in US dollars. That only came about when Nigeria passed the responsibility for paying the Air Wing to where it rightly belonged, the Sierra Leone government.

> The home-made problem came about because everyone who had a hand in signing our payment papers wanted a slice of our money for themselves before they would process it to the next department. The Chief saw the President a few times to tell these people involved to desist and sign these request forms because we risked our lives and still did so and we deserved every penny we earned. But even Kabbah's instructions were disregarded. We were helped at one time by an expatriate man recruited by Dr. Jonah to resolve the Sierra Leone Finance Department. But once he left, we went back to the 'delay' and phoney excuses until we agreed to their terms. That was life in a 'brown envelope' country. It was so bad that even the British High Commissioner was involved by directly asking Kabbah to help in releasing our pay.

Juba might put it in the category of WAWA [West Africa Wins Again].

> WAWA has so many facets to it. One simple example is a West African busy drowning, with only his arm sticking out above the water, and you come to rescue him. You're about to grab his arm, when he pulls it back and says, 'What's in for me?'[3]

At a wider level, when Fred and Juba considered what they were risking their lives for, in moments of gloom it all seemed futile: the government's progress towards disarming the rebels was getting nowhere; unbelievably, the RUF leader, Foday Sankoh, who was said to have already amassed millions of dollars for himself from the sale of illegally mined diamonds, was now chairman of the Commission for the Management of Strategic Resources, National Reconstruction and Development, and it was widely known that illegal diamond mining was still going on in rebel-held territory.

What was missing was leadership and insight at the top. President Kabbah lacked both. It was frustrating for High Commissioner Peter Penfold to see the shortcomings and guess what the consequences might be.

> He had no way of being able to deal with a person like Sankoh. I mean the way that he treated Sankoh, I mean, it made your stomach turn. He was flattering to him, and he kept on kidding us all; he would invite Sankoh round to the residence

late at night, just the two of them would chat, and then I'd go and see Kabbah the next morning, and he'd say, 'Sankoh's really changing; he's changing, he's really trusting me now. He's really going to follow through with the disarmament.' He was so gullible when it came to things like that. Maybe it was because he sincerely wanted it to happen. But he did not have the political nous, he did not have the experience of security matters; he did not have the ability to make decisions.[4]

And stoking the incredulity of one that served with the 200 men of Executive Outcomes who defeated the RUF on the battlefield, news that the United Nations, custodian of international peace and security, was finding it necessary to increase the UNAMSIL force from 6,000 to 11,000 men was the last straw.

Fred's rare outburst came on Saturday 5 February. He already had a good few drinks under his belt in Paddy's before moving on to the bar at the Cape Sierra. There, with Juba, some British members of UNAMSIL, a few ECOMOG personnel and in the company of some of Kabbah's people, he took the floor. Usually a man of serene stillness that masks great physical strength, he silenced the august gathering by declaring that they had risked their lives to save this government, and delivered himself of the considered view, 'The President is nothing but a fucking weak shit, and Gen Khobe is a fucking thief.' Immediately, there was a move by Kabbah's people to call the police and have him arrested, but the ECOMOG Chief Air Officer, Gp Capt Easterbrook, stepped in and quietened things by saying it was an Air Wing matter; they would deal with it. Next day in his diary Fred dolefully recorded the events of the night before and noted that he must apologize to Rod Stewart, the RAF officer attached to Air Wing.

However, the one who could have taken offence was not Rod Stewart but the President; and not surprisingly his minions dutifully told him about this drunken outburst on the part of a friend of Hinga Norman's, because some time later the President challenged Hinga Norman about it.

The Chief told me that Kabbah mentioned the incident to him at one of their meetings one morning. He played it down by saying that Fred was a military man and talks straight as they do in the military. We both laughed, and I promised never to embarrass the Chief again.

But before that though, Fred had to face the music at work on Monday morning. The political drama of Saturday night was discussed; Fred simply recorded in his diary, 'Not very pleasant.' He was to keep a low profile for a while, so he decided to take a spell of long overdue leave in the UK; and the following Thursday he met Chief Hinga Norman and told him his plans, and flew home the next day for a long break. He had not been home all that long before Juba phoned him and reminded him of the absurdity of the situation now when he said that Neall Ellis and Cassie had flown the President and 'Killer Sankoh' to Bo and Kenema.

Then, in Sierra Leone, Brig Gen Khobe, the Nigerian who had been appointed as Chief of the Defence Staff, became ill. It seemed to Peter Penfold that the security situation was deteriorating; there would be a vacuum as ECOMOG withdrew from the country and the UN were slow to deploy; and his tour of duty as British High Commissioner was coming to an end. He contacted the Foreign Office and made a number of suggestions: he should stay on a little longer to help ease tensions; Col Dent should temporarily move into the Sierra Leone Ministry of Defence; Britain should bring forward the arrival of a brigadier who would head the UK military training team; and finally, they should ask Brig David Richards, who was visiting the country at the time, to stay on for a week or two and give military advice to President Kabbah – both Brig Richards and the President were in agreement with this idea. 'The FCO turned down all my suggestions.'[5]

To make matters worse, Gen Khobe was airlifted to Nigeria in a coma. He was treated in hospital there and, it was reported, died on 18 April as a result of complications that had set in to an old shrapnel wound. Khobe, it will be recalled, had been slightly wounded at the storming of State House in Freetown when ECOMOG ousted the AFRC junta two years earlier; and at the time Juba and Fred had flown him to Lungi so that he could be airlifted for treatment in Nigeria. But that had been two years ago, and now, in Sierra Leone, rumours were rife of an alternative cause of death: it was said that he had been poisoned over a period of time. As a foreigner in charge of the military of the country, he may well have had enemies – among Nigerians as well as Sierra Leoneans (there was bad feeling among some senior Nigerian army officers that Khobe's perceived new status was above theirs). But whatever the cause of death, Fred's response to the announcement was unambiguous,

> I was in London when I heard the news that Khobe was dead. I went and bought a few bottles of red wine and celebrated his death as a rat! Much blood of innocent Sierra Leoneans was shed because of his greed and selfishness.

Who knows, Fred's intemperate assessment at the Cape Sierra bar may indeed have been a case of 'in vino veritas', for about the time of Khobe's death, Maj Gen Jetley, the Indian commander of the UN peacekeeping force in Sierra Leone, was crafting an early draft of an explosive memorandum to the UN – that would not become public knowledge for some months until it was printed in the *Guardian*, but was circulated among Security Council members – accusing senior Nigerian army officers of prolonging the war in Sierra Leone, being secretly in cahoots with the rebels and amassing a fortune for themselves through the sale of illegally mined diamonds in the rebel-held areas. In his memorandum, Jetley singled out the late Brig Gen Khobe for being known as the 'Ten Million Man', on account of Khobe's allegedly having made $10 million from the sale of diamonds.[6]

However, Khobe's death prompted a crisis for President Kabbah. It looks as though, in desperation now, he asked Britain to provide a senior army officer to be Chief of the Defence Staff. The British Foreign and Commonwealth Office Secretary of State for Africa, Peter Hain, told his parliament's Foreign Affairs Committee that while Britain would supply arms and ammunition for the pro–government forces fighting the rebels he was turning down the request to provide a Chief of Defence Staff. Using uncharacteristically blunt language for a politician referring to the head of state of a friendly country, he 'called Kabbah's proposal a "crazy idea" which would have put a British officer in charge of an army "which did not in effect exist"'.[7] In addition, Britain also decided to send a small team of military advisers.

In Sierra Leone, the peacekeeping process turned into a fiasco: about three days after Peter Penfold departed the country, the RUF attacked Magburaka, Makeni and Kenema. They surrounded a disarmament camp in Magburaka and forced the UN peacekeepers to dismantle it; on 5 May rebels seized 13 of the 16 armoured cars of the Zambian contingent of UNAMSIL; the following day an RUF force of between five hundred to a thousand captured Lunsar, using vehicles captured from the UN; and by this time an estimate of the number of UN troops captured by the rebels was as high as 500. But there was further horror in the streets of Freetown: on 8 May, thousands of peace demonstrators massed and converged on the house of Foday Sankoh protesting at the slow progress of the peace process. Sankoh's bodyguards opened fire on them killing and wounding more than twenty people, while Sankoh escaped from the building.

Hearing about the events in Sierra Leone on BBC news, Fred phoned Chief Norman from London in the evening. The Chief judged that the situation was now calm but tense; and Fred said that he would return there right away. Although on leave, Fred had been engaged in discussions about possible future training projects in Sierra Leone, and he phoned a contact to find out if he could get a flight out with the RAF. He got the answer the next day – it was 'no joy.' He then phoned Hinga Norman again and asked him to organize a landing visa for him. The following day he received it by fax, and booked his flight.

The security situation continued to deteriorate in Sierra Leone: a contingent of UNAMSIL troops was forced to withdraw from the strategic crossroads town of Masiaka after coming under fire from unidentified gunmen.[8] In the light of the UNAMSIL's loss of control, Sam Hinga Norman, Deputy Minister of Defence announced, 'Our security in Sierra Leone was in the hands of the United nations but surprisingly we have come to the conclusion that the United Nations has not been able to protect us any longer.'[9] He indicated that Kamajor militia and loyal Sierra Leonean troops had been sent to Masiaka to halt the RUF advance. Britain, in the meantime, ordered an evacuation of its nationals, and Operation Palliser was set in train with the arrival of the advance party of the 1st Battalion of the Parachute Regiment, whose role was to secure Lungi airport to which the bulk of the regiment would be flown directly. Royal Naval warships converged on West Africa.

Within days of sizing up the situation on the ground, the commander of the British forces (who, interestingly enough, turned out to be), Brig David Richards, realized that UNAMSIL could not contain the rebels by playing the role of the village bobby, whose presence alone, it is supposed, reassures the law abiding and deters the potential law breaker; speaking on Radio Democracy 98.1 FM, he urged the UN force to become more belligerent, and alongside pro-government forces 'take the battle forward.'[10]

The underlying folly of the agreement that had given the RUF what it was unable to attain on the battlefield was spelled out forthrightly by the chairman of the US senate's powerful Appropriations sub-committee, who blocked the US contribution to pay for one third of the UN peacekeeping costs. He argued that the Lomé Peace Accord was an abnegation of responsibility on the part of the west in forcing the Sierra Leoneans to accept it, then leaving them to their fate.[11] Although Foday Sankoh was captured later in May, it made no real difference as far as the RUF in the bush were concerned, for it had been without his leadership for some time; and as far as the results of the cynical expediency in railroading through the Lomé Accord were concerned, the damage was already done.

On 14 May, Fred was back in the country; he met Hinga Norman the same day; and he was in action with the Air Wing two days later. Juba was long overdue leave, and was in South Africa. Fred's first reconnaissance and fighting patrols were to the Makeni and Lunsar areas. A pattern was established where they flew every day or every second day. On 20 May, after a reconnaissance flight to the Mange bridge, they picked up Chief Norman after his return from a short trip to Nigeria; then next day, not far from the Madina Junction, Fred attacked a transport vehicle that burst into flames when tracer rounds hit it. Although they were resupplying troops, the Air Wing gunship team were certainly taking 'the battle forward' in a way UNAMSIL was not. And so, on 22 May,

On our way back from Bumbuna resupply, we came out to follow the road just before Binkolo, looking for any stolen UN vehicles used by RUF commanders, heading towards Makeni and Lunsar, rebels strongholds. Nothing at Binkolo nor Makeni town, even the market square was quiet. And passing Makeni following the road, we saw a white pickup caught in a cutting on the road. I asked Neall to orbit, which he did, giving me direct view to the target, which I blasted with my GPMG. That operation left 3 bodies on the ground. One guy escaped from the initial burst of the gun and tried to climb up the steep embankment but I brought him down without any regret whatsoever. Years of experiencing the cruelty and senselessness of their atrocities to the unarmed civilians made me immune to any feelings. In actual fact, I enjoyed it very much.

Further down the road, we came across a deserted green pickup with a 12.7 anti-aircraft gun, and I shot it up with nearly all the rounds left – bar 300 rounds for protection – but could not completely destroy it. Point of interest, even though they had the AA gun, when faced up to by someone who could shoot back, they ran like the rats they were.

Rebel groups kept in close touch with one another by radio; they had done so since the early days of the RUF insurgency – Foday Sankoh's previous life as a wireless operator convinced him of the need for good radio communications in running a guerrilla war – and they used it extensively. Their radio messages were intercepted and monitored by the UN force as well as by ECOMOG. ECOMOG had already announced that it would cede its role in Sierra Leone to the UN, but until that happened it was still interlinked with Air Wing. Its Chief Air Officer, Gp Capt Easterbrook, was in charge of the Air Wing operations; Juba and the team ran the day-to-day operations, but tasking was done by the CAO, assisted by his Liaison Officer, Flt Lt. Wakili. And what ECOMOG picked up in the intercepts was the rebels' complaining that the gunship's attacks were killing numbers of them. That day's attack, for example, had killed the Makeni rebel commander.

The following day they flew first to the Mange bridge area, from Lunsar to Port Loko; then on a Lunsar–Makeni axis with guest observers from UK forces on board. That evening though, Fred had a drink at Paddy's and the Cape Sierra with their guests. But next morning, the crew had to be clearheaded when they were fired on during a battle at Rogberi Junction. Two vehicles carrying journalists and Sierra Leonean soldiers were ambushed. An American and a Spanish journalist, as well as four soldiers, were killed, and two journalists were wounded during the engagement.[12] There had been a military checkpoint there in the past with a makeshift building. This was the location of the firing.

They shot at us from inside the house, but because of the speed we were flying, we passed it before we could react. We could not orbit and shoot it up in case we killed some civilians.

The principle Fred operated on was that he either had to be able to eyeball the shooter or be under continuous fire from a source before he could return fire.

More of the same followed over successive days with reconnaissance and fighting patrols. Not, however, on Saturday 27 May when they had to change a blade on the Mi-24, but they made up for lost opportunity with marathon flight times the next day: they went first to Lunsar and Konta areas and attacked both locations; then they flew Chief Hinga Norman to Bo; their third sortie was to fly top-cover for their own troops advancing towards Lunsar; on a final flight they attacked retreating rebels and, as the weather worsened, shot up two trucks. Fred's diary entry sums it up – 'very long day.' Foul weather continued the next day, but they again flew top-cover for their troops who were now established in Lunsar.

A break from the intensity of these patrols would have been welcome, and indeed one was to come his way; but the prompt for it was concerning: when Fred phoned Hawa, she told him that their little daughter, Maliaka, was very sick. He had to continue with his immediate commitment; he flew to Bo to pick up Hinga Norman before making a night flight. The rebels had been under attack during the day when they tried to move in force along the Makeni – Lunsar road, so they waited until dark. And so did Fred and Neall Ellis. They were over the target at 2000 hours.

> We flew along the side of the road giving me space to observe any lights of vehicles moving along the road. The area was strong, rebel-held territory, and because they suffered using the road in the daytime, we received information that they were moving at night, which made sense to us, hence the night flight. You only have a shot at the target lights, but once they were off, you have lost it. The area we flew over was pitch black. Because we flew without lights, we were at the target before they knew it. Then shots started flying. But they learned very fast. But at least we stopped the night movement in that area.

On 2 June, returning from Bumbuna, they came across a hijacked UN truck and shot it up with 'Big 3', the gunship's 3inch rockets.

> It was beautiful to watch. These were the vehicles that were stolen from the 600 plus troops who surrendered without a single shot fired because they were not there to 'fight'! Indian Troops would never have surrendered their weapons without a fight and the rebels knew that very well. But African troops were a different story.

Later that day, Fred had pepper soup with Chief Norman and told him that he was due some leave and he would like to go to the UK for two weeks as his young daughter was quite ill. Chief Norman, 'agreed with me wholeheartedly. He thanked me and hugged me and wished me and my family the best, so I left Sierra Leone.'

Little Maliaka was very resilient and recovered quickly, and two weeks later Fred returned to a hero's welcome. Air Wing was about the only credible force carrying the war to the rebels; and this was widely perceived to be the case. On his first night back Fred went for a drink, and was overwhelmed at the reaction when he appeared.

> Received a standing ovation from everyone at Paddy's as if I was a hero. It was because of what we as a group had done to help the country and the people during their most difficult time that I received such an unearned applause. I was very humbled by their instantaneous reaction. I felt very humble indeed.

But the conditions for bringing back stability to what, in effect, was becoming a failed state were being put in place, thanks to the role of the United Kingdom. Britain's unique contribution to its former colony began with a Short Term Training Programme for the Sierra Leone army, but it became much broader based than that, and was part of an overall counter-insurgency policy that the UK had developed over decades. Nonetheless, close co-ordination was required between the British High Commissioner and the Sierra Leone government, and neat footwork by British military commanders on the ground. Brig David Richards later summed it up like this.

> What transpired ... was a fascinating example of modern day intervention operations in an uncertain environment. It started as a NEO [Non-combatant Evacuation Order] but developed into something that has characteristics between counter-insurgency and small-scale war-fighting operations. I found myself directing a campaign at the operational level.[13]

At one level it was a low intensity military operation with patrols being sent out and information being gathered, at the same time as the training programme was underway. At another level, the Department For International Development (DFID) was to be engaged to train the Sierra Leone police, so that, when the rebels were defeated or neutralized and disarmed, the vacuum that existed in law enforcement in up-country areas could be filled. And at international level, Britain took a lead in pressing through sanctions in the UN against the trading of diamonds from the rebel-held areas of the country. In all of this it was essential to have the close support of the Sierra Leone government. Indeed the role of the British commander on the ground gave him direct access to the Defence Ministry.

> In appearance, the British Force commander worked for the GoSL [government of Sierra Leone]. This was important to maintain the GoSL legitimacy. In reality, the system placed the British commander in a position where he could directly influence the Sierra Leone Ministry of Defence.[14]

Fred was in a pole position at this time: he was a friend of Chief Hinga Norman, Deputy Minister of Defence, who trusted him; he had extensive experience in the SAS; by now he had worked in Sierra Leone for almost six years, several of them serving in combat against the rebels, so he was respected; and he had access to people of influence. It is not surprising, therefore, that he was sought out. On 19 August Fred recorded in his diary that he had, 'a very useful and fruitful discussion with British military advisers.' These were two of the team of 15 military advisers that the British Defence Secretary had earlier promised would be sent to Sierra Leone.

> The meeting that I referred to was with the two military advisers at the Defence HQ. They explained their views of how the rebuild was going to be carried out in a very thorough and professional way, and the parts each party would play. I saw the Chief afterwards and mentioned my meeting with the two military planners, and he smiled. His remark was, 'Yes they are doing a very good job indeed. Fred, you will see a change in the Sierra Leone Army.' The Chief was very proud of his British army training and always believed that the British would bring back the pride and professionalism that was once there. Today the Sierra Leone

Army are very well disciplined, smartly dressed and regularly paid with their accommodations and welfare improving yearly.

By late August, the short-term training programme for the Sierra Leone army was in the second tranche of trainees. The first cohort had been put through the course by men from the Royal Anglian Regiment, who then handed over to the Royal Irish Regiment. But there was still a long way to go: in the wider bailiwick of the UN (whose numbers now amounted to some 13,000, shortly to be authorized to increase to 20,000) lawlessness reigned. Even Kamajors, the former bulwark of the CDF, were reported by the BBC to be carrying out criminal acts in the Kenema area. Vice President, Albert Joe Demby, led a government delegation to the area and warned them to desist from lawlessness and work for peace. Sam Hinga Norman, Deputy Defence Minister and National Co-ordinator of the CDF warned that, 'the Civil Defence Forces are not an organization for sheltering criminals, adding that anyone caught involved in any criminal activity will face the full force of the law.'[15]

Full force of the law did not mean much to a group of rebels who styled themselves the West Side Boys. They were a motley assortment of young, motiveless killers looking for a motive; they had no political objectives; their reason for being was banditry; there were ex–RUF as well as former AFRC members among them – and they were volatile and highly dangerous, equipped with an impressive arsenal, thanks to what they had captured from UN forces. Their local leader was Foday Kallay, and if they needed some figurehead at a national level it appeared to be Johnny Paul Koroma, the former AFRC leader. But he soon renounced any affiliation with them.

They took control of movement on the Freetown – Masiaka road, although that route had been cleared by a UNAMSIL operation and came under the surveillance of the Jordanian Second Battalion. The West Side Boys devised a sideline by charging illegal taxes on motorists: they stopped cars and charged a rate of SLL 2000 per vehicle. The Jordanian Second Battalion adopted a relaxed attitude to this highway robbery (thereby giving the impression that there was a two–way benefit from so doing) and claimed that 'the presence of armed West Side Boys militia on that road is merely a confidence-building measure and not at all a security threat.'[16]

In their fiefdom, though, the drug-fuelled West Side Boys were really in a fool's paradise. Not since Executive Outcomes had a military force successfully attacked and destroyed a rebel stronghold: ECOMOG had not been able to do it – although it had cleared Freetown – nor had UNAMSIL. There seemed little likelihood of it now with the general lacklustre performance of the UN forces. But then, by their own actions on 25 August, when they surrounded and took hostage a reconnaissance patrol of 11 Royal Irish and a Sierra Leone army liaison officer, the West Side Boys set in train a response that would not only destroy them but have a demoralizing effect on the wider rebel movement.

They took their hostages and their three Land Rovers to the area they had selected for a stronghold. Like that of the RUF leader, Foday Sankoh, in which Swiss

Consul-General, Rudi Bruns was held hostage five years earlier, the site of the West Side Boys' stronghold was cleverly chosen. It was only about seventy kilometres from Freetown, and it lay in the Occra hills on the north side of the Rokel Creek, in Gberi Bana. To the east was swampland, to the north and west dense jungle, an approach track ran along the north bank of the creek. But as part of intuitive defensive planning, they established a position in Magbeni on the south bank of the creek to block movement coming from the Freetown-Masiaka road. They were experienced jungle fighters; it would have been a mistake to under-estimate them.

Because they had no rationale that could be fitted into the pattern of other insurgency groups, it meant that, from a negotiating stance, they were unpredictable. Five years earlier, the RUF knew what they wanted out of taking expatriate hostages: international awareness-raising as a stepping stone to assuming power. Not so the West Side Boys. From the start they used their prisoners as bargaining tender for food and medicine, then for the release of one of their commanders, Brigadier Bomb Blast (aka Brigadier Papa). They separated the Sierra Leone officer from the others, and tortured him. On 3 September, they released five of the soldiers as a goodwill gesture, but they subjected the others to beatings, mock executions and daily humiliation – quite unlike the disciplined regime that Foday Sankoh imposed on the management of the RUF's hostages, which, as we saw earlier, Rudi Bruns experienced.

The omens pointed to a final scenario where, with nothing to gain and not much to lose, the West Side Boys would kill the remaining hostages out of hand. Direct action would be necessary; planning was already well underway for an attack to release the hostages. British Special Forces infiltrated two observer teams along the Rokel by assault boat,[17] and they were passing back high grade intelligence.[18] A land-based assault was not viable because of the location, so it would be a complex undertaking, involving high risk in an unpredictable situation. The rebel camp at Magbeni on the south of the creek would have to be attacked as well as the site at Gberi Bana, where the hostages were held. The raid would be carried out by men from the 1st Battalion the Parachute Regiment and Special Forces.[19] And such was the complexity of this operation that, as the MoD later confirmed, it would involve all three services. In addition, 'Assistance was also provided by the Sierra Leone army.'[20]

Uppermost among the elements of the Sierra Leone Armed Forces to provide assistance was the Air Wing. And so it came about that Fred, only three months from his sixtieth birthday, and contracted by the Sierra Leone government, would play what he describes as a minor part in Operation Barras. Juba was in South Africa at the time, so the Mi-24 gunship crew would consist of Fred and Neall Ellis.

Our involvement was because the West Side Boys had a twin barrel 14.5mm anti-aircraft gun, and if the ground forces were to fail to destroy it, we would be called to destroy it with the rockets. We had two pods of 16 x 7" rockets, which are much more powerful than the 3" ones that we normally carried on patrol, plus we had the 12.7mm Gatling four-barrel gun that fires up to 5,000 rounds per minute.

An RAF liaison officer had been attached to Air Wing at the time of Operation Palliser, and now a British army electronics engineer arrived and worked on the Mi-24, so that it was provided with a secure communications systems for its part in the operation. As part of his Air Wing duties, Fred continued with the practice that had been established when they supplied the ECOMOG bases of noting in his diary their flying times and routes, which were then written up at the end of the day in the pilot's flying log book. He sometimes included the odd cryptic comment. On Thursday 7 September, two British soldiers, X and Y, arrived and the electronics specialist handed over liaison to X, the senior of the two. Fred's laconic entry in his diary that day, 'Nice to see the guys.' Meanwhile the Mi-24's Gatling gun was still malfunctioning; they test-fired it the following day. Then on Saturday 9 September, Fred and Neall were briefed on Operation Barras, 'but based on need to know. Must carry on as normal.' They had been warned to be prepared for an early call out over the week-end.

Throughout all this, the rumour mill was grinding away at full tilt in Freetown's bars, spreading scenarios galore of imminent rescue missions. And since Fred, Juba and Neall frequented those same bars, and three months earlier Fred received a hero's reception on behalf of the work of Air Wing, all that was needed was one chatterer to float the suggestion of their involvement to put them on the defensive. But it was Saturday night; if they did not turn up, it would lead to speculation; so they went out to the bars and put on an act.

By then the rumour machine in Sierra Leone was rife that something might happen that week-end. To counter that Neall and myself went out to Cape Sierra, Paddy's and other beach bars to be seen drinking. But what they did not know was that for every half pint of shandy, we had at least 2 or 3 of lemonade or tonic. We stayed till about 11pm and then left and went home. To any casual observer, we went home drunk, which was what we wanted them to believe.

Next morning at 04.25 hours, Fred's phone rang. He recognized X's voice, and he heard the code word: it was D-day for Operation Barras. Neall must then have been contacted, for he in turn confirmed with Fred at 04.35. Ten minutes later, Fred made a cup of tea, and left his house at 05.15 hours and drove to Cockerill, where there was a quick up-date brief before departure. Operation Barras went in at 06.16 hours,[21] and Fred, Neall, X and Y monitored everything in the Mi-24 on the ground at Cockerill. Then came their clearance to take off, and at 06.32, the Mi-24 was airborne with a crew of four: X in the front cockpit, operating the radio, Y in the back with Fred. They headed straight for the operational area, but not right in to its centre. The gunship was kept at a holding point where they could see the activities of the helicopters as they listened out, as prearranged, for any call for assistance from the commanders on the ground.

On the ground, the surprise, overwhelming firepower and speed of the assault was matched by its precision. The British Special Forces had the hostages free and unharmed and had them, and the Sierra Leone army liaison officer, on the Chinook in a matter of twenty minutes. But the West Side Boys fought fiercely, and the raiders took casualties.

In the air, in their holding position, the four-man team waited. And when the request for assistance came from one of the ground commanders, it was for a rocket attack. Neall fired a salvo of rockets at the specific target given by the ground commander. From his position at the gun port, Fred saw the spectacular result: one rocket severed a palm tree, the others exploded where their target was but the results were lost from sight because of the dense canopy. That was their only involvement in Operation Barras. In all they flew two sorties – with a brief refuelling at Lungi – and were in the air over the area for about three hours until they were given permission to leave when their assistance was no longer required and the operation was being wrapped up.

They flew back to base, the rest of the day was theirs. Before they started celebrating, they got a preliminary account of the casualties: of the West Side Boys, 25 dead and 17 captured, including their leader Foday Kallay; British forces suffered one dead and (at this stage it was thought) 8 wounded. Fred noted it up, 'Regret very much the death.' Then they celebrated the success of the operation all day. Fred's evaluation was as follows,

> Operation Barras once again demonstrated not only the professionalism and courage of the British forces but also the determination to achieve the impossible through the 7 Ps (Prior Planning and Preparation Prevents Piss- Poor Performance!)

Final death count of rebels was higher. The group was shattered. However, this operation had perhaps a greater psychological impact on the rebels throughout the country. Britain had the resolve to risk its soldiers' lives and the capability to attack any rebel stronghold.

After the raid, it was not a case of business as usual for Fred; there was some follow-up to it. On 12 September, he was briefed on the operation, and wrote in his diary that he had been 'very proud of their success.' The same evening, he had a drink with Stefan Cajrell, a young Swede, who worked for the UN in logistics, and one or two of the SAS raiders; he learned that the British soldier who had been killed in the operation was to be buried at Hereford. Almost immediately, post-operation activities began, and Fred was in the Mi-24, flying over the areas that had been attacked, dropping leaflets for the rump of the West Side Boys who were still in the areas with their families. This too was part of a comprehensive anti-insurgency strategy: after the fist of steel, a psychological operation. One leaflet contained an image repeated of Foday Kallay, leader of the West Side Boys. He had been captured, not with weapon in hand but hiding among the dead, as the raiders checked them over. The left of the two images shows him from chest up, in a trendy, long sleeve Calvin Klein T shirt; the right image is a close-in shot. He looks rested, rather placid and anything but a humiliated PoW. The leaftlet's heading reads, **West Siders … Where is Kallay now?** Then alongside the images the statement **You Fought – He Hid**. And underneath the images the message, **He is safe now / Why should you still fight? / The British-trained SLA is coming / Hand in your weapons and you will be safe**. So it was a reassuring communication. Become part of the Disarmament, Demobilization and Re-integration [DDR] process and you too can have a designer T shirt. Because you're worth it.

As leader of the West Side Boys, Kallay felt he was a high flyer among insurgents, for, at the age of twenty-four, he styled himself 'Brigadier'; as a captive of the British (he had not yet been handed over to UNAMSIL along with the other prisoners en route to the Sierra Leone police) he may well have thought that he made the smart move when he hid in the dawn hours that Sunday morning; now, happy to be alive, Kallay was co-operative with his captors. The three Land Rovers of the Royal Irish patrol had been retrieved and air-lifted out when the operation was being wrapped up, but two of the vehicle-mounted radios had been removed by the West Side Boys and were still in Gberi Bana. Kallay told his captors where they were located.

About ten days after the raid, intelligence reports indicated that Gberi Bana had been abandoned by the remnant of the rebels. The Air Wing gunship took off with Fred, forsaking his bright coloured civilian shirt, wearing British army issue DPM (destructive pattern material) that Britain supplied for the Sierra Leone army and four SAS men who had been on the operation. Their flight path was along the course of the Rokel creek. They circled Gberi Bana, which seemed deserted from the air. However, there was the risk of diehards in the area. This time it was not a case of fast-roping down; if something went wrong, there was no back-up, the gunship would have to touch down to extricate them. Neall Ellis brought down the Mi–24; the soldiers and Fred, carrying his GPMG, jumped down, and immediately Neall took-off. He orbited overhead while the others stayed on the ground. The place was indeed deserted; and the radios were located. Fred described his response not to the sight but the feeling he had: 'eerie, knowing that many lives were sacrificed here.'

Operation Barras turned out to be a watershed: as far as the West Side Boys were concerned the former AFRC leader, Johnny Paul Koroma, to whom they had looked at one point for leadership, said of them, 'With the attack from the British (to rescue British military hostages) I think that is over now';[22] as for the wider rebel movement, bereft of charismatic leadership, the implications of what happened at Gberi Bana and Magbeni sapped their resolve. Britain also provided a powerful military background presence that boosted the UNAMSIL force in its peacekeeping role; in addition, it deployed a Royal Naval task force in Sierra Leone waters as a gesture of support. And it had taken the lead in piloting through the UN an embargo on Sierra Leone diamonds, thus undercutting the illicit trade in blood diamonds that had fuelled insurgency for years.

An indicator suggesting that rebel activity was being contained by UNAMSIL is that Fred flew fewer combat sorties for the Air Wing, and instead became more involved in activity concerned with a stable future for the country. He had many meetings with Chief Hinga Norman, or *Oscar Lima*, as his diary has it – the phonetic alphabet first letters of Old Lion, his cryptic code for the Deputy Minister of Defence. For a while, there was the possibility of work with Ray England, another former member of the Regiment, in training the Sierra Leone police, but it did not come to fruition. At the end of September, Fred went to Mongeri, the home town of Hinga Norman, to the opening of a new school that the Chief had lobbied to have built. Fred supplied the funds and the food for the opening ceremony. But the past was not yet in the past and the training of the CDF continued. They watched a passing out parade of recruits; the drill was done using sticks, and the formation movements were carried out without spoken commands. It was impressive. Some UN observers attended, but Hinga Norman told them not to bring their weapons into the chiefdom, the war was over.

In its aftermath, there would be a bleak future for those had suffered most from the ravages of a brutal insurgency war, especially the young. There were the young boys that the RUF traumatized into becoming killing automatons in the Small Boys Unit, who, as Rudi Bruns felt when he was their captive, had lost their childhood. And there were the victims of terror, the amputees and the orphans. What would be their future?

Aminatta Forna, in her fine book, *The Devil that Danced on the Water*, describes the plight of Mohammed and Salamatu, two young amputees who had married shortly before the rebels struck. They lived in Makeni. When the rebels attacked, they cut off his feet, and abducted his wife. She tried to escape from them and they hacked off her feet above the ankle. Now she was ashamed to go out, and would not wear crutches. And a baby had just been born to them.

She was not more than about twenty: skin unblemished, hair woven into neat braids. Salamatu and Mohammed must have made a striking pair on their wedding day, it occurred to me. She sat with her legs stretched out in front of her and inadvertently I glanced down. As I did so I saw she made a move to pull her *lappa* across her legs, but not before I had seen the horror that contrasted with the serenity of her face. These were not neat amputations performed by a surgeon's knife. One foot had been sheared off below the shin, the other sliced diagonally across the ankle bone. The skin around the wound was rough, the flesh chapped and grey – the appearance was more of hide than human skin. Above the missing feet the flesh was thick, dense and splayed as though she had, at some point, tried to walk and the body had compensated by building up layers of tissue. They looked like the feet of an elephant.

Mohammed retrieved the baby and handed her to me. She was a few weeks old, with skin only the newest babies have: shiny and wrinkled like a fresh leaf unfurling in the early morning.[23]

Mohammed had been a panel beater to trade; now he begged for them both and the baby. But he was relatively lucky compared to others like him, for he had won a wheel chair donated by a western charity.

For the younger victims of the war it would be harder. Hinga Norman discussed some ideas with Fred. 'I suggested for us to set up a fund and call it "The Norman Foundation for War-Affected Children of Sierra Leone", namely the orphans, amputees, handicapped and the blind.' Hinga Norman liked the idea but he pointed out that neither of them had the money to set up a foundation. Profits from a security company was the idea Fred came up with, but then he was given the chance of a short-term contract which put him in touch with people who had money.

However, at a time like this, the international community, particularly the powerful western nations that had remained on the sidelines (apart from evacuating their nationals each time the rebels attacked Freetown) would now surely channel resources to the greatest priorities and help rebuild lives; national politicians would pull together, setting aside personal aggrandisement and focus on restoring the country to something of its former status. And pigs might fly.

Part IV

Chapter Ten

Last Enemy

> Hinga Norman was an honest leader and a great man. He meant more to me
> than Nelson Mandela would ever mean to me. Mandela was also a good man, but
> Hinga Norman, he suffered a great deal.
>
> Col Roelf van Heerden (formerly of Executive Outcomes)

Elephants, so lore has it, never forget; for a certainty, though, political figureheads
who have been outperformed as leaders by a subordinate in a time of national crisis
do not; nor do peers who have been eclipsed by a charismatic colleague. When the
armed conflict was over and he was returned to office for a second term, President
Kabbah's deft flash of stiletto was intended to finish off Hinga Norman's political
life, but in no way imperil his person: he offered him the post of high commissioner
to Nigeria. To a man without wealth, who had endured privations to the point of
existing on starvation diet in his fight to restore democracy, the offer must have had
its attractions. He and his family would be well-provided for, and he would enjoy
the style and trappings that go with representing one's country. Did he agonize over
his decision and discuss in detail with his family his reasons for turning the offer
down?

> Not really, but he had been an officer mind you, and he felt that going to become
> an ambassador was not helping the country; he wanted something that was
> actually active and hands-on to help the nation.[1]

Confidential though such soundings out are supposed to be, rumours get around.
Besides, a special envoy from Nigeria was airlifted from Lungi to Freetown by
helicopter in which Fred was a crew member. So Hinga Norman touched on the
subject with him.

> Normally the Chief and myself would walk on the beach; usually the beach was
> empty, nobody there, we could sort of meander and the driver would be driving
> along the road while we walked along the beach. And we were talking and he said
> to me this day, 'Fred do you know that they wanted me to go to Nigeria as the
> high commissioner?' I said, 'Yes I heard sir.' He said, 'Of course, you heard.'

The reasons he gave Fred for his declining the job developed along the same lines as his family deduced: he felt that he could better serve his country at home. On that basis he was given the government post of Minister of Internal Affairs; and he shifted his energies on to this new remit, unaware that he was being set up.

Until, in a nightmare, he saw danger emerging.

I had a dream – President Kabbah said he was tired of my business, he was therefore going to get rid of me. He drew a machete from the sleeve of his gown to strike, but before he could, I automatically woke up.[2]

But, when Hinga Norman wakened, the nightmare still continued: he was in solitary confinement in prison, indicted as a war criminal.

A Kafkaesque coil began to encircle him at his desk in the Ministry of Internal Affairs on the morning of 10 March. President Kabbah allegedly phoned to speak to him, for no other reason, it seemed, than to establish that he was in his office. Shortly after putting down the phone,

I was arrested in the Ministerial Office of Internal Affairs and led away in HANDCUFFS (as a Minister of the SLPP Government) to the Cell of an old SLAVES' DUNGEON in Bonthe, on the 10th of March, 2003, on the orders of a Judge of the Special Court for Sierra Leone, His Honour Justice Bankole Thompson, who signed the single Indictment against me, dated 7th March 2003 and on which Indictment I was held in very deplorable and inhuman conditions for a considerable period of time before I and others were transferred to the present Special Court Detention Facility in Freetown, where I am still being held awaiting Trial and being forced to use a Plastic Bucket in the Cell for toileting purposes at night.[3]

The statute for the Special Court was set up by agreement between the United Nations and the government of Sierra Leone to consider responsibility for violations of human rights and crimes against humanity since 30 November 1996, the date of the Abidjan Accord. Another institution with a short-term time scale was established to complement it, a Truth and Reconciliation Commission. 'These two institutions were to employ different procedures and, to an extent, different objectives in the hopes of achieving peace, justice and reconciliation.'[4]

An American military lawyer, David Crane, was appointed Chief Prosecutor for the Special Court. Matching the sharpness of perspicacity of his president, who had identified an axis of evil on a world scale, he announced that,

This is the most black-and-white, good-versus-evil situation that I have ever seen in 30 years of public service.[5]

But then, however, before the indictments, the clarity of focus dimmed: he would bring in members of the CDF as well as the rebels. Peter Penfold commented,

Crane said at the time that he felt that he had to be seen as even-handed in his indictments — rather like a referee, having red-carded a footballer for a brutal tackle, sending off a member of the opposing team in order to keep the sides even.[6]

And indeed the pattern of violations by alleged perpetrators show the massive imbalance among the combatants: the RUF plus an unidentified group of rebels account for almost 70%; the AFRC almost 10%; the Sierra Leone army almost 7%; the CDF almost 6%; a category termed unknown 5%; and ECOMOG almost 1%.[7] The broad-brush approach to indictments was in keeping with a what-we-say-goes hegemony that Peter Penfold came across early on.

My view on the Special Court was this was the western world appeasing their conscience for not having done anything in the first place, and I specifically said to Crane — and this is in relation to fighting — , 'As a result of what you've just done, and if there is any trouble, you're going to be one of the first people to jump on a UN helicopter and get out of here, leaving us again to pick up the mess.' I really felt very angry about that. There were too many people who came in 2000 and afterwards who had not been there before, had no idea what we'd all gone through before; we'd gone through one helluva lot, and it had been a real struggle, and there had been a lot of sacrifices, and what we were handling was a very delicate sort of peace and democracy. And then these people suddenly fly in from around the world who had no idea about what had happened, and were imposing all their concepts of what constituted justice and democracy.[8]

From the start, statements by Special Court officials did not always meet their face value: misinformation, disinformation and fact were co-mingled. On the day that Hinga Norman was arrested, Special Court Registrar, the Briton, Robin Vincent, 'disclosed that Hinga Norman would be held in a country outside of Sierra Leone.'[9] In reality, he was already on his way to a cell in Bonthe. And, as to the scope of the Special Court, Prosecutor David Crane intoned,

No one — no one — is above the law, regardless of their power, stature or wealth. It must be seen that justice is open, impartial and fair.[10]

High ideals — let justice be done though the heavens fall. Except it was not true. The land of the free, home of the brave had just made sure that its citizens would continue to enjoy their liberties by exempting them from the powers of the Special Court. Having already withdrawn from participation in the International Criminal

Court (ICC), the US government was negotiating a bi-lateral arrangement with the government of Sierra Leone excluding its citizens from the scope of the Special Court. Ratification in the Sierra Leone parliament was awaited; and a civil rights group, Campaign for Good Governance (CGG) urged the parliament to reject the agreement, which, it said,

> Seeks to reverse recent advances in internal justice and seeks to endorse a two-tier system on international justice – one for US nationals and another for the rest of the world.[11]

The political context in which the Special Court was set up was resonant of George Orwell's satire on totalitarianism, *Animal Farm*, where the pigs pronounce that all animals are equal but some animals are more equal than others. Changed days from when the US Chief Prosecutor, Robert Jackson, declared at the Nuremberg war crimes trials after the Second World War,

> If certain acts and violations of treaties are crimes, they are crimes whether the United States does them or whether Germany does them. We are not prepared to lay down a rule of criminal conduct against others which we would not be willing to have invoked against us.[12]

Political finagling behind the scenes shaped the parameters within which the Special Court for Sierra Leone would operate. Only crimes committed after 30 November 1996, the date of the Abidjan Accord, would be considered, but actions by ECOMOG forces, however, would be excluded from consideration. Nor would Foday Sankoh's responsibility for earlier crimes committed by the RUF before November 1996 fall within the scope of the Court. Peter Penfold pointed out that,

> The US Government's position in this saga has been somewhat duplicitous. It was the Americans who had encouraged Kabbah to make Sankoh the de facto Vice President as part of the Sierra Leone peace process, against the wishes of the Sierra Leone people, and then scarcely a year later turned around and pushed for Sankoh to be tried as a war criminal.[13]

This was the political background against which the man many people in Sierra Leone regarded as the champion of democracy was arrested in his office on 10 March.

But the Chief Prosecutor, before deciding whom he would indict, must have taken advice from a range of people; one of whom was Peter Penfold who advised against indicting members of the CDF.

And I said, 'Hang on' I said, 'the CDF are the good guys' I said, 'they are the guys who were fighting for the restoration of Kabbah's government; they were fighting for democracy.' And Crane said, 'Yes but I've got to be seen to be even-handed,' these were the exact words he said, 'when I come to issue the indictments.'[14]

It certainly is surprising that such consideration by way of even-handedness came into the reckoning in the aftermath of such a brutal war and the overwhelming imbalance of violation of human rights. But then there were some in Sierra Leone and further afield who benefited from the blood diamond wars.

There are others, and there are always others, who have their own agenda for wanting the conflict to continue. There were clearly people in the country who were living off the back of all the turmoil created by the RUF, not least when it comes to diamond mining and so on. Now in that group as well there will be some of those do-gooding NGOs [Non-governmental organization] who, because they would want to work in say RUF areas, would turn a blind eye to all the nasty things that the RUF were doing. But equally, they would focus more and more on the nasty things that were being done to the RUF by these Kamajors. So this created a bit of a lobby so that when it came to looking at the human rights violations people would be saying, in the corridors in New York and London and so on – it's not just the RUF, there've been terrible things committed by the other side as well, so that if you're going to set up a court, make sure that you get everybody.[15]

In his prison cell, the man who had cause to feel wronged and abandoned was allowed a notebook and pen; his first entry was made four days later. In it, and in the earliest entries, he writes not expressing feelings of self-pity or outrage at his plight: he describes his dreams. And in some of them, he goes into great detail. In the first dream he had in prison, he was looking for directions.

I dreamt I was walking, and finding me looking at many roads in a green field and while wondering which way to take, I saw some people far away from where I was standing. I enquired from the people which way to take and someone among them told me that whichever way I took would take me to where I was going, and as soon as I started moving, I woke up.[16]

It was only after he had been there 30 days that there are entries of draft letters that show the conditions at Bonthe. On 10 April, he wrote to the registrar for the Special Court, through the Commander Detention Unit Bonthe, headed – Request for Legal Action. He argued that it was exactly 30 days since he was arrested and,

taken into detention under very appalling conditions 22 hours 20 minutes of continuous lock-up in a very hot cell with very small vent holes, no fresh air and in ISOLATION in blatant contravention of the following (A) Rules of Detention.[17]

He lists rules, 5, 25, 43 and 47; then (B) Article 17 (3) of the Statute of the Special Court, arguing that he is being treated worse that a convicted person. The paragraph of the Statute he referred to simply stated that defendants were to be presumed innocent until proved guilty.

There had been allegations in the press, and in an interview that Hinga Norman's daughter gave to the BBC, that he was being mistreated while in custody. These allegations were refuted by the registrar, who, it was reported, in a statement insisted that those in custody were being treated in accordance with international standards.[18]

Well, from what Hinga Norman recorded, it is evident that international standards had slipped over the years: top Nazi officials awaiting trial in Nuremberg at the end of the Second World War received more consideration for their spiritual needs than did Hinga Norman and his fellow detainees. In 1945, at Nuremberg,

Before the beginning of the trial, the defendants remained in solitary confinement, their only whispered contact during the half-hour walks around the prison courtyard, one behind the other at a distance of four feet, or during the Sunday church services which all of them (except Hess, Rosenberg and Streicher) attended.[19]

But in the case of the detainees of the Special Court for Sierra Leone, a different regime operated; it comes to light on the approach of Easter, when Hinga Norman took it upon himself to make a request for an Easter service. The tone of his draft is less a complaint and more an assumption of oversight on the part of the Special Court officials. On 14 April 2003 he wrote,

Dear Sir
Urgent Request – Spiritual Welfare

Today makes me 34 days in detention and although none of us has met with the other detainees, but I believe that the others may also have been held for as long as 34 days to date without attending common religious services, neither among ourselves nor by any qualified religious authority or representative. I have recently forwarded a request for common prayers and I am still awaiting response. I am however making this URGENT REQUEST for the services of a Religious Representative (Christian) Non Roman Catholic to hold an Easter Sunday (20/4/03) service at the Detention Unit between daylight and darkness.

We missed the Palm Sunday (13/4/03) service probably because there was no request.

Although, as a prisoner, my status is no higher than my colleagues, being a Government Minister and a Traditional Ruler and being 63 years of age, I believe I bear some responsibility under the Geneva Convention and, while in detention, the additional Protocol II, to seek the welfare of others considered subordinate.

In light, therefore, I am appealing to you to make arrangements for us (Christian Detainees) to attend a Common Easter Sunday service on 20ᵗʰ April and to continue attending religious services thereafter.

My highest regards
Sam Hinga Norman[20]

His urgent request was replied to; and from his response to that reply, it is clear that lack of provision for religious services was not an oversight but official policy. His letter had prompted action, and a solution was contrived which could be said to provide for a person's spiritual welfare without allowing the detainees to meet for common worship. He refused to accept the compromise, and wrote to the Registrar, through the Commander, Detention Unit.

Dear Sir
Religious Services

This is to acknowledge receipt of your letter, Ref DET/-/2003 of 16/4/03 received 17/4/03 at 1645 hours.

I wish to inform you that if the Chaplain is to pray for us on an individual basis, then I will refuse to accept that condition and shall advise my solicitor to publish your letter with the newspapers for this nation to know the type of conditions we are subjected to just to make sure that we are held in segregation and in isolation for more than 10 hrs during daylight.

May I inform you that I have already posted (through the SC) a copy of this letter to my solicitor for public information and to obtain his advice to a court action on this particular issue.[21]

Bureaucracy is always strong when it comes to blunt rebuttals, but revelation in the newspapers from an official's letter is its soft underbelly; quickly, policy was changed, and common worship was permitted. The change may have taken place on 27 April, because he wrote an order of service, including hymns, psalms and readings from the Old and New Testament.

It becomes clear over the ensuing months that his stand was not a ploy to get the detainees together. What comes through from his writing in prison is that he was a complex man: certainly he was a fighter who believed in the rightness of what he had done, but at the same time he was a deeply spiritual man who walked humbly with his God. His fight against the AFRC and the RUF, he would have seen as being vindicated under the principle of the just war. He was a man who, as we shall see, was able to lead others in worship, even his former enemies. Certainly, prayer was an important part of his day. He wrote, 'Prayed naked and put my case and the nation's plight before God and asked for a message every night, 28/29/30 April.' Indeed, he himself, as he told his friend the Rev Alfred SamForay, felt that all three of his names predestined him to be a both a warrior and a man of God: the biblical Samuel; then Hinga, which in Mende implies a male protector of the clan or village; and Noorma, anglicized to Norman, which again in Mende means one who persists in a cause.[22]

For about the first two months of his record, he gives no expression to his thinking about the political reasons for his being where he is; he simply relates his dreams, and two of them are interesting. On the night of 3/4 May, he tells us,

> I found myself in front of a crowd of people as if it was a church or a religious gathering, where I was invited to the front towards what appeared as an altar, and I was given a bowl of oil (like an olive oil) and I was told to pour the oil on my head, but a hand took the bowl and poured the oil on my head and in the cup of my palms joined together. I poured the oil which had been poured into my hands on my head and automatically the crowd sang out loudly this song, 'When the battle is over you shall wear the crown, you shall wear the crown.' And I joined in the singing. I was singing until I woke up singing the song in my bed. This was now Sunday (4/5/03) morning I realized then that I was in jail.[23]

Certainly the dream he recorded on 21 May is a rich source for interpretation.

> I dreamt I found myself in a car driving on a highway and at a point, the car turned left and headed down a very steep fall towards what looked like the Atlantic Ocean – the view of the ocean was without limit and there seemed no turning opportunity for the car. At that point, I felt like urinating. The car stopped and I attempted climbing down another steep fall down to the water's edge of the wave–slapping ocean.
>
> But, at a point in my attempt to stop and urinate I found that the rocks on which I was standing were giving way under my feet – as if the next thing that would happen to me was to fall into the ocean. I was terribly afraid and I realized I was alone and struggling for something to hold on to. After some struggle, I managed and turned round and grabbed some rocks and suddenly found myself standing up on the steep pavement having been saved from falling into the sea. I then walked up to the level top of the pavement where I met two white men in military dress; one was carrying a gun and he seemed to be arguing, saying, 'If you make that announcement we will shoot them', pointing his gun at the back of the other white man who was already moving towards a stationary car, black

in colour. We all moved to the car and I was told to go into the car. I made an attempt to enter on the right side of the car but, I found human faeces (shit) on an old palm log from the tail end to head of the car, and could not enter on that side of the car, so I passed to the other side of the car to enter on the part of the main road.

The door behind the driver was opened but the backrest of the driver's seat was flapped down and I couldn't enter. While I was still trying to get the seat rest up so I could enter, I took a look into the car and saw to my surprise, that President Tejan Kabbah was in the car, but trying to conceal his face and identity. There was also another person sitting in the back seat of the car. I never quite entered the car when I woke up.[24]

That dream inevitably raises the question, how much did Kabbah know in advance about his former Deputy Minister of Defence being indicted, and did he raise a hand to help the man who had done more than anyone in the government to restore him to power. Hinga Norman told both the Rev Alfred SamForay[25] and Peter Penfold about the phone call before his arrest.

And he told me on the phone that it was about an hour beforehand that Kabbah had rung and didn't have anything at all to say. And the way that Sam interpreted it, and I do as well, that he knew. It was obvious. The point that I always made was – and of course Kabbah denied it – that, in a way it doesn't matter whether he did know or he didn't know, in my view: because Kabbah is damned if he did know or he didn't know, in my view. Because, if he did know, then he was obviously acquiescing – and that was terrible, because he knew it was happening to a person who he owed his position to; if he didn't know, as far as I'm concerned, he's damned because he's the president of this country, it's his own policemen who were going to arrest and drag out his Minister of Internal Affairs, and he should have known. So as far as I'm concerned, he had no excuse either way. He's damned if he did know and he's damned if he didn't know. And he's damned because, when it did happen, he didn't say a thing. He didn't say a thing. And it went on and on without him saying anything. All you could get out of him when I tackled Kabbah about it, he said, 'Oh, I mustn't interfere with the judicial process of an independent court.' And all this sort of thing. Now, when he's told me that, then I thought – you're clearly quite happy for it to happen.[26]

The inaccessibility of Bonthe island meant that there were few visitors. Mostly contact was made by letter or by phone call, which was permitted. Hinga Norman had a letter from Peter Penfold on 25 May, along with several from friends abroad. Fred was in touch with the Chief by phone, and then sent him some books. And on 16 July, Hinga Norman wrote to thank him.

Fred

Thanks for the reading materials. Please assist bearer to enable him to copy the documents and transportation to distribute.

If in doubt, please try and ring.

Highest regards
Chief Sam Hinga Norman[27]

Fred had left Air Wing the previous year and set up a security company, Vanguard International Protection West Africa (VIPWA), registered in the UK and in Freetown. Fred was Managing Director, and his partner with a limited amount of money was the American actor Jeffrey Wright. Fred had been invited, when he was still with the Air Wing to carry out a reconnaissance in Mozambique for the shooting of Michael Mann's film *Ali*. Fred spent ten days in the country in November 2000; he went back again for about six weeks the following year, and provided security for the director, Michael Mann. After the shooting wrap, Fred took Jeffrey to see Sierra Leone. The upshot was that Jeffrey was interested in investing some money in the country, and so the company was formed, but with a modest level of financing. Fred also asked his friend from Lifeguard days, TT De Abreu, to join them. The new company was in a strong position; Fred knew the country and he knew a lot of people; and they won an important contract with BHPB (Broken Hill Proprietary Billiton Ltd); and, ironically, they won the contract to provide security for the Special Court of Sierra Leone. That is, until, after Hinga Norman's arrest, Fred's relationship with him was discovered, when, quite properly, it was revoked. Perhaps it was just as well; had the contract gone ahead, over time, with Fred's sense of commitment to the Chief and TT's experience of leading a break-out from AFRC/RUF-held Kono, it might have landed them in deep trouble.

Among those who contacted Hinga Norman by phone was Col Roelf van Heerden. Executive Outcomes had been disbanded as a private military company, and Roelf was back in the country again, working for a mining company, African Gold and Diamond SL.

I called him while he was still in Bonthe Island and had a brief chat with him, as the guards were all over him; and he and I could not say much. He was sad, but still had hope and was very much encouraged by the call.[28]

A few days after he wrote to Fred thanking him for reading material, Hinga Norman came across in it a statement by Benjamin Franklin that he found relevant to his own situation, for he chose to write it up that afternoon of 19 July at 3.45pm in one of the blank introductory pages of the notebook he had started writing in four months earlier.

Those who would give up essential liberty to purchase a little temporary safety deserve neither liberty nor safety.

Although he felt abandoned by president and party, he had many supporters. The international action group, SLAM-CDF, was reactivated under its Secretary-General, the Rev Alfred SamForay, to set up the Hinga Norman Defence Fund of SLAM. As early as 24 March, the group had established where he was being kept prisoner and, in a press statement announced that, through his counsel, Hinga Norman indicated that he would not accept any financial or legal aid from the government of Sierra Leone or the SLPP (Sierra Leone People's Party); he would rely entirely on 'support from his friends and relatives at home and abroad to finance his legal defence.'[29]

Meanwhile, the Truth and Reconciliation Commission (TRC), the separate body created with a specific role in the post-conflict, was taking statements from interested parties; the Commission wanted Hinga Norman to appear, and he very much wanted to speak to the Commission in public as others had done. Judge Thompson of the Special Court ruled against it. His interpretation was that the TRC could take statements from three categories of people: perpetrators, victims and interested parties. He ruled that because Hinga Norman was a central figure in the conflict, it must be interpreted that he would come under the category of perpetrator and if he made a statement it would offend against the basic principle that an indictee is innocent until the court proves him be to be guilty. His judgment went to appeal.

In what looks like a first draft disputing the Court's decision, Hinga Norman, takes the role of leader for all the other detainees in his position – CDF, RUF and AFRC – and argues that the right to be heard and recorded by the Truth and Reconciliation Commission was negotiated by representatives of the parties to the conflict in Sierra Leone, whereas the Special Court was imposed by an agreement in which representatives of the conflict did not participate. And he concluded his thoughts:

> Since for many reasons the impartiality of the SCSL is in serious doubt and that there are clear indications that the Court has every potentiality of being biased, we, the indictees, having no faith in the fair trial and justice, have decided on the following, a) that until we are allowed to appear and publicly testify before the TRC we have decided not to appear before the SCSL.[30]

The appeal against Judge Thompson was heard by Judge Robertson. He partly accepted that Hinga Norman could give testimony to the TRC, but it had to be through a sworn affidavit, supplemented by an *in camera* meeting and not broadcast. Hinga Norman refused those conditions: unless he was allowed to appear in public and make his statements like the others, he would not make a written statement.

Judge Thompson's ruling and Judge Robertson's decision on appeal have been subsequently critiqued in an academic law journal on the basis that the two bodies, TRC and SCSL, were intended to have complementary roles – the SCSL was not the superior body, that while it had primacy over the courts in Sierra Leone, it was contentious to assume it had primacy over the TRC. Furthermore, Judge Thompson's view that Hinga Norman's 'centrality' implied that he was in the category of perpetrator, thereby compromising his right of assumption of innocence, has also been challenged. That he was a central figure in the conflict is clear, but that this was interpreted by the Judge as putting him in the category of perpetrator, suggests, it has been argued, a pre-existing presumption of guilt.

> Viewed in this light, the result of Judge Thompson's decision is to inadvertently bring into question the independence and impartiality of the SCSL. Without further evidence beyond what was present here, such as facts evincing the coercion of the Accused or a legal requirement that the Accused testify against himself at the TRC, this disposition should not be followed in the future.[31]

Fate, it would seem at that point, was conspiring against him and his fellow detainees. Sierra Leone was the first (and to date, only) country to have both a Truth and Reconciliation Commission and a Special Court operating at the same time, and the implications of their interacting had not been sufficiently thought through in advance. In hindsight, a common belief is that the TRC was not strong enough to stand up to the Special Court, but an articulation mechanism between the two should not have had to rely on something as tenuous as the leading personalities in the TRC.

Given the robust tone of the papers that would flow from him in prison, it is most unfortunate that Hinga Norman did not contribute to the truth and reconciliation process; he would have given unique insight to the TRC on the operation of the CDF, and would certainly have had something to say about one damning statement against him. It is contained in paragraph 839 of the TRC final report, and concerns an attack by Kamajors on a bus during the Black December campaign, a campaign agreed on by the Sierra Leone Government in exile. The attack took place on 2 November 1997, and at the time, it was reported that there were atrocities. An anonymous survivor of the attack stated to the TRC that he was travelling from Kenema to Bo in a Government bus which was attacked. Afterwards the Kamajor commander made a call on his mobile,

> And communicated to Hinga Norman, who was in Monghere [sic] at that moment. According to their conversation, I understood that Hinga Norman gave them the order to execute everybody.[32]

Of course it did not matter where a decision by phone was taken, whether it was Mongeri or Mombasa, but the survivor's insistence on pinpointing Hinga Norman in Mongeri (his home village) is interesting, because, as we saw earlier, in the letter he wrote to Fred on 8 November 1997, requesting supplies to be dropped off at Base Zero on their next flight with Bokkie, Hinga Norman explained, 'we mistakenly dropped a bag of mine at Gendema on our way on Wednesday [5 November].'[33] So the attack on the bus took place on 2 November; but on 5 November, Hinga Norman was in Gendema; the means by which he got about in Sierra Leone was by helicopter. As Fred put it, the claim, 'was a lie because we moved the Chief and his people by air.' However, the survivor's account gets even more interesting; and it is a pity that the TRC short-changed him by concealing his identity: he could have made a fortune for himself, his family and supported his community by performing for the media the accomplishment hitherto achieved solely by the oozlum bird that flew round and round in ever decreasing circles until it disappeared into a place where the sun doesn't shine – for he concluded his statement.

> I was the last person in the men's row. As they were about to kill me, I used mystical power and disappeared.[34]

Despite the legal ruling and Hinga Norman's refusal to contribute to it under conditions different from those accorded to the president, in the TRC final report there is a paragraph (673) written in the first person, and obviously in Hinga Norman's words (an extract of which appeared earlier in chapter four in connection with the May 1997 coup). There is no introduction to it or explanation for its being there. However, the source text from which it was taken is a statement he wrote in his notebook in prison. It is the longest entry in the notebook, and is an address he makes to be presented to the Special Court, not the TRC. He introduces the statement as, 'Pursuant to Article 6: 3 of the Statute'. Paragraph 3 of the article deals with the overall responsibility of a superior.

> The fact that any of the acts referred to in articles 2 to 4 of the present Statute was committed by a subordinate does not relieve his or her superior of criminal responsibility if he of she knew or had reason to know that the subordinate was about to commit such acts or had done so and the superior had failed to take the necessary and reasonable measures to prevent such acts or punish the perpetrators thereof.[35]

Following on from that heading, he wrote a first draft of a statement, laying responsibility on the president for not acting on the warnings of his deputy minister of defence that the 1997 coup was imminent. He amends his wording as he goes, but the lay out is systematic and he has clearly marshalled his thoughts; the draft reads easily with one exception. He interpolated the paragraph he numbered 3 later, after he wrote what follows it, and so he had to cram it into the margin at the top of the page. He was forced to use a shorthand that worked for him but which, for another reader, in places, is illegible. Maybe his reasoning for including it was to forestall the question, why not have a private word with his boss before confronting him in the presence of witnesses, two of whom would subsequently be executed for their part in the coup? It seems he had first spoken to him privately.

1. Pursuant to Article 6:3 of the Statute that Dr Ahmad Tejah Kabbah, Minister of Defence, Commander-in-Chief of the armed forces and President of the Republic of Sierra Leone, while holding positions of superior responsibility and exercising command and control over the government, armed forces and the entire nation of Sierra Leone, is responsible for the criminal acts of the armed forces in that he <u>knew</u> that the armed forces were about to commit such acts and he failed to take the necessary and reasonable measures to prevent such acts.
2. That his failure and deliberate refusal to take necessary measures to prevent such acts caused untold number of deaths, injuries to human beings (men, women and children, young and old) and destruction to public and private properties across the entire nation of Sierra Leone.
3. That some time in April 1997, through the assistance of some senior officer, I obtained the working parts of some dangerous military copies [?] which I gave to HE informing him of my suspicion of the Army and I told him in the event of any coup, with those parts the Army could not play havoc in the city. The [omitted] gave those parts back to the CDS and to the Chief [illegible] which were later used in the coup. After this incident, I now decided to the following in the presence of witnesses.
4. That in the afternoon of Friday the 16 May 1997, I Chief Samuel Hinga Norman, then Deputy Minister of Defence in the Government of Sierra Leone, obtained permission of HE to invite the following persons to his presence:

   a) Dr Albert Joe Demby, former Vice President of Sierra Leone now residing in Bo, Sierra Leone.
   b) Mr Teddy Williams, former Inspector General of the Sierra Leone Police – I understand he his now living in Freetown.
   c) Commander A B Sesay, the former Navy Commander, now the Deputy CDS of the Sierra Leone Army at the Ministry of Defence Sierra Leone.
   d) Brigadier Hassan Conteh, former CDS of the SLA. Executed by firing squad.
   e) Col Max Kanga, former Army Chief of the SLA. Executed by firing squad.

And in the presence of these five, I informed HE the President that there was a planned coup to overthrow the GOSL [Government of Sierra Leone] and to cause serious destruction to life and property and that the CDS and the Army Chief, Brig Conteh and Col Kanga knew about same.

HE the President said to the CDS and Army Chief, gentlemen did you hear what Chief Norman said? They said, yes sir. The President further asked, do you have anything to say? They said, no sir. The President then said, Chief Norman the gentlemen say they do not have anything to say.

I was shocked. I said, your ex [Excellency] I invited these men to tell you in their presence their involvement in a grave situation facing the nation, but I do realize you do not intend to take action to prevent their plan. Well, I am requesting Your Excellency to tell them not to execute their plan; that if they do, I, Chief Hinga Norman will join the people of Sierra Leone and we shall fight these and those who shall take part in the coup, we shall defeat them, reverse the coup, take power from their hands and restore the government and Your Excellency will be bound by the Constitution of Sierra Leone to sign their death warrant after due process of the law. Since it appears you do not believe me and you are reluctant to take the necessary action to avert this fast approaching troubles [sic], I will pray God that you survive the coup to witness eventual consequences.

We left the State house and HE never referred to the matter again until the coup struck on Sunday May 25th 1997.

Well, ladies and gentlemen, Mr Prosecutor, the President and Chief Hinga Norman who bears the greatest responsibility now that you have heard from me? Or is this matter still to be dealt by you as a Special Court decision – meaning you did not come here to prosecute the President but Chief Hinga Norman as may have been decided upon by some people at the UN?

Again, I have been charged for unlawful killings. Well people were tried in court and found [guilty] but were never allowed to appeal and were executed [a reference to those found guilty of treason after the 1997 coup was crushed].

My question Mr Prosecutor is this.

The President and his former Attorney General now Vice President of Sierra Leone on one part and Chief Norman on the other who to your honest and moral knowledge unlawfully killed in Sierra Leone?

Finally, the test of your honesty, morality and sincerity Mr Prosecutor is now at hand.

The neutrality and impartiality of the Special Court is now under test.

That if the action expected is not taken in the next seven days of this disclosure, I shall refuse to participate in this matter and shall ask my sympathizers in Sierra Leone and the world to start a non violent demonstration.

Finally, I wish to apply as at now to request another neutral organization or nation to responsibility of [sic] my detention as I do not feel safe in the hands of the Special Court officials – I am in grave fear for my life. Starting now (this very moment).[36]

How a shortened version of this text found its way into the TRC final report is not known.

Then, in a short, undated piece, he returns to the theme of the president's culpability and muses on reasoning for setting up the apparatus of a Special Court.

Tejan Kabbah's refusal to take necessary action to prevent that coup – being the Minister of Defence, the Commander-in-Chief of the Armed Forces of the Republic of Sierra Leone was immoral, unconstitutional, dishonest and to say the least reckless and criminal.

Look at the result and the consequences. Now he designed a Special Court for what? To cover up his failure or create by design a commercial activity for them [sic] in the UN to open yet another avenue for employment for their friends, relatives and contacts for 3 years.

Money which should have gone to the TRC to move with speed and recommend compensation for the victims.[37]

However, this entry does not seem designed to link to anything wider; it may have been for a paragraph in a letter.

A new year began in prison. By now his notebook was full. However, he had a very small pocket diary for 2004 that did not have room for extended thoughts; but he managed to write over the last day of the previous year and the first of the new year, 'The future of this nation is hugely going to depend on pursuing: – prosecution – reconciliation.' When accommodation was ready in Freetown, he and the other detainees were transferred to the Special Court Detention Centre there.

Peter Penfold was one of the early visitors; indeed he was flown by UN helicopter to Bonthe the previous year; and after the switch to Freetown, he came on three occasions at the end of February and the beginning of March. On the date of his first visit, Hinga Norman, giving Peter Penfold his honorary title, wrote, 'PC [Paramount Chief] Komrabai.' Peter Penfold had no difficulty in being allowed to visit. It was a different story when Roelf van Heerden tried.

I tried to visit him on two occasions. Firstly they, the Special Court, said I must make a booking and could not see him as a friend, within 14 days. I came back but was refused. I tried to use the influence of Neall Ellis, working for the government at that time as their gunship pilot, but still in vain. I decided to drop it as Neall Ellis told me that some politicians 'told' him to stay out of their politics. Neall then said to me I must drop the issue.

I can remember Fred; he would always go to serious lengths to try and make things better for Hinga Norman, especially in later days when he was locked up and it became really a political prickly pear: you didn't know whether you should mention his name in public because they were just looking for people to interrogate and also to lock up. And it was really a messy thing. But Fred always kept straight, supporting the man. Yes I think that Fred was really a great friend of the Chief.[38]

The reason Hinga Norman had earlier been in contact with Roelf, then working with African Gold and Diamond SL, was because there was a gold project in his area and he wanted the area developed like other districts; he told Roelf that the mineral licence was expiring and that there was no development; he had asked him if he could find investors. But Roelf later learned that there were other government ministers with an interest in it as well and, in his view, they conspired,

> to keep the Chief away from developing it as it would not bring bribe money into their pockets. It was, according to me, a corrupt government network to sideline him. He had true intentions for this development.[39]

No obstacles were put in Fred's way at this stage, and he went to visit the Chief as often as he could, and responded as best the could to requests for help. For example, on 14 April, at the bottom of a page of a sheet of A4 paper, torn from a pad, on which, written in blue ink by the same hand, was a list of 15 names. At the bottom of the list, in black ink, the Chief wrote:

> Fred
>   Please receive these names of some of the un–employeds [sic] I have around me – see what you could possibly do for them.
>
> Many thanks in advance.
>
> Your brother
> Sam Hinga Norman
> Chief Norman[40]

The 15 men were former members of the CDF, and they were out of work. Fred made efforts, but,

> the company could not afford to recruit any more people because of shortage of funds. This was after we lost the BHPB contract because we could not maintain the safety standard required by BHPB management.

And two weeks later, the Chief's financial worries increased: he was supporting his family, and from now on it was going to be more difficult. He wrote to Fred.

Dear Fred

I am sure you have also heard about my replacement at the Ministry of Internal Affairs.

Please be informed and also explore the possibility of approaching the (your) organization if it could be possible to arrange the relocation of my family to some other (less expensive) address until I am released.

Please, let me hear from you on the issue at your earliest convenience.

Yours
Sam Hinga Norman[41]

This time something could be done – or so it appeared at first. Fred asked Mrs Norman to find accommodation,

I would pay the rent if it was reasonable, because if I found a place, it would cost a lot of money. We did find a nice compound with three bedrooms, but when I went to pay for it, the landlady gave the house to a tenant that was willing to pay more because they were from the UN; so we lost out. We never did find one that I could afford to pay because I was not getting paid from my own company.

Apart from his family, his legal team, friends like Peter Penfold and Fred, few of his political colleagues visited, it would seem.

Anyone who was going to visit the Special Court, your photograph had to be taken to go to the State House for them to see. That is why after my dad was arrested all the ministers refused to visit him, because when you go and visit you'll be sacked the next day. So everyone who wanted their job refrained from going to the Special Court. All those, close party members, they all neglected to go there; no one was friends with Hinga Norman any more. As soon as you would mention his name, they would move away.[42]

His son, Sam, had been living in the UK since 1995; he went back home and visited his father.

We sat down. And I said, 'Why? It's hard for me to understand why are you here? You walk around Britain and people that do good, they have statues.' I said, 'You're not the Bad Guy, you fought for the country.' He said to me, 'You don't understand what life is like.'[43]

Although he understood what life was like, he showed in his notes no indication of being beaten; he had reserves, inner resources and the moral fibre to fight. His capacity for the former is evident to a surprising degree.

Despite not being allowed to give a statement to the TRC on the same conditions as others, in the week before Easter 2004, it becomes apparent that he was making a remarkable contribution to reconciliation among the detainees of the previously warring parties. On 4 April, he conducted the Palm Sunday mid-day service in the detention centre in cell 10; Bishop Sannoh conducted the main Palm Sunday service.[44] Of the RUF leadership, Foday Sankoh had died in May 2003 while in detention, and Sam 'Mosquito' Bockerie, who had been on the run, was shot dead by Liberian troops during the same month; so the Interim leader of the RUF was Issa Sesay, and he was in the detention centre. It was not possible for the Special Court to indict everyone in RUF, only those in positions of power; and he,

> had been pressured by the UN and Kabbah to become 'RUF interim leader' in order to ensure that the RUF complied with the disarmament and demobilization of the RUF as part of the peace process.'[45]

Now labelled as a leader, Issa Sesay was arrested. And on Easter Sunday, Hinga Norman wrote, 'Easter Service – I preached to Issa Sesay in the morning.'[46] He preached to him – not preached at him. Some sort of reconciliation seemed to be at work, because three month later, he wrote, 'Chief Norman met with the 3 SCSL (RUF) indictees and offered prayers and had discussion with them.'[47] Then later in the year he, 'went and prayed with my Moslem colleagues.' On 2 May, he conducted a service and preached, 'about four parts of the man called Peter.' He was emerging not only as the leader but a spiritual mentor to the group of detainees. And in the evening of a day that he spoke out strongly in court for what he saw as his rights, only to have the judges refuse him, he wrote:

> Later at evening prayers God reminded me of (S. M. & A.) in the Bible [Shadrach, Mishach and Abednego, tested in the fiery furnace, Daniel, 3.][48]

At various points in his notebook or diaries, he brought his own situation to his reading of the Bible: in one place he wrote of God's assurance, 'His forgiveness for wrongful acts with genuine intentions. Math 12: 1–5'; and on 16 May, he wrote, 'God gave me psalm 62 as my personal psalm.' Certainly the psalm contains poetic expressions that he applied to his situation: 'For God alone my soul waits in silence/... He only is my rock and my salvation/... How long will you set upon a man to shatter him, all of you, like a leaning wall, a tottering fence?/ They only plan to thrust him down/... They take pleasure in falsehood.'

But hand in hand with his belief in a merciful God there runs a very strong fighting spirit. The court process had begun, and he was intent on defending himself. He had no legal training, but he was adamant. The existing papers for much of what follows come from Fred's collection and are typed, because, for some months of 2004, Hinga Norman was given access to a computer and printer as part of his defence requirements. He could not pass these papers to Fred directly when he came to visit, for Fred was searched on the way in and out, so Hinga Norman gave them to an Investigator, who had been allocated by the Special Court to the Defence to contact witnesses; the Investigator was instructed to pass them to Fred.

Hinga Norman's first major hurdle was faced on 15 June 2004; though the signed copy passed to Fred was dated 23 July. It is headed'

'The Address.'

I am Samuel Hinga Norman

The facts about me are that I joined the Army at the age of fourteen and a half years and at the interview before the General Officer Commander-In-Chief, West Africa, I said this; that I was joining the army to defend Her Majesty's Empire. I was asked, at this age what can you do? I said I will grow up and I would do a lot of things. I am in the process of doing those things.

I have been under tremendous stress, like I was when I was deciding to take up battle against my colleagues, the soldiers and against my brothers and sisters, the RUF, for the honour of Sierra Leone. In the process, I am standing here again in that same way, taking up to defend myself in response to what is facing Sierra Leone today.

I cannot, I should not and I will not respond to anything the Prosecution may have said before this Court as constituted and before your Lordships sitting as a Trial Chamber of the Special Court for Sierra Leone under the presidency of Your Honour, Justice Itoe, and Your Honours, Justice Bankole Thompson and Justice Boutet, as members of the Trial Chamber for the following reasons:

1. There is or are no charge or charges legally placed before this Chamber against me. If there is or are charges against me before this Chamber, then I submit that by law I have not taken any plea before this Chamber, or on any Indictment against me before Your Honours. I will state the reasons when I hear the response from Your Lordships.
2. This Court, operating as a Trial Chamber of the Special Court for Sierra Leone, does not have the Constitutional Authority to try me and indeed, any Sierra Leonean, pursuant to Article 8 of the Statute of the Special Court for Sierra Leone over all the courts of Sierra Leone, which, in effect, has taken away the constitutional powers of the Chief Justice of Sierra Leone, which is entrenched in the Constitution and cannot, I repeat, cannot be taken by any other means except the means provided for in the Constitution of Sierra Leone.
3. Whatever took place in Sierra Leone as an incident since 1991 to the date under review, has not been defined whether it is war or conflict. If it is war, What type of war; Conventional or Civil? If it is conflict, what type of Conflict; International or National?

This much I know, as a soldier, well trained in the British Army and as a Minister of Internal Affairs in Sierra Leone, having privilege to documents, that Sierra Leone acceded to the Geneva Convention in 1986. And in that Convention under Protocol 1, the conflict in Sierra Leone would be well described as International and so, if International, then, the Geneva Convention stipulates that Article 90 of Protocol 1 should be applied and that a Commission of Inquiry should be instituted in Sierra Leone to investigate the happenings in Sierra Leone and submit a conclusion, with recommendation for those who did WHAT and to WHAT EXTENT and at WHAT GRAVE LEVEL; for Parties to the conflict to compensate Sierra Leoneans who may have lost lives, limbs, blood, property, dignity and opportunity and those Parties to the conflict are Governments and Organizations that sent their Agents, the Armies/Auxiliary Forces, that dealt with the situation in excess of the fire-power that was required. Any other way of doing it will be a CYNICAL MANIPULATION of the process of law in Sierra Leone.

For these reasons I have chosen to defend myself, that in the area of self-defence, there is no time limitation whether you should start it or, you should apply it in the middle or in the end. There is no age limit, whether you are a baby or an old person or a young one; that there is no qualification, whether you are educated or not.

These are my reasons for not responding to whatever DRAMATIC THESIS the Prosecution had proffered here before Your Lordships and this court intending to incite your sentiments on issues that they are sure, as I am, that they do not have any reason to hold against HINGA NORMAN!

I thank you, Your Lordships.

SAMUEL HINGA NORMAN – JP
Self-Defending Accused
15th June, 2004.[49]

When he returned to his cell after his appearance in court, he wrote in his diary:

Self-Defending Accused.
I delivered my speech to the Bench at the SCSL, which lasted for not more than 15 minutes, and received thunderous applause. But, the Judges forced the start of the Trial by calling the 1st witness a Mr I. Bah. Later at evening prayers God reminded me of (S M & A) in the Bible.[50]

And so he persevered, and recorded in an entry on 23 June, 'A mixture of yes and no composed the decision on my defence requirements.' The Special Court went into recess until 8 September.

Two days before the proceedings were due to resume, Peter Penfold was in touch with him by phone. When the proceedings got underway, Hinga Norman was forthright as before in his next statement to the Court bearing his name and role as Justice of the Peace. Long before the political undertow dragged him into the shoals of the Special Court, at a time when there was widespread admiration for his initiative during the 1997 coup, Hinga Norman had been asked in an interview about the contribution of the CDF in restoring Kabbah's government; and perhaps unsurprisingly for someone of his age trained in the British army, he compared it with an allusion to Winston Churchill's tribute to the RAF during the Battle of Britain – 'the few'. However, Hinga Norman developed it:

> Now in Sierra Leone I would go further to say 'never was so much owed by so many to so few for nothing'. In the case of Britain, these were men who had been hired on salaries, they were paid. They did more than their salary required. In Sierra Leone they did more than what the ordinary man could ever do for another person – laying down your life not on any bet or any favour whatsoever – just laying down your life so that the other man can live in freedom. That is what the Civil Defence has been doing.[51]

Now here, before the Special Court, his own words in his second paragraph have a Churchillian ring to them. The paper is headed

NO ONE IS ABOVE THE LAW

I believe it was under the Rule of Law and NOT by FORCE OF ARMS or INFLUENCE of any sort from any quarter whatsoever, that I was arrested in the Ministerial Office of Internal Affairs and led away in HANDCUFFS (as a Minister of the SLLP Government) in the Cell of an old SLAVES' DUNGEON in Bonthe, on the 10th of March, 2003, on the orders of a Judge of the Special Court for Sierra Leone, His Honour Justice Bankole Thompson, who signed the single Indictment against me, dated 7th March 2003 and on which Indictment I was held in very deplorable and inhuman conditions for a considerable period of time before I and others were transferred to the present Special Court Detention Facility in Freetown, where I am still being held awaiting Trial and being forced to use a Plastic Bucket in the Cell for toileting purposes at night. Several complaints for inhuman treatment have been lodged in the form of Court Motions before the Trial Chamber but the Trial Chamber has done nothing to address the situation to Date. We still continue to [have] the Toilet Buckets in our Cells which we know and believe is inhuman under Fundamental Human Right Law.

I believe in the STAND that I and the CDF/SL (KAMAJORS) took against our Brothers and Sisters of the RUF and my Colleague Soldiers of the SLAF, in the STRUGGLE to REINSTATE the Presidency and Restore DEMOCRATIC

RULE in Sierra Leone which is <u>A DUTY EXPECTED OF EVERY CITIZEN OF Sierra Leone and THE FREE WORLD</u> – a struggle in which many other Sierra Leoneans and other nationals joined and for which I extend thanks and appreciation to all those who offered sacrifices of all kinds. I also extend my heartfelt sympathies and APOLOGIES to all those who suffered unnecessarily in the conflict. I wish to urge all and sundry to accept what has happened to all of us as worthy SACRIFICES in the course of our Nation's HISTORICAL JOURNEY.

My respect for the Rule of Law and acceptance of the fact that NOBODY and NO ORGANIZATION is ABOVE the Law is profound – hence, my determination for the Rule of Law to be forever respected in Sierra Leone is non-negotiable.

Therefore, if the Rule of Law has been accepted and respected by me, equally so, I would expect the same Rule of Law to be accepted and respected (with the greatest of respect to their Honours) by the Judges of the Trial Chamber of the Special Court for Sierra Leone.

I was arrested under the Rule of Law and I am now requesting under the same Rule of Law that the JOINDER INDICTMENT against me should be SERVED on me pursuant to RULES 50 (A) & (52) of the Rules of Procedure of the STATUTE of the Special Court for Sierra Leone, to enable me proceed to Court and pursuant to Rule 61 (ii) of the Rules of procedure, be arraigned before the Trial Chamber to enter Plea on the charges against me, so that my trial could commence. <u>THIS IS THE LAW</u> and these are the LEGAL and LAWFUL conditions which should be RESPECTED by the SPECIAL COURT – remember, that <u>no one is ABOVE THE LAW</u>; NOT EVEN THE SPECIAL COURT FOR SIERRA LEONE.

If justice is the mission of the Special Court, then, I am simply requesting for:

a)   The APPLICATION of the LAW.
b)   The IMPLEMENTATION of JUSTICE.

Let Justice be Done and be Seen to be Done by the Special Court.

Samuel Hinga Norman
Self-Defending Accused
28/9/04[52]

Around this time he wrote to some former colleagues who had served with him in the CDF and who were now either turning their backs on him or changing sides and becoming witnesses for the prosecution. His letter to a paramount chief goes on to say,

This bearer has been to see you several times only to be told on each occasion that you were out and could not be reached. This time round, I have advised him to drop this letter which, I am sure will reach you in his stead.

You were the Chairman of the War Council of the Kamajors at Base Zero just as President Kabbah was in Conakry and for which service you were decorated; both of you holding those positions until Parliament of Sierra Leone passes another resolution to dissolve the Civil Defence Force CDF/SL. You should therefore please be in readiness to be available at any time you may be called upon to testify in court about events (criminal or otherwise), relative to CDF and Kamajors' defensive activities in Sierra Leone for the period under review.[53]

But another, whom he addressed as 'My Good Friend and Brother' he challenges on the grounds that having been a senior member of the CDF/Kamajors, he is now an agent for the prosecution, and frequently visited the Detention Centre, but kept away from the principal CDF defendant.

During the war you were, and you still are, the Chairman of the Appointments & Promotions Committee and a member of the 'Base Zero War Council' your responsibility being that of recommending the most suitable members of the CDF/SL for senior commanders' position in the battle field.[54]

He too was told to hold himself in readiness to be called by the defence.

Set-backs and successes marked the end of the year. On 2 November, the computer and printer were removed from him as part of the judges' decision revoking his self-defence; however, next day, buoyed with ideas, he spoke to Charles Margai, the son of Sir Albert Margai, a former prime minister, about the politics of the country and the formation of a 'third force political party.' Then on 8 November there was a prison break at Pendemba Road jail, which led to a tightening of security at the Special Court Detention Centre with all visiting banned for four weeks. Towards the end of the month he was told to expect a decision on his 'Motion of Non Service & Arraignment.' His diary entry for Monday 29 November reads:

The long awaited Decision was given in favour of Hinga Norman.

a) Majority Decision was partial
b) Minority Decision was totally against the Prosecution and TOTALLY in FAVOUR OF HINGA NORMAN.[55]

Below he wrote, 'Messages of congratulation flowed in with prayers for total victory. Long victory prayer; Hymn 82; Psalm 3.' The year ended for him with two visits from Peter Penfold.

Another year in prison began, and resulted in far fewer diary entries. One of the topics that recurs is his country's politics: issues about contesting the SLPP (Sierra Leone People's Party) were raised; an injunction was taken out against hosting the convention of the party's delegates in Makeni; again there are references to the possibility of forming a new political party; and on 25 September, a meeting was held of representatives of the former warring groups: AFRC, RUF and the CDF with the purpose of 'working together in a united political set-up.'[56]

The Special Court continued at its own pace, but Hinga Norman writes little about its deliberations. On 16 May he wrote of the Appeals Chamber releasing a confused decision; and nine days later he simply recorded that a Consequential Order was given by a majority of judges and a separate dissenting order was expected. For whatever reason – he gives no background on it – on 6 June his visits and outside communication were suspended; and a month later he writes, 'Start of hunger strike if …' Over the months he met with quite a few people, continuing discussions on the political framework of the country. One of his last entries for the year was on 16 November when he had another visit from Peter Penfold.

Thus far, Fred had experienced no difficulty in being allowed to visit the Chief. But that changed not long after a visit when he had a set-to with the security at the detention centre.

Your photograph was taken and a card kept on the number of times you visited your friend/relative. One day as I was coming in to the office to check in, before being searched, the security was very arrogant, and the visitors were sitting on breezeblocks because there were no chairs. I was so mad that I told the security that the visitors should have chairs instead of what was happening now. Also I said, 'If it was not for Chief Norman and the CDF, you would not be sitting here where you are today. You all owe your freedom to the man that you have kept as a prisoner.'

They must have been recording this by a hidden camera or microphone because shortly after the exchange, an American security guy appeared and asked me what was the matter. I asked him, 'Why do you make these women and children sit out in the sun on breezeblocks or stand out in the sun while the security sit on chairs? Where is the shelter and chairs for the visitors?' Next time I came to visit with the Chief's two daughters and niece, they allocated a room in the building for the visitors to wait for their turn before being called forward to be searched. Bravo!

Fred knew several people in the business community in Freetown, and one businessman he was on very good terms with was Benjamin (Benjie) Blair, a Sierra Leonean who had had a successful career in the United States and who was invited to return home by President Kabbah to channel his energies and skills into regenerating business as the country recovered from years of conflict. Benjie was an effective operator, and he had been helpful to Fred's company on a number of occasions. He was also a relative of Tejan Kabbah's deceased wife, Patricia, who had died in a London clinic in 1997; he lived in the lodge with Kabbah. Shortly after Fred had visited the Chief, he and Benjie met. Benjie raised the topic, and he put the matter subtly, but unambiguously.

> Not very long after my last visit, as we were talking, Benjie said that maybe it was best for me not to visit the Chief if I wanted to help the family. Nobody could accuse me of political interference. I took the warning.

Fred was in no doubt; Benjie had handled it lightly, as a friend – but the import was clear. Fred's work visa could have been revoked at a stroke. And he was providing some financial support for Hinga Norman's family at the time, so what he did from now on was communicate with the Chief through Mrs Norman.

This is about the third allusion to the government of Sierra Leone – if not the actual gatekeeper for access to Hinga Norman – having, perhaps through informal and unofficial channels, knowledge of who was visiting him. If that was the case, there was one visitor who had too high a profile to risk inhibiting: Paramount Chief Komrabai, the retired former British High Commissioner, Peter Penfold. He was a staunch friend throughout to Hinga Norman, and had written articles supporting him. For example, after Charles Taylor was arrested and detained, Peter Penfold wrote that,

> it does nothing to negate the injustice of the continued detention of Chief Hinga Norman. The trial of Norman and his two fellow CDF indictees continues at a snail's pace with a number of high level witnesses being called, such as the former Vice-President, Joe Demby and Lt Gen David Richards, the British soldier now commanding the NATO forces in Afghanistan. Other witnesses to be called include President Kabbah himself, for whose restoration the CDF were fighting. At present Kabbah is refusing to appear, ironically on the ground that he is a head of state, the same reason why Taylor had initially refused to accept the Court's indictment. The Court over-ruled Taylor's objection; it has yet to rule on Kabbah's.[57]

Dr Joe Demby and Peter Penfold appeared at the Special Court and spoke in defence of Hinga Norman. So did Gen Sir David Richards, currently Chief of the General Staff of the UK, whose testimony appears as Appendix 3. Considering the responsibilities and pressures on Gen David Richards, Commanding Officer of NATO forces in Afghanistan, who was prepared to travel to Sierra Leone and give evidence that he saw Hinga Norman obeying the rules of war regarding treatment of captured enemy at the time of the rebel incursion into Freetown in 1999, and witnessed him later dissuade a CDF group from using boy soldiers, it should not have over-taxed even a weak president's frail sense of moral duty to say something in the court on behalf of the man to whom he owed his position. Even although he seems to have spoken bold words in the beginning, in the end he would have had to be dragged there against his will.

Oh yes, when the Court was being set up, he said that he was prepared to face the Court. And yet he wouldn't even consent in the end to being a defence witness for one of his own ministers. And when we pressed hard – we who were involved in Sam's case – to try and get Kabbah to appear, they had a special hearing to decide whether Kabbah should appear before the Special Court; and the judges ruled that he shouldn't be brought before the court.[58]

No diary exists for 2006 among Hinga Norman's papers. There is a statement, however, written by him (and passed to Fred) entitled, 'Exhortation to Kamajors By Chief Samuel Hinga Norman', the first two paragraphs of which rehearse his membership of and sufferings for the SLPP in the 1960s and 1970s, then the paper continues:

3. And when the SLPP government was overthrown in May 1997 after only fourteen (14) months in office, President Ahmad Tejan Kabbah fled into exile and made a passionate plea to the people of Sierra Leone to do everything in their power to restore his government back to power. You and many others, including my humble self even as his Deputy Minister of Defence, eagerly took to the bush for several months and finally succeeded in bringing back the President and his government in March 1998, a job we selflessly did without any prior conditions of remuneration or other reward.

4. The government subsequently made an agreement with the United Nations to establish a Special Court for Sierra Leone. And today, three of us who were among the most instrumental in securing that restoration are standing trial before that Court right in the heart of Freetown, where we have been detained for over three (3) years now, all in proxy for your own alleged activities during the war.

5. Neither the Party (SLPP –Palm Tree) nor you as its members are responsible for what is happening to me and my colleagues. The Party, as a party, has not done anything to hurt me. And so I will never take any action against the Party or anyone who has not hurt me. Our reward lies in the bosom and contemplation of the Lord Allah, and will surely come.

6. You may be aware that I have taken two judicial actions in recent months in respect of the Party, one of which is still pending in the Supreme Court. Time will tell that both actions were taken for the protection of the Party itself, so that other political parties do not invoke the national Constitution against it at an inauspicious moment to the detriment of the Party, especially considering

its twenty-nine (29) years in the political wilderness from 1967 to 1996. After the Supreme Court decision, hopefully in the next few weeks, you will hear again from me as a matter of URGENCY.

7. Until then, PLEASE, in the name of God and the dear lives that were lost in the defence of our country and our Party, I repeat PLEASE DO NOT JOIN ANY OTHER POLITICAL PARTY (new or old) for the purposes of the next general elections.

8. WAIT! BE PATIENT AND STEADFAST!

Date: 26 August 2006.
Sam Hinga Norman[59]

However, energetic and determined as he was, over the time he had been in detention, health problems developed, particularly pain in his leg. He first referred to having it seen by a doctor on 28 March 2003, shortly after he was arrested. Then in early 2004, he had to have his cervical collar examined at a medical centre. This may have been a recurrence of a problem he had treated in a clinic in Pretoria (courtesy of Executive Outcomes) when Roelf van Heerden was escorting him at a UN conference in South Africa. By the end of 2004, he was recording a very painful groin and leg; and the following year he required treatment for his right leg, back and neck. Finally, the recommended treatment was hip replacement surgery, which was unavailable in Sierra Leone. The Special Court asked some other countries to provide such medical assistance, and only Senegal volunteered.[60] However, Hinga Norman did not know this; the venue for his treatment was withheld from him as preparations were put in hand for both him and the Interim Leader of the RUF, Issa Sesay, who also required surgery for some problem, to be taken to Dakar, Senegal early in the new year.

Meanwhile, Fred and his company came up against the consequences of endemic corruption at official level. His company, VIPWA, submitted the first proposal to the government for a contract to provide security for Fishery Protection in Sierra Leone. It was a well-crafted tender; they felt they were in a strong position to win. But at ministerial or official level the company's bid was released to rival security companies, enabling them to undercut Vanguard, and of course, give a kick-back to ministers as part of the arrangement. Faced with the realities of government contracts, Fred's partner with the finance, Jeffrey Wright, put other irons in the fire and, as Christmas approached, he was negotiating a partnership with a South African mining company. The omens looked promising as Fred booked his flight to the UK for a vacation.

A fourth New Year's day in prison began for Hinga Norman, and two weeks later he was informed that he would be transported to another country for medical treatment. He had a brand new notebook, and he immediately began making a record of events. On 16 January at 9pm, 'I was informed of my travel to elsewhere for medical treatment.' And the following morning, 17 January, he began charting the sequence of events in numerical order, under the heading, 'the process for the treatment of my hip replacement started', beginning at 5.30 when the door of his cell, number 3, is opened. His packed belongings were carried to 'the just-landed helicopter'. From the style of the way he wrote this record, he anticipated that it might later be read by a third party, or in the event of his death, because while written in the first person (singular and plural), there are times when he includes his own name. For example,

07.45 Issa Sesay and I, (Chief Hinga Norman) were taken by a waiting jeep to the waiting helicopter.[61]

They landed at Lungi airport and boarded a fixed-wing UN aircraft. On landing at 11.10, he was informed that they were at the Military Wing of Dakar International Airport. The immigration formalities carried out, he and Issa Sesay were taken in two ambulances in a 'long motorcade'. By now his numbering of the sequence has reached point 11.

11. 12.00 The 2 ambulances entered a Victorian-looking courtyard where [we] alighted and were escorted by a large number of uniformed men with pistols who, I was later informed, were prison officers of Dakar-Senegal. I was taken into a just-renovated tiny room with a door marked *Cabine* 10, referred to as self-contained with a very small shower-bath and a toilet bowl with a wash-hand basin all jammed together, so-to-speak.
     In the room were:-

     a) A bed with only a single bedspread with no pillows.
     b) An air conditioner with no remote control
     c) A local TV with three local stations only
     d) One empty fridge.
     e) One empty wardrobe.

12. 2pm. Food was served but we refused to eat. We stated that if we did not get in touch with our people back home to report our plight, we will refuse to eat anything and we will eventually refuse treatment.
     Later, I got in touch with my daughter to whom I narrated my (our) plight and we thereafter took our food and ate; other events followed later.
13. 11pm I retired on the bare bed and soon thereafter, fell asleep and woke only the next morning.[62]

He was in L'hôpital Aristide Le Dantec, Dakar, and, according to Special Court officials, in 'the VIP (Very Important Persons) wing of the same top military hospital where Senegalese Ministers of Government get treated.'[63]

For ten days after his arrival there is no entry in his notebook until 27 January, when he wrote that he received $500 US from his daughter Teteh by Western Union Dakar-Senegal. He needed the money: arriving as he had at such short notice, he was unprepared for the local custom where VIP patients brought their pillows with them to this wing of the hospital, so he was now able to make good his deficiency. And he certainly required a pillow, because four days later he wrote,

> We quarrelled about the continued constant lock-up which we (Issa Sesay and Hinga Norman) considered a mental torture.[64]

Life seemed a bit better the following day when he heard from a few people, and again the next when he linked up with Mahmoud Kamara Jr, a grand nephew who lived in Dakar. And it is clear too that the regime of being confined to his cell had eased a bit, he wrote that he,

> visioned a brown belt with a gold buckle lying on the ground in front of me as I was sitting in the court yard of Hospital Aristide Le Dantec in Dakar-Senegal.[65]

But the time for his treatment was close, and the doctors informed him that they were going to carry out his hip replacement surgery on 7 February. Then there was some aggro over his grand nephew, Mahmoud Kawara Jr not being allowed to be around to inform Hinga Norman's family immediately after his operation.

On the morning of 7 February, he wakened early, he writes, and got himself ready for the operation. The Special Court-appointed physician, Dr Harding, was waiting for him along with a Mr Walt Collins; he requested a phone call to his daughter Teteh; and then they waited. Around 10.30, the surgeon confirmed what they had already begun to suspect, that it was impossible to go ahead with the operation, 'because of an unannounced strike today by all the hospital nurses of Senegal.' So the operation was rescheduled for the following day.

It was now almost four years since he had been arrested in his office at the Ministry of the Interior; the Court's decision was anticipated sometime in the course of the year; and he seems to have been as strong in himself, and as free in the power of his mind as he had been during the first hellish months in Bonthe. In that former slaves' dungeon the first dream he described was of finding himself in a strange place, asking for directions, and being told that whichever path he took it would lead him to his destination. Nonsensical in the physical sense, yet the dream's meaning echoes what the philosopher, Kierkegaard argued, that it is not a case of one particular route as opposed to another; in the spiritual sense, 'the way is: how it is travelled.' And Hinga Norman travelled according to his lights: a statesman, a resistance leader carrying an AK-47 rifle and a Bible; he risked his life to restore democratic rule; he made no wealth for himself or his family – as some of his political colleagues had – ; and he stood his ground before men for what he had done.

In his cell on the night before his surgery, he recorded what is surely a fitting journey's end for a soldier who bears no personal animosity towards his enemy: hostilities over, two former enemies, the National Co-ordinator of the CDF and the Interim Leader of the RUF, Issa Sesay awaiting medical treatment together, and he wrote, 'Took communion with Issa before midnight.' Then at midnight they spent time on,

> Some meditation reading from Mark 11: 23–25, reading Psalm 67 followed by prayers and we retired into our *cabines* to sleep, wake up and look forward to the day's events.[66]

Next morning he was up early.

> Again, Dr Harding and Mr Walt Collins showed up around 8:30 am to join me and Issa who was also informed shortly after midnight to prepare himself just in case they may decide to do his operation as well.[67]

And these were the last words that Chief Hinga Norman wrote.

The operation was successfully carried out, and Hinga Norman's adopted son, Lansana Jawara, arrived in Senegal to be of support; and he wrote a short account of what transpired. He turned up at L'Hôpital de La Dentec, only to be told that his father had not been admitted there but at Hôpital Aristide Le Dentec. There he met Hinga Norman who confirmed that the operation had been successful but he was suffering severe pain at night, and he asked him to find out why there were 'no nurses at night to attend to him.'[68] Lansana was informed that the nursing staff had to go home, 'because security closed the wing where Chief Norman was admitted at night.'[69] From 15 February through until 19, there was bleeding from the wound. The following day, Hinga Norman collapsed and required a transfusion of two pints of blood. And the next morning, after breakfast, he seemed to be on the point of collapsing again. Dr Harding, the Special Court's doctor was there; other doctors were called, and one suggested the patient be moved to intensive care.

> But Dr Harding said the hospital needed to go through security procedures first before transferring Chief Norman to the intensive care unit. At this stage I asked Dr Harding which he thought was his priority, the security clearance or the life of my father, but he simply ignored me.[70]

Lansana was then asked to leave the room, but he refused. A few minutes later, *Oscar Lima*, the Old Lion, was dead.

Chapter Eleven

Paying Back the Shilling

In the SAS we used to say that when you join up the Queen gives you a shilling. But when the Queen asks for the shilling back, you've got to pay back the shilling.

Fred Marafono

That same day, in London, Fred received a call from Lansana Jawara in Dakar with the news that Chief Sam Hinga Norman had died around 11.00 am.

Apparently, the Chief had already prepared a list of people to be contacted in case anything happened to him. It included Peter Penfold and myself. He was always a thorough man in everything he did.

I sat down and cried. I spoke to him only two days previously, when he told me he was looking forward to going back to Freetown to have some pepper soup, which was one of his favourite dishes. Hawah used to cook it for us when he came to visit me and to discuss anything he wanted me to do or anything he wanted me to pass on. We used to laugh afterwards because the soup was so hot that we were both sweating at the end of the meal.

Hinga Norman's death had a profound effect on Fred, for his life had been intertwined with the Chief for years in the fight against insurgency, and, after that period, his loyalty held firm.

A sense of duty arising from inner prompting can be a very powerful driver in some people. Fred repaid the Queen's shilling many times over in the SAS, and after he left the army his sense of duty was directed by a warrior's code. When Hinga Norman asked him why he stayed to support him, rather than move on to a more lucrative contract with a PMC in another country, he replied,

'Chief, if I was to turn my back on you, every time I heard something about Sierra Leone on the news, especially you fighting the war, I would feel very guilty for leaving you when you most needed me. I would carry that burden for the rest of my life and I would rather not.' We both laughed and never talked about it again.

The constitution of Sierra Leone did not lay extra responsibility on Hinga Norman's shoulders compared to those of the president or fellow ministers in respect of defending democracy, yet he responded as though it had. And his reasoning:

I got the inspiration from the simple fact that this is the only country that I have. If I lose it, my very belonging – I will be ... be dispossessed of belonging to a nation. Even the bird perching on the tree would be better than me.[1]

Another on the list of names that Hinga Norman had drawn up of those who should be contacted in the event of his death was that of the former British High Commissioner. Peter Penfold too had made a commitment, and that commitment came from a deep moral awareness. The sacrifices that many Sierra Leoneans made to have democracy instated, and then reinstated, in their homeland made an impact on him.

In my experience, these people grasped the essence of what all this means much more than in the sophisticated countries. So I was inspired by all that.[2]

But Peter Penfold's support for that country cost him much in his professional life. Robin Cook said in the House of Commons that there would be no scapegoat over arms to Sierra Leone; yet as long as Peter Penfold continued working, the Sandline affair was never allowed to become a closed chapter. After his tour of duty in Sierra Leone was over, although he had been assured of another posting, he was turned down for 16 posts that he applied for, and forced to take early retirement.[3] His actions, which, in time, were interpreted as being completely compatible with the UN resolution, had temporarily inconvenienced some politicians and officials. And for that his career suffered. But in the long run, what he set in train through his support for Sierra Leone led on to all the other elements of a successful British foreign policy initiative: financial and military support within a counter-insurgency strategy that concluded logically in a military intervention at Rokel Creek, smashing a rebel stronghold, and the defeat of the RUF that brought a lasting peace.

However, Hinga Norman, defending democracy in his country, paid the highest price. His was a tragic end. He was, as Col Roelf van Heerden put it, 'an honest leader and a great man.' Perversely, however, it was his charisma that brought him down: it was threatening to some. His final enemies were not among the RUF − the night before his operation in Senegal, he was leading an RUF man in Bible study − and there were very crude attempts to make something stick that would impugn his motives. One venomous idea was spread, insinuating that he was disloyal and had political aspirations to depose the president. This line was further refined and introduced at the Special Court. Gen Sir David Richards, Chief of the General Staff of the UK testified [see Appendix III] on Hinga Norman's behalf at the Special

Court, and he was asked if he had been able to assess Hinga Norman's attitude to the government. He said, 'It rather surprises me, your question.'

> Well, it never occurred to me to have to assess it, in that he was clearly absolutely devoted to what he was doing, which was defending the government and defending the country's rather fledgling democratic process. I never even – I mean, it just didn't occur to me to question it. He was very often at some personal risk. He was defending the country against the country's enemies, and would always defer to the President when he – sometimes he'd say, 'That's an issue for the President,' or whatever. So it rather surprises me, your question.[4]

And when it was put to him that there were allegations that Chief Hinga Norman and the CDF were inclined to overthrow the government, Gen Sir David Richards said that in his professional opinion, in both 1999 and in 2000, 'if that is what they had wanted to do, they could very easily have done it.' When he was asked further, he answered:

> Yes, I'm very clear. So far as my direct observations are concerned, at no stage did Chief Norman say anything that suggested he was anything but completely loyal to the President in my hearing. Or any actions... If I may, picking up Your Lordship's point, I infer from the 18 months or so of observing Chief Norman over those five visits that he lacked intent from my perspective. Because, in my professional judgment, over an 18-month period, he could have done what was being suggested a minute ago. He had the military power to do it. That is, I hope, the answer that you were seeking. But specifically, in terms of fact, I also can confirm that at no stage did he say anything that would even hint of anything but loyalty to the government of which he was a part and specifically to the President.
>
> I mean, it was well understood that Chief Norman, as Deputy Minister of Defence, was playing a key role in the defence of the country. But why I said I'm rather surprised, from my narrow perspective, that you even asked the question. It wasn't a topic of conversation at all. He was absolutely a key partner in what we were all doing.[5]

And in return for that fidelity, he was abandoned. So, it was entirely appropriate that the Norman family should ask Peter Penfold, a man who had displayed great loyalty to the former Deputy Minister of Defence, to be their representative in dealing with the United Nations and arranging the funeral, along with Dr Albert Joe Demby, former vice president of Sierra Leone. Peter Penfold immediately demanded that an independent pathologist from the United Kingdom be allowed to carry out a post mortem examination of the body.

Part of the problem, and Fred will know this, the UN gave me a helluva time. I've got a lot of contempt for the United Nations over the funeral arrangements of Sam Norman because you had all the young European lawyers – no experience whatsoever of Africa – and they're all saying how the Norman family has been very unhelpful to them, and they're not co-operating. And I said, 'Let's get something straight, Sam Norman was a typical African and had a typical African family, in other words, he had more than one wife; he had several children, and it's not surprising that they will each have different views on different things.' I said, 'That's why the family collectively have asked me and the ex-vice president to co-ordinate all the funeral arrangements, and to liaise with you. We're here to help you. But at a time when they are all grieving, you're imposing all these bureaucratic burdens on them; you're expecting them to fill in.'

We asked them to delay the autopsy so that an independent pathologist from the UK, Dr Mike Buller, could be there, and they refused. And I was trying to identify an eminent pathologist in Gambia to see whether he could slip across to Conakry, but we failed to do that. In the meantime, I had spoken to Joe, and he agreed that he would go up anyway, although he was not a pathologist, but at least it would be good to have him there with his medical background. And so they carried out the autopsy. Ostensibly the UN would say that they agreed to a pathologist being around and they agreed to pay for him, but when they contacted him – we'd already said he wouldn't be available until the Sunday – the UN travel people had booked for him to fly out on the Saturday; and then he got in touch with us and said, 'I told you I can't go on the Saturday because I'm committed.' And all this ate up time and time and time, so the end result was we had no pathologist there.

It was a very, very difficult time, and the UN bureaucracy didn't help. Staff like lawyers and so on, people on the UN gravy train for lawyers. Interestingly enough, the people who had the most sympathy, were the security staff. They developed quite a close bond. Walt Collins was very friendly, and he was the one who was helpful to us during the funeral arrangements. They say that prisoners and prison guards often develop a very close relationship.[6]

The cause of death, according to the autopsy report, was myocardial infarction, a heart attack. Dr Joe Demby attended the autopsy, and he concurred, but he went beyond the final cause of death in his report to the Special Court [see Appendix IV]. He noted that,

Mr Norman bled from the day of the operation, i.e. 8/2/07, not knowing how much blood he lost during the operation, until the day he died i.e. 14 days. During all this period his haemoglobin was tested only once and two days before he died. After that one blood transfusion of two pints, he developed High Fever and Rigor… Why was the patient continuously bleeding from the day of the operation to the time of his death? In my opinion, if this patient was admitted in a well-equipped hospital all these anomalies would have been detected before it was too late… In my opinion therefore, while I do still accept the autopsy findings, yet I do record here that Mr Sam Hinga Norman died due to **medical negligence and the failure of the Special Court to provide the enabling environment i.e. proper medical facilities for his treatment (hospital)**.[7]

The Special Court appointed Justice Renate Winter to head an inquiry to look into the circumstances of Hinga Norman's death. Her report found that proper care had been taken by the Special Court for Sierra Leone in furnishing and providing medical care for Sam Hinga Norman.

'I therefore, find no reason to believe that the concerned authorities of the Special Court for Sierra Leone have failed in providing the best possible medical treatment available.'[8]

However, while the learned justice found the authorities of the Special Court to have been impeccable, she apportioned a degree of blame to the deceased: he was responsible for his own death.

Mr Norman refused the doctor's advice to follow a healthier lifestyle.[9]

Bearing in mind that a few years earlier Hinga Norman, who was a non-smoker, had been game enough to get into PT shorts and exercise along with the CDF at Base Zero; that during the last four years, his BMI would have gone up, living in such a restricted environment, nonetheless, it appears, he received – and wilfully ignored, according to Justice Winter – the standard advice from a doctor to a patient in his mid-sixties with regard to the areas of input-output in his lifestyle that (in normal circumstances) he can control: change your diet; eat more healthily; and exercise, exercise man! Get out and about more!

Peter Penfold and Dr Albert Joe Demby carried out their responsibilities thoughtfully, and were able to arrange and oversee what one newspaper described as a state funeral without the state.

The Norman family asked Dr Demby and me to coordinate the arrangements for the funeral which included the Special Court signing the body over to us from the UN helicopter on its return form Senegal, the laying out of the body in the Victoria Park in Freetown (where thousands filed past the coffin), taking the body by The road to Bo, with stops en route, the church service in Bo, where I delivered the eulogy, taking the body to Mongeri, for traditional service with Chiefs, and finally the burial at the family home. The family asked us to respect Sam Hinga Norman's wish that the SLPP government should NOT be involved in the arrangements. I persuaded the family to expand this to the non-involvement of any political party – any individual was welcome to attend and participate, but not on behalf of any political party. (You will recall that this was in the run up to an election and all of the parties wanted to take advantage of Sam's death and funeral in order to attract votes – many claim that Sam's death had a big say in the defeat of the SLPP at the election.)

And so it was a state funeral without the state! Dr Demby and others such as the CDF and Civil Society Movement must take most of the credit for the arrangements. I found the whole affair very moving and emotional, especially the scenes in Bo, passing through the villages en route to Mongeri and then leading the body on foot into the village hand in hand with the family.[10]

For Peter Penfold, what happened to Hinga Norman, 'his arrest and death was a huge travesty of justice for which I remain very annoyed and sad.'[11]

So, for a time, the destinies of Fred Marafono, Hinga Norman and Peter Penfold ran together and focused on a cause, which, in the absence of commitment on the part of the west, required the use of former professional soldiers, as well as local militias loyal to the government, to have hope of being realized.

In the same way that a phone call from Ian Crooke, twenty-two years earlier, brought Fred into the world of private security work, so that call from Lansana Jawara ended what became an extension of his military career. After the death of the man he had crossed the river for, he never went back to Sierra Leone. His son Duncan took his place with the company Vanguard International Protection West Africa. At first Fred felt anger that a great man who put his country before himself and his family had been set up and abandoned by less worthy men.

However, about a year after Hinga Norman's death, Fred began to collaborate with the author to have the story of his twelve years in Sierra Leone in book form, not because he felt his role was all that worthy, but because it would be a means of having on the public record some small part of the Chief's contribution to his country.

Without a doubt though, Fred's own part is noteworthy. A modern–day warrior; a master of arms, with years of experience in Britain's elite force, yet he was endowed with the hallmark of an earlier chieftaincy code. It characterized him, from his first job in KAS and his respect for David Stirling to his outstanding loyalty to *Oscar Lima*, the Old Lion.

It was this combination of high professionalism in arms and a warrior's zest for action that made him, within a week, not just a newcomer to Executive Outcomes, but a front man, much older than most of the others but a man Roelf van Heerden had to hold back. What Simon Mann wrote to Fred of his contribution to Executive Outcomes sums it all up,

All reports are that you have done a great job, as I knew you would, and are the man for that job.[12]

With between 180 and 190 men in Sierra Leone, the company Executive Outcomes stands out as the classic example of what a highly trained, mobile force operating under tight military rules can achieve compared to what, hitherto at least, the wider international community can muster. A comparison of the rough financial costs of EO's contract in Sierra Leone compared with the cost of UNAMSIL is outlined in Appendix 2, but what cannot be computed is the cost in human life of the political decision to terminate the company's contract. Basically, Executive Outcomes ended a war in Sierra Leone, and it would have remained that way, instead of continuing for another four years. Each time the rebels entered Freetown, unknown thousands of Sierra Leoneans were to die and hundreds of children were abducted. Unconfirmed estimates put the cost of the 6th January 1999 invasion of Freetown in terms of property destruction and lost growth as high as one billion dollars. Doug Brooks is currently the President of IPOA – the Association of the Stability Operations Industry. In 2000 he was an academic fellow with the South African Institute of International Affairs. He made two research trips to Sierra Leone where he did scores of interviews with Sierra Leoneans, politicians, UN officials, labour leaders and contractors; he would later make clear,

Executive Outcomes was remarkably popular among Sierra Leoneans, a popularity that genuinely came from their military effectiveness and discipline. The war was essentially over at the end of EO's tenure in 1995–96, and when their contract was shockingly cancelled it resulted in an almost immediate resumption of the conflict – and literally tens of thousands of unnecessary deaths.

Whether the task of ending Sierra Leone's horrific conflict should have been left to a small private company is a larger policy question that perhaps says more about the international community's shameful lack of will, but EO was certainly far more effective and professional than the 17,000 UN peacekeepers that would follow. And they did their job without the massive sex trade, black market schemes and endemic military frailty. EO was a bargain in humanitarian terms, it was paid to end Sierra Leone's conflict, not to kill people, and in fact their presence virtually ended the violence and allowed democratic elections, all at a fraction of the cost in money and lives of the subsequent UN operation.[13]

Yet the term *mercenary* tends to give rise to moral opprobrium in political quarters in the west. However, writing in September 2000, Doug Brooks disputed one particular claim:

It's a fallacy to claim that PMCs 'kill for money'. PMCs are for-profit companies that are contracted to do a task, such as end a war, and they are expected to use violence to achieve that end. In the past PMCs have killed fewer people and caused far less damage than typical African military factions. And of course, even UN troops are paid for their services.[14]

And what must not be forgotten is that fewer than 200 men of Executive Outcomes had an impact on the rebel war in Sierra Leone that no other military outfit equalled until Britain's Operation Barras hit the West Side Boys.

But a holier than thou posture by politicians persists. Peter Penfold gives an illustration.

> That's right, I've said that you have two scenarios: in one you have this country with a despot of a dictator, ruining the country, killing lots of his people and so on, is totally undemocratic. And you decide you want to get rid of him; in Country A, we mount this huge international operation, with thousands of American and British troops who go in and remove this guy, and we call that a success and a triumph for democracy. And in Country B, because you can't get any governments that are prepared to do it, this handful of guys go in and they end up getting arrested and knocked out and we say nothing about it; and they're the bad guys. One thing I've always been annoyed with is the lack of even-handedness when it comes to dealing with some of these issues. If a principle is right it's right for those circumstances; you can't just chop and change.[15]

The professionalism and effectiveness of even smaller PMCs may exceed what some countries' militaries are able to accomplish. Against heavy odds, Juba, Fred and Sendaba succeeded in keeping the air bridge open between Monrovia and Lungi in a way that is redolent of the legendary Roman officer, Horatius, and two comrades defending a bridge over the Tiber against an army. The team of Juba Incorporated, who, in the Sandline helicopter, daily risked their lives for small wages, sustained the task force that would liberate Freetown; their achievement adds to the annals of PMCs – and must include honourable mention of Bokkie, the gutsiest of Mi–17s.

Although Fred's commitment finished with the death of Chief Hinga Norman, and at the end of the day he reaped no riches for his work, this is not a story of failure. Fred's record is a record of strengths, both professional and moral; he performed signal service and gave of his best in every engagement for a good cause. You cannot ask more of a soldier.

Appendix I

Hostage of the RUF, Swiss Honorary Consul-General, Rudiger Bruns

Rudiger Bruns, Swiss Honorary Consul-General in Sierra Leone, was taken captive on 18 January 1995; he spent three months in the hands of Foday Sankoh and the RUF. Fifteen years later, he has long assimilated the experience and can write freely about it.

Hostage of the Revolutionary United Front

One target of the RUF was to cut the economic and financial backbone of the government, which was the mines: diamond, rutile and bauxite. While the diamond areas in the northeast of the country had already come very early on under the control of the RUF, the two biggest companies in the country, Sierra Rutile Ltd (rutile/titanium) and Sieromco Ltd (bauxite) in Moyamba district in the southeast, remained untouched, mainly because the RUF at the beginning did not have enough manpower, and the two mines had their own security arrangements.

The first attempted attack on Sierra Rutile was on Christmas Eve 1994. We, at the mines, were aware of the rebel activities. However, they were considered to be far away and we were not supposed to travel to these areas anyway. Christmas I spent together with my wife in Freetown, staying in one of the company's bungalows at the Cape Sierra hotel and enjoying life. During the early afternoon of 24 December, we suddenly noticed many friends and some people we knew from Sierra Rutile arriving at the Cape Sierra. What had happened? There had been an attempted attack on Sierra Rutile by the RUF the day and night before. The RUR commander, 'Dennis' (a popular name within the RUF), was killed by government forces, and the RUF withdrew.

Returning to the mines after the holidays, our life continued in the normal way. The expatriate and local families stayed, children went back to school and there was no panic or fear.

We at Sieromoco had security arrangements with the Sierra Leone military and the paramilitary unit, the SSD. We were led to believe that everything was under control and the RUF would not dare to come close to the mine. This was totally misleading, and turned out to be an error. And anyway, we had our own security contingency plan: phase one – women and children to be evacuated, and so on up to phase four – everybody should leave the area. But we started with the unplanned phase five – too late!

While we were continuing with our work, and while life was more or less normal, we could hear the sporadic gunfire. News arrived about one week before the attack on Sieromoco that Njala University complex, about 20 miles from the mine, was under attack by the RUF. We saw helicopters flying over our compound and smoke coming from the direction of Njala University. However, the Sierra Leone army commander, Capt Yajar and Inspector Gblah of the SSD, both in charge of the security of the mining area, assured us that we were safe and had nothing to worry about.

In the early morning of the day of the attack on Sieromco, Wednesday 18 January 1995, we could hear the gunfire coming closer. Later we learned that Kabaima village, just 5 miles away, had fallen into the hands of the RUF. We continued with our office work, children went to school, and the wives did their work at home. The three auditors of KPMG were checking the annual accounts; two British computer consultants continued cleaning our computers, but, luckily for them, by 10:00 hours they decided that they had completed the job, and one of our cars took them back to Bo. My secretary, Brimah, joined them to settle some family matters in Tajama and afterwards return to the mine. Unfortunately, the car was ambushed by the RUF on the way back not far from the mine, and Brimah was killed.

About lunch time, the Managing Director, James Westwood, and I were busy preparing a presentation to the Board of Directors to be given the following Monday at our head office in Zurich, when we heard gunshots only about 200 yards away. One hour earlier, Capt Yajar and Inspector Gblah reassured us that everything was under control. That was the last we saw or heard from them. Outside the camp, government soldiers stopped our vehicles from leaving the mine to travel to Freetown. We were trapped. But they all ran away when the RUF was approaching. Inspector Gblah was probably the bravest of all. He left last, while his SSD men and all the military soldiers had already run. I still see Inspector Gblah these days, but we do not talk much about the past. Capt Yajar was later promoted and transferred as Chief Military Officer to the diamond area in Kono district.

When the gunshots came closer to our works' compound, I had already packed my briefcase with documents, some cash and personal items, for example, my Nikon F3 camera – which I saw later in the hands of Foday Sankoh! I rushed in my company car, a Citroen 2CV, to the main gate to enter our residential compound, just next door, to support my wife. Too late! Groups of RUF 'boys' with red headbands, firing gunshots into the air, were blocking the main gate. What to do? Back to the office! Within a few minutes, about eight of my colleagues assembled in my office, probably because my office was the last one of the whole block and considered to be safer.

Suddenly, it was dead quiet. No voices, no shooting, no birdsong. This continued for approximately ten minutes. These minutes were terrifying; no way to escape; no place to hide. We had heard stories of RUF burning houses while people were inside, committing atrocities or just killing innocent civilians. Then we could hear the noise of breaking doors by force – we had wooden doors. It started at the other end of the office block. They were coming closer, door by door. There was no screaming or shouting! My wife called me from the residence, asking what to do and what to pack. 'Just keep calm and pack what we enjoyed most, and things to remember.' She did very well. My office door split within seconds. We were expecting the worst. In came a boy of about 15 years, an AK–47 in his hands and obviously surprised to meet so many people in the room. We immediately raised our hands and whispered 'surrender'. The boy looked at us and replied, 'Don't be afraid, I am your friend. Please come out and join me.' This was the beginning of a ninety two–day journey across Sierra Leone of about 250 miles, walking in the shoes I was wearing, mainly at night over long distances for 12 hours or more with no rest, and in between, long periods of idle time in various RUF camps.

It was obvious that the RUF had good information about our village, Mokanji, and our works and residence compounds. When we were taken out of the compound and met our other colleagues from Sieromco, who were also taken: eight Sierra Leoneans, including the three KPMG auditors, who later had to serve special functions and training, and five Europeans. We feared that the rebels would enter the residence compound where the women and children were, but luckily they passed by, obviously by instruction of Foday Sankoh. Later we learned that he had given orders to take only a few, maximum four, hostages. Apparently his men on the ground were too enthusiastic.

The government representative at the mine, Mr Sannoh, was not so lucky. He was in the office of our vehicle workshop together with the Swiss engineer and some other people during the attack. The RUF fired into the door and Mr Sannoh was killed by a stray bullet. He was the only casualty.

The whole 'exercise' from the attack to our being taken – and this meant the closure of the bauxite mine in Sierra Leone, with its 1.5 million tons of export and a turnover of US $30 million – took less than two hours.

The first night we were locked up in a small house in the village of Ngerihun, about two miles from Mokanji in the direction of the Sierra Rutile mine. On the way to the village, there was some confusion and sporadic gunfire with a few Sierra Leone army soldiers. I tried to escape twice, hiding in the bush, but I noticed that two SBUs (Small Boys Unit) were taking personal care of me. No chance! I remember one boy saying, 'Please Papi, don't do it again.' It also became clear to me that these SBUs had lost their childhood. The gun was the family. One of my 'caretakers' found a little toy car in the village; he looked at it for a few minutes, and then destroyed the toy.

Early the following morning, Thursday 19 January, we had to walk toward Sierra Rutile about 15 miles from Mokanji. It was very hot, no food or water. One of our hostage colleagues, Raman Abdullah, the Chief Chemist of Sieromco, who was heavy and overweight, found it very difficult to continue walking, so he just lay down in the grass, pleading that he couldn't walk anymore. A young SBU came up to him, saying, 'Papi, you either get up and walk or I'll shoot you.' You can imagine how fast Raman got up and continued walking. He made it to the very end of our journey and his physical condition was much better afterwards than before.

On the way to Sierra Rutile, we saw abandoned military equipment left by the Sierra Leone army. When we were passing through the villages of Moriba Town and Mobimi, people were watching us but couldn't do anything. As we came closer to Sierra Rutile, we found ourselves facing some resistance from the army. Rocket propelled grenades were flying over our heads, and I remember Eldred Collins, one of the RUF commanders, saying, 'Ah that's music, let's go to the fire.' We feared that the RUF would use us as human shields, but luckily we were covered among themselves. After one hour's fight, the Sierra Leone army abandoned their position and ran away. The Sierra Leone army commander was the Naval Wing officer from Bonthe (Sherbro Island) Capt Gilbert, a known and disliked figure. He was later executed by the Kabbah government for treason, together with the AFRC/RUF helicopter pilot, Victor King, and some others when they were intercepted in an Ukrainian-piloted helicopter close to the Liberian border.

We were taken to the hills, covered by thick forests just outside the Rutile mine, where we spent five days. More hostages from Sierra Rutile joined us. Among them were: Personnel Manager, Peter Wight (British); Chief Security Officer, Andrew (Andy) Young (an ex-Rhodesian Police cop, who gave us many problems during the journey); old Alfred (Alf) Conte, an ex–Sierra Leone Police officer, who was known to many RUF boys; Dr Wai, the company doctor; Koji, the electrician, who later died in captivity due to malnutrition and starvation; and some others. At Rutile we lived quite well. The company supermarket provided enough food. I personally preferred the food from the Malaysian food store (there were about 50 Malaysian contract workers on the mine to build up a dredge). New clothes came from the looted residence houses. We could even submit shopping lists to the RUF boys and they supplied promptly. Only the beers and whiskies they kept for themselves – and not to mention that a close look at the RUF girls was also taboo during the whole journey.

On Friday 20 January, the Sierra Leone army under the command of Col Tom Nyuma, with the support of the Guinean army, regrouped and tried to recapture Sierra Rutile. Heavy gunfire and artillery started early in the morning. During the day air support came from Ghanaian and Nigerian Alpha jets. The fighting was concentrated on RUF positions at the mine site, but stray artillery shells often landed very close to our bush camp. In our Rutile camp we foreign hostages were separated from the Sierra Leonean hostages. Among the Sierra Leonean was the Sieromco Company Doctor, Mohamed Barry, a German-trained physician. Before he was employed by Sieromco, he worked and lived in Kailahun, which was the first area in Sierra Leone occupied by the RUF. Dr Barry obviously knew some of the RUF boys, one of whom was a huge man known as 'ECOMOC', who provided personal security to Dr Barry. Not surprisingly, Dr Barry later became the unofficial spokesman for the RUF.

We were also introduced to the second in command of the RUF, who was responsible for the Sieromco/Sierra Rutile operations, Mohamed Tarawally, a short man, about 30 years old, Libyan-trained, and always very friendly to us, much like Eldred Collins. Tarawally was later killed by Executive Outcomes (I think) during their attack on the RUF main camp, 'Zagoda', after our release.

It must have been the third day at Rutile, when it suddenly became hectic and there was great tension in the camp. The commanders were not around, they were engaged in combat. A group of RUF soldiers came to us non-Sierra Leoneans, shooting live bullets around our feet, and ordered us to undress naked, and pointed pistols at our heads. What had happened? Apparently one of the Alpha jets had a well-targeted strike, killing 'ECOMOC' and several other commanders and RUF soldiers. Mohamed Tarawally escaped by inches. We, the white hostages, were blamed for having directed the Alpha jets to the target, using the small FM radios which were given to us by the RUF to listen to the RUF success story on BBC Focus on Africa. These were probably the nastiest moments during our captivity. Particularly the behaviour of the women was very aggressive. Some of my fellow hostages fainted away as some rebels presented broken glass bottles in front of them. I attracted the attention of a young RUF soldier, from the shape of his face, he must have been a Malian or Burkinabe. He was sharpening his long bush knife in front of me, obviously to cut off my head, which I found to be a bit nasty. Luckily it did not come to that and we all survived. The commanders came back later and apologized. We had long and, in a way, amazing discussions and arguments with the RUF soldiers afterwards:

-   you white people are supplying the aircraft,
- =   but your black brothers are flying the aircraft and dropping the bombs,
-   you are responsible for the killing of our brothers,
- =   what about the AK-47 in your hands, made by white people but you are shooting with them,
-   that's different.

Any form of discussion was impossible with these people. Only some commanders, for example, Tarawally and Collins were different and more educated.

With the ongoing artillery shelling and aircraft bombardment, the situation was not safe for us. Upon instruction from Foday Sankoh we left the Rutile camp after five days and the long march started.

We were passing deserted and destroyed villages, many of them well-known to us from before: Taninahun (the home village of Maada Bio; we saw the RUF burning Maada Bio's family house), Serabu, Sumbuya and Koribundu (I think the camp was called Camp Cuba, with Morries Kallon its commander. He was recently sentenced by the UN Tribunal and is now serving a long imprisonment in Rwanda). Interestingly, the Nigerian army had a military base not far from the RUF base, and occasionally we could hear the sound of their vehicles. There must have been some kind of gentlemen's agreement between the two parties, don't-disturb-me-and-we-won't-disturb-you. We were passing Blama until we reached the RUF headquarters, Camp Zagoda, south of Kenema. Here we had the pleasure of staying for seven weeks.

Before we entered the five-mile security zone of Camp Zagoda, the three KPMG auditors were separated from us and transferred to an RUF training camp located in an abandoned agricultural training complex, approximately 20 miles south of Camp Zagoda. These three KPMG auditors were supposed to be the future financial brains of a Foday Sankoh government in Sierra Leone. They had to spend almost two years in captivity.

Passing through the five-mile security zone, we saw many human skulls stuck on wooden poles, a warm welcome to Foday Sankoh's military headquarters. The camp was cleverly located at the end of a V-shaped chain of hills south of Kenema. A river fed from a spring was flowing through, providing good water for drinking and washing. In the camp, we were first met by two young British VSOs (Voluntary Service Overseas), Robert (Bob) de Cruz and Calum Murray, who were both kidnapped in Kabala in November 1994. They had had a hard time walking all the way from Kabala to Camp Zagoda, most of the time blindfolded and with no proper shoes, sometimes even barefoot. Calum had only arrived in Sierra Leone two weeks earlier, and it was his first time in Africa. What an experience and shock. Calum was quiet, but a great guy and respected.

We were directed to huts with six bamboo stick beds in each. We made ourselves comfortable – as much as we could; although even today I still prefer a spring mattress to the bamboo mattress.

At the beginning of the journey I organized myself with a military backpack, toothbrush and toothpaste, soap and towel, blanket, toilet rolls, metal cup, water bottle, some spices to make the food tastier and, the most important item, **a spoon**, commonly called 'ID-Card'. Before an item was finished, I put it on the shopping list and within a short period it was delivered, either from the Sierra Rutile stores or from an ambushed vehicle on the Bo-Kenema road.

Late afternoon of the day of our arrival we met Foday Sankoh in person. Some of us were of the belief that he was already dead, but here he was, fit, cheerful and lecturing us about himself and the better life we would have after had had taken over power in Sierra Leone. This lecturing and also discussion took place almost every day, following the morning and evening prayers. He was obviously in need to talk about politics, his time in the British army and the aim of the RUF. His own soldiers were not the right partners for this kind of discussion.

After five days, another hostage joined us, Roger Graf, a Swiss national working with Panguma Sawmills, north of Kenema on the way to Tongo Fields.

Roger was ambushed and kidnapped on New Year's Eve 1994, on the way from Panguma to Kenema, where he wanted to buy drinks for the New Year's Eve party. Unfortunately, he had given a lift to one SL army soldier, which made the RUF decide to ambush the car. The soldier was killed instantly.

Since officially, we all were Foday Sankoh's VIP guests, they had problems feeding us accordingly, because we were just too many. It also created jealousy and tension with the RUF people in the camp. In the morning we normally had some tea, one tea bag for ten cups and dry bread. The evening dinner, served around five o'clock, comprised a tray of rice with the normal cassava leaves, sometimes with small pieces of unidentified meat or fish, to be shared among ten people. Each corn was counted. The enjoyment of the morning tea was rotated – whoever had the tea bag first in his cup for a few seconds. The RUF people lived much more simply. We saw them eating rats and mice.

Camp Zagoda was quite a big camp, although we could never figure out how many people were actually living in the camp. It had a hospital where wounded fighters were treated. It was well equipped, considering the circumstances. Before our Dr Barry volunteered, a trained nurse was in charge doing all kinds of surgery. I wonder how many have survived? The camp had a school for the many young children of the female auxiliary soldiers and wives. These women were also in charge of preparing our food.

There was not much for us to do. We could not leave our section of the camp unless we had to fetch water, bathe or wash our clothes. Guards were permanently around us; even when we took our daily bath, a guard with an AK-47 was watching.

We knew that Camp Zagoda was not the end of our journey. Foday Sankoh obviously wanted to keep us alive and at the end to get rid of us as fast as possible. Some of us volunteered to fetch the water every day from the river, a few hundred yards down hill. Physical exercise was on the programme; we improved the living conditions in our huts; the rest of the day we were playing cards or resting. Two or three of us, including the ex-Chief Security Officer of SRL, took it too easy and just lay down, smoking self-made cigarettes: tobacco was supplied by the RUF, and an old bible was misused to provide the paper. Shame on us! When we finally had to leave the camp and walk all the way to Kailahun and the river Moa, our ex-Chief Security Officer was more or less unable to walk. The RUF organized a small motorbike, but it did not work out. A funny episode was the sedan chair: eight RUF men were allocated our ex-CSO in a sedan chair, four carriers at a time, with a change-over every ten minutes – it was not easy to carry 119 kilos or more for a longer period. When we were a good distance away from the camp, the carriers stopped: 'No more; the times are over for carrying white people in a sedan chair! You either walk or we shoot you.' Andy made it finally, but he delayed our release by more than a week.

Foday Sankoh was in regular contact at specific times with his commanders. His radio station, powered by solar panels (probably stolen from SierraTel transmitter stations), was not far away from our huts and we were able to listen to his communication. We even heard him one day talking to Charles Taylor. He was using an old British military code system when he was giving commands and instructions. His strategic military chart was a Shell Road Map of Sierra Leone, available in most book shops. Coloured stickers marked the position of his troops. The same Shell map with coloured stickers I was to see later in the office of the Nigerian ECOMOG commanders at 1st Battalion Wilberforce Barracks in Freetown.

By the way, the communication system and the solar power panels at all RUF positions in the country were installed by a captured Russian sea captain. His coastal tanker was supplying fuel to the probably illegally operating fishing trawler off the coast of Sierra Leone. He and his hand, a Ghanaian seaman, went ashore on the coast of Sulima, not far from the Liberian border. There were different stories of why they went ashore: a) they had technical problems with the ship; b) they were looking for food supplies; c) they were going to invite some girls on board. Anyway, they obviously were not aware that the RUF was in that area. Both were taken hostage and later released to the ICRC at river Moa, the same location where we left captivity.

Thanks to Roger Graf we had the radio frequency of the Panguma Sawmill office in Freetown. Foday Sankoh allowed us to establish contact. It was great to talk to our old colleague, Joe Blume, on the radio. Our families at home were relieved to hear that we were alive.

Halfway through our time at Camp Zagoda, we had a surprise visit from a Ghanaian special envoy to a London based NGO and his RUF bodyguards. I understand the purpose of his visit was to negotiate our release. This NGO was a specialist in this type of conflict solution. He apparently had been in contact with the RUF for some time, and the RUF organized the safe walking trip from Liberia to Camp Zagoda. At the end he had to walk back to Liberia since the Sierra Leone authorities did not allow him to depart from Sierra Leone to Europe because he had not entered the country legally. He took many photographs. One with myself in it I found later in the West Africa Magazine. His visit was a blessing for us. Chocolates and, more important, letters from our folks at home. My wife, Beatrice, was great. Her supportive and positive words were encouraging. To let me know that she was well, she included her ski-lift tickets of the previous week's skiing in areas close to our home in Switzerland, which I knew so well. It was still winter in Europe. I wished I could be there.

Foday Sankoh's main contacts were Dennis, commander of the RUF troops in Kambia and Mohamed Tarawally at Sierra Rutile. His men at SRL must have had a good time, particularly since the SL army had given up trying to recapture the place. For a long period, electricity was available, as well as food, drinks and fuel for the cars; everything was there, and even the odd girls were around. Foday Sankoh's plan was to use his Rutile troop for the attack on Freetown. The RUF troops in Kambai had just captured eight catholic foreign nuns, and were controlling the road to Guinea. We had a smile when we heard the permanent excuses of his boys at Rutile about why they could not leave the place, which they obviously had no intention of doing. After a few weeks they finally left, but their move to Freetown was stopped at Newton, 20 miles outside the capital, Freetown.

At the same time, the SL government had engaged the London-based company, J&S Franklin Ltd, to provide mercenary support in the form of Gurkhas under the command of Bob McKenzie. One of their first assignments was to free the eight nuns in Kambia, which ended in a total disaster. Unfortunately, a good friend of mine from the Freetown Hash House Harriers, A D Tarawali, a major in the SL army, was also killed during this exercise.

Still in Camp Zagoda, we were able to witness Foday Sankoh's strategy. Since Mohamed Tarawally and his troops had to draw back at Newton, Sankoh wanted the Kambia troops to join Tarawally's troops for the attack on Freetown. The eight nuns were a handicap. Sankoh wanted the release of the nuns within a few hours. He radioed Primo Corvaro, head of the delegation of the International Committee of the Red Cross (ICRC) in Freetown to collect the nuns. However, the ICRC required 48 hours to go through all the formalities, which was too long for Sankoh. Through our radio station in Freetown, Sankoh established contact with Bishop Beguzzi. Procedures were agreed on between Sankoh and Bishop Beguzzi, and the eight nuns were collected by the bishop himself and taken to Freetown. They had gone through hell and were traumatized.

Otherwise, there was not much to do and we were desperately waiting for the next steps in our captivity. Once it happened we had to get ready for the next destination, but where it was we didn't know. A personal handshake from Foday Sankoh and off we went. Even at this stage, he didn't know my name. It was absolutely advisable to keep a low profile under those circumstances. The Sierra Leonean hostages were given the choice to continue walking with us or stay with Foday Sankoh's RUF as hostages, not as part of them. I recall that at this time some of us had the so-called 'Stockholm Syndrome', named after a hostage situation in Stockholm some years ago, where the hostages, after a while, identified themselves with the ideas of their kidnappers. And some were also of the belief that the RUF would enter Freetown within a month, and this was probably preferable to staying in a refugee camp in Guinea.

We stayed at various RUF camps and deserted villages, but we felt safe because we were in the middle of RUF controlled territory: no more the sounds of Alpha jets or gunfire. The food was getting better every day. We were fed 'de luxe'; obviously Foday Sankoh wanted to put some lost kilos back on us.

Only after a while, my shoes were slowly falling apart. These were the same shoes I was wearing at the time of being captured in my office. Being creative, with some nails I found in burned down villages and resin from trees, I was able to maintain my shoes and they are now in a cupboard in our home in Switzerland.

We were passing Segbwema, Daru, Pendembu, Kailahun, Buedu and finally Koindu. Preparations were in progress to hand us over to the ICRC at the river Moa, the same location where the Russian sea captain and the Ghanaian seaman were handed over to the ICRC earlier.

When we arrived at the spot, the procedures were formal and professional. We were on the Sierra Leone side of the river while the ICRC delegation was on the Guinean side. A small team of the ICRC came over in canoes. The first person who contacted us was the ICRC medical doctor. All of us were asked the same questions. Have you been tortured? Are you well? How do you feel?

Official handing over protocols were signed by both parties, RUF and ICRC. The responsibility of our welfare was handed over from the RUF to ICRC at this moment. The deal was done and we were canoed across the river Moa. We were free! Only at the other end two Guinean soldiers stopped us and asked us for entry visas and customs declaration. Well, this was solved within seconds.

The ICRC is a very thoughtful organization. My highest respect! Being in the bush for three months, not thinking of women apart from our wives, no beer or other beverages, what did we find in the ICRC vehicles which took us to Conakry? Lady drivers, soft drinks and beer in the boot. I immediately placed myself in the front seat. A beer can was passed on to me and, thanks to the efficient air conditioner of the vehicle, within a few minutes we had our first cold beer in three months. Everybody was happy.

On arriving in Conakry, the official part started again. Everybody was met by his country representative. In my case it was the German Ambassador himself. The first question: have you been tortured? A protocol was signed between the ICRC and the respective country representatives. The responsibility was handed over from ICRC to our national countries. New clothes were waiting for us to make us fit for the return flight to Europe. Later that evening, we boarded an SN-Brussels flight. It was also interesting that the German Ambassador accompanied me all the way to the steps of the plane's gangway, informing me that, with my first step on the gangway, his responsibility would end and responsibility would be taken over by our employers.

In Conakry when we arrived was also the first time I met Fred, not knowing that we would become close friends after my return to Freetown in October 1995.

The following morning, Sunday, we landed about six o'clock at Brussels airport. Whom did I meet on the tarmac? The German Ambassador to Belgium and his Deputy. First question: how are you, have you been tortured? After confirming that I was all right, I apologized for waking him so early on a Sunday morning, and I wished him a pleasant day. He had done his job.

At the airport hotel we were re-united with our families, and I started a six-months leave. Some of my clothes at home, which I had grown out of for some time, suddenly fitted again. However, it didn't last, and before long I had the lost kilos back on.

After returning to Sierra Leone later in 1995, I travelled across the country and visited some of the places we walked through. I could remember some houses we stayed in quite well, but I never met the people, civilians or RUF again.

I was alive and happy, and I had some wonderful times with Fred and his EO friends later in Freetown.

Rudi Bruns
November 2009.

Appendix II

Comparative Costs: Executive Outcomes, Sandline, Juba Incorporated and UNAMSIL

Executive Outcomes with fewer than 200 men were in Sierra Leone for about a year and a half. They effectively stopped the rebel war. Sandline's contract, as a result of international pressure, was not allowed to be fully implemented. Juba Incorporated with 3 men and Bokkie, for five months, were in support of ECOMOG to restructure ECOMOG's position in Sierra Leone and prepare for the build-up and retaking of Freetown and Sierra Leone from the junta. The UN Security Council Resolution 1270 established UNAMSIL with a peacekeeping force of up to 6,000. It eventually rose to about 17,000.

Comparative Costs

Organization	Cost	Purpose
Executive Outcomes	$31 million USD[1]	Defeat RUF, create stability.
Sandline	$10 million USD[2]	Train, equip and mentor forces loyal to the government to allow them support ECOMOG in defeating RUF.
Juba Incorporated	$1 million USD in 5 months[3]	Support ECOMOG Forces on all levels to defeat Junta and retake Freetown from rebels.
(UN) UNAMSIL	$600 million USD per year[4]	Ensure security of movement and afford protection to civilians.

Appendix III

Testimony at the SCSL on behalf of Chief Hinga Norman, General Sir David Richards, Chief of General Staff, UK

Testimony on behalf of Chief Hinga Norman at the Special Court for Sierra Leone Freetown, Tuesday 21 February 2006. (Legal argument and questions edited for brevity, and overlapping dialogue excluded.)

General Sir David Richards, Chief of the General Staff of the UK

My job at the time was – I think it's best described as a military troubleshooter. I worked in the headquarters near London whose task was to monitor unstable situations anywhere in the world, one of which was Sierra Leone. As far as London was concerned, in January 1999 all communication with the country appeared to have been severed.

In my trouble-shooting role, I was ordered to go to Sierra Leone to establish what was happening here and to see if there was anything Her Majesty's government could do to help. I flew to Dakar in Senegal from London. And with a team, a small team of staff officers, and a Royal Navy ship, a frigate was diverted from another task in the West Indies to come and pick me up in Dakar. We then sailed from Dakar, via Conakry, to the Freetown area, off the coast.

There was still very heavy fighting here when I arrived, and we had some trouble establishing communications with anybody here. Our understanding was that ECOMOG was the principal defender of the government, assisted by the Sierra Leone army and the Civil Defence Force, who were acting together to try to push the RUF out of Freetown.

[Question: his coming ashore]
Yes. As I said, there was a lot of fighting and indeed a number of corpses in the water as we approached the coast. And Nigerian Alpha jets were still dropping bombs quite visibly from the ship – we could see this – on, we assumed, RUF positions near Freetown. We had some problems getting ashore safely. But we did so in a helicopter, once we had established communications with ECOMOG forces.

I actually lived on the ship and came ashore daily. For an eight-day period I lived on the ship. But every day we would come ashore to liaise, find out what was happening, and draw up my report for London. And on that first occasion, I remember there was a lot of excitement around, because the RUF were still quite near where I landed, which was in Cockerill Barracks.

I first met General Shelpidi, he was commander of the ECOMOG forces here. He then took me to meet in the cellars of Cockerill Barracks Chief Hinga Norman, very briefly… Well the car park, the garages in the base of Cockerill Barracks, where there was a rudimentary, what we would call a command post [and met there] Chief Norman and Brig General Maxwell Khobe. And that was a brief meeting, but I then went up to see President Kabbah.

[Question: whether he knew who Chief Hinga Norman was at that time]
Not really. We had not picked up his role with the country as much as I then discovered it was. So I was more focused on ECOMOG and Brig Gen Khobe at that time on that first day.

[Question: whether he had further encounters with Chief Norman]
Yes. Remember my primary task was to make a military assessment of the situation here in this country. That meant me talking to all the major parties to the crisis on the government side. I had to decide whether to recommend to the British government that Sierra Leone was able to be helped, to be saved, if you like, from a ferocious attack on the capital. So I met everyone, as I said, from the President two or three times in that visit; [I] did a lot of work with ECOMOG, with Brig Gen Khobe who had tactical control of the government forces, and also Chief Hinga Norman who was the Deputy Minister of Defence.

There was one occasion that stands out in my memory. And that was when Gen Khobe took me to observe some fighting on and around a bridge, Congo Cross bridge. That was essentially as far as the RUF reached as they advanced through Freetown from east to the west.

On that occasion, I stood behind some cover, because there was quite a lot of firing going on, with a pair of binoculars, and we watched the government forces who were a mixture of SLA and ECOMOG – a few ECOMOG were there – and CDF. Khobe explained to me that if the RUF got over the bridge, they would then be able to fan out. And there was also an armoury that contained arms and ammunition which they would try to capture.

I observed the government forces successfully stopping the RUF advance and they got across the bridge – the government forces got across the bridge and took some prisoners. I had observed 10, 15 minutes before that, through my binoculars, the killing of some people on the far side of the bridge, the RUF side of the bridge, which everyone had seen from the safe side, if you like. It was clear that the government forces were very excited and angry when they captured the prisoners and I think I remember the atmosphere. It was very dynamic, a lot of shouting, excitement. There were still bodies on the road from the fighting. All this sort of thing. And I saw a group of people go across the bridge to where the prisoners were being held. And I said to Khobe, 'What are they doing?' and he said, 'That's Chief Norman.' And I remembered that I had been introduced to him on my first day here. And he remonstrated with the government forces, the group I'd say there were about 10 or 12 of them, who had captured the RUF or AFRC, I don't know which they were, … I mean, basically the RUF and the AFRC were on one side of the bridge and the government forces on the other. They [government forces] had attacked across the bridge and another group came down the line of the river or stream. And they had – it was a very neat little operation. And they had captured – there was a fight and they had captured some of the RUF.

[Questions: Judges ask details of who was doing what to whom]
Sorry, I misled you. And there were – it is difficult to know but those who were actually holding weapons, guarding the prisoners, were probably about the same number, but there were many more around. And I saw Hinga Norman – well Gen Khobe said, 'That's Hinga Norman,' because I said, 'What's he doing?' and he went up to the group and, through my binoculars and from what I could hear …
Hinga Norman went up to the group and remonstrated with them. And it was clear that he was, even from what I could see, telling them that they must behave and stop getting so excited. And they were threatening to shoot these prisoners.

[Judge clarifying it was government forces Chief Norman remonstrated with]
Yes, remonstrated with the government forces who were very excitable. They had seen some unpleasant sights and some of their friends had been killed. So my impression, no more than an impression, was that they wanted to kill or mutilate or do something angry against the prisoners they had taken. And from what I saw, the impression I gained was that Chief Norman prevented that abuse from happening.

[Question: elucidation of abuse]
Yes. I mean, during the fighting I and everyone had seen at least one apparently innocent person killed by the RUF group on the far side of the bridge. They were firing their weapons indiscriminately. And so everyone was very angry. I was very angry. I couldn't believe what I was seeing.

[Responding to question]
Yes, I think he was a civilian, sir. He was a male. But they not only – I have to get rather gruesome, if I may. They not only killed him, they then chopped an arm off him. I don't know what actually led him to die. And we had all seen that happen.

[Responding to question]
It's only my impression, because I was 200 yards away, but there was a lot of shouting with the group; a lot of pointing at the prisoners and people pointing their rifles at

them. And to remind you, there were dead – there were bodies around. So it was a very febrile atmosphere. And the impression I gained was that they were going to dispatch them themselves, because of their anger.

Well, that was it, really. The situation was calmed down. I didn't speak to Norman, Chief Norman at that time, because Gen Khobe wanted to take me to another area of fighting. And apart from that occasion and the final conference, I suppose would be the right –

[Responding to request for clarity]
Yes, I saw the prisoners being marched away and the situation was definitely calming down.

[Responding to question]
Well, in my judgment, Chief Hinga Norman calmed it down. Because if he hadn't gone across the bridge, what might have happened, I don't know. So I say, in my judgment, it was him that calmed the situation. I then went with Gen Khobe to the barracks near the presidential lodge – I forgot the name of the barracks – which is where ECOMOG were based. Wilberforce Barracks. And from there I went round the town, making a judgment on what was happening. But I didn't see any more close-quarter fighting in my time there. Not at 200 yards. Maybe a half a mile away, but no more than that.

[Asked if he had anything else to tell the Court]
Well, two things if I may. First of all, as far as the nature of the fighting was concerned, I think it was a very chaotic situation. There were groups of armed men – as I've said, ECOMOG, some ex-SLA and CDF – working to a sort of common plan, which was to push the RUF out of the city, and they were successful in that. By the time I left I think they had been evicted from the city completely. But they had – there was a lot of destruction, particularly in the east [of] Freetown. I would say it was a – and this, I do not mean to be rude about some very brave people. But as a professional soldier, it was not a well-organized operation. It was quite, as I said, chaotic. There were groups that were often doing as they wished, as far as I could see, but working to a common plan, which was to push them out.

And, if I may, there's one other thing which I think is pertinent. That is I was sent here to make a judgment on whether the British government should provide material assistance to ECOMOG and to the government and, specifically to the Sierra Leone army. And my judgment, which was fully accepted in London, was that the country merited support, logistic and other support, from the UK and they agreed a package of approximately, and I can't remember the exact amount, but approximately £10 million, to be matched by another £10 million from other international donors. One of the reasons the government accepted my advice – beyond a natural desire to help the country that is held in high affection in London

−, beyond that [was] because they had confidence in President Kabbah, the Deputy Minister of Defence, Chief Norman, and in ECOMOG's determination with them to defend the country and to bring the RUF to some sort of peace process.

I came back in February because my government gave me the privilege of coming to report to President Kabbah that this aid package had been agreed and, because I had established good relations with him and with some people here, they let me come back, and also to help co-ordinate how that money would be used. ...I also brought back in the British High Commissioner, because by then I was able to say it was safe enough for him to return to the country. I stayed on board another ship for most of that, but I seem to remember spending one night with Mr Penfold to prove with him it was safe enough for him to live here.

[Question: any encounter with other leaders in Sierra Leone on second visit]
Yes. Obviously with the President, primarily. He was running the country and it was to him I was reporting. But I had a team of about seven or eight staff officers with me who did the detailed work of how the money should be spent. Most of that work I led personally with Brig Gen Khobe and with Chief Hinga Norman. So they were the two people I dealt with mostly on what they would need, weapons, lorries, all the sort of things that make an army effective; radios, for example.

No decisions were taken without me being there to confirm the staff advice, although I do know that the staff dealt particularly with Brig Khobe who had tactical control of the government forces, whereas Chief Norman was the Deputy Minister of Defence. So he might establish policy, but how it was spent in detail, how the forces were organized, that was all Gen Khobe's job.

[Question: did he observe participation of Chief Norman in those transactions]
Yes. We must have had two or three meetings. [I met] with him in a collegiate atmosphere. But one of our concerns was that the equipment we provided would leave this country when ECOMOG left, whereas we wanted it to remain behind for the Sierra Leone army. So we had to build in safeguards in our negotiations to ensure that ECOMOG understood that, while the equipment could be used collectively for as long as necessary, ultimately it was for the Sierra Leone army. And Chief Norman was robust in making sure that ECOMOG knew that it was for the Sierra Leoneans, not for ECOMOG. So he was fully involved in the policy. The detail, i.e. how many radios, how many lorries, that was something we dealt with primarily with Brig Gen Khobe over.

[Question: his assessment of effectiveness of Chief Norman in those discussions]
He had military acumen. He was very determined. Kept talking about this was for everybody, not just for ECOMOG. And did have a view on some of the detail. But I suppose I had already formed the opinion on my first visit that he was a very effective minister. He was dynamic. He took decisions and had the courage of his convictions,

if you like. What's very difficult for a soldier is when people keep changing their mind. And although that's something we get used to, in Chief Norman there was a minister who understood not to get involved in the tactical issues, but to keep at the right level for him, and he let the military get on and run their own affairs in line with the policy that had been agreed by the government. So it was refreshing.

[Question: did he observe children under age of 15 on the side of any fighting]
To be certain they were under 15 would be difficult. I saw some at the fighting at the bridge that I told you about. There were certainly some very young people, young men on the other side, on the RUF side of the bridge, and the group – amongst the group of prisoners that I mentioned, who Chief Norman intervened over, there were some there who were young. How old, I don't know. I never saw them at that time. I never saw anybody on the government forces that would be – I could say was that young.

[Question: whether he had any problem about child soldiers]
Yes. Even in February of '99, there were strings attached to the aid package. One of them was an absolute no acceptance of child soldiers and any suggestion of child soldiers in the government forces would put the aid package at risk. I came back in May of 2000 and two occasions spring to mind where the subject of child soldiers came up. One was when I went to the CDF headquarters here in Freetown, very near here, in an old hotel, I think it was. Brookfields Hotel, which the CDF were using as a temporary headquarters. I went down there for a meeting to talk to the CDF who, in May, were again fighting on behalf of the government under our overall co-ordination. And Chief Norman gave a talk to a group of CDF there, quite a large group, who I had gone along to meet to thank, actually, for all they were doing; fighting the RUF. And in his speech to them he emphasized how, colloquially, what an own goal any use of child soldiers would be, because international support would be put severely at risk. He said, 'This must not happen.' I remember physically then reinforcing that point from my perspective. So irrespective of any ethical issues, there was a very clear practical issue also at stake. The only other time I was involved practically with child soldiers was when we went to a home to visit a centre where there were a number from upcountry and we talked to them and Chief Norman talked to them and, you know, they were a very sad group of people.

[Responding to whether this was April or May/June 2000]
No, April I only stayed for a week, less than a week and went back to England. It was a routine visit which I conducted to a number of trouble spots. But I went back and said, 'There's trouble brewing in Sierra Leone again.' But I then came back in May. When things got very bad, they sent me back.

   Would it help if I explained roughly what we did in that period to set it in context? The UN had a number of units up in the country and the RUF had taken a lot of them hostage. Again, things looked very difficult here, because the force that the UN, that had been sent to protect the government and to further the pursuit of peace had themselves been – was starting to be captured by the RUF. Therefore, the UN had become a neutered organization in military terms. They weren't capable at that time of doing their job. Mr Kofi Annan had asked a number of nations if they would go to Sierra Leone to see if they could help. The UK said they wouldn't act as part of the UN operation, but they would send a team to find out what was happening and to see how they might help unilaterally. I commanded that team and I arrived here I think on May 6th, Saturday, May 6th May. And we found again a very troubled country.

The RUF had not disarmed after the Lomé Accord of the previous year, whereas the government forces, the Sierra Leone army and the CDF had disarmed, give or take, and that would have been fine if the UN had filled the vacuum, but for a number of military reasons, the UN were not able to do that and, as I said, a number had been taken hostage.

So I arrived in May: one to be prepared to evacuate British nationals and others that might want to flee the country, but also to try and stabilize the situation for sufficiently long to allow the United Nations to recover, reinforce themselves and to become more focused on what they were doing. So the British government felt that they were acting in line with Mr Annan, Kofi Annan's request, albeit not as part of a single UN operation. Over the next five or so weeks we conducted an evacuation because on, I think it was Monday 8th May, there was a riot, is the best description, up near Foday Sankoh's house. There was a riot and it was sufficiently serious for the British High Commissioner to request me formally to initiate an evacuation. There were a lot of excited people running around the town, some armed, mainly with clubs and things and machetes. But it was a very frightening atmosphere and I agreed with the High Commissioner it was appropriate to start an evacuation. Over the week-end the 6th, 7th and again on the 8th, I had a lot of British troops arrive to enable me to conduct the evacuation. And four Chinook helicopters, without which we couldn't have done it. Because we had to secure a point on this side of the estuary and Lungi airport on the far side because we were flying them out. So we did that. It became clear to me with the full support of my government that we could do more than just do an evacuation. We could actually stabilize the situation and I then got permission to go ahead and do that. We moved British troops into key places to the east of Freetown and to the east of Lungi airport. And along with the SLA, a small number who were still prepared to come back in, really, because they were being reformed at that time, the CDF and largely Nigerian troops who had remained behind from ECOMOG to become part of the UN, we conducted an offensive operation the RUF. That allowed the UN time to focus on what they were doing to reorganize and to be reinforced. I left, as I said, in mid-June, having bought enough time for the UN to start again, effectively.

[Question: whether, in his encounters with Chief Hinga Norman, he had been able to assess his attitude to the civilian government.]
Well, it never occurred to me to have to assess it, in that he was clearly absolutely devoted to what he was doing, which was defending the government and defending the country's rather fledgling democratic process. I never even – I mean, it just didn't occur to me to question it. He was very often at some personal risk. He was defending the country against the country's enemies, and would always defer to the President when he – sometimes he'd say, 'That's an issue for the President,' or whatever. So it rather surprises me, your question.

[Counsel for the accused explains context was allegation in some quarters that Chief Hinga Norman and some CDF were inclined to overthrow the government.]
Okay. Well, all I can tell you in my professional judgment is that both in '99 and in 2000, if that is what they had wanted to do, they could very easily have done it.

[Judge asking for a direct answer.]
Okay. They clearly didn't.

[Legal argument follows: was the question designed to elicit opinion.]
Yes, I'm very clear. So far as my direct observations are concerned, at no stage did Chief Norman say anything that suggested he was anything but completely loyal to the President in my hearing. Or any actions… If I may, picking up Your Lordship's point, I infer from the 18 months or so of observing Chief Norman over those five visits that he lacked intent from my perspective. Because, in my professional judgment, over an 18-month period, he could have done what was being suggested a minute ago. He had the military power to do it. That is, I hope, the answer that you were seeking. But specifically, in terms of fact, I also can confirm that at no stage did he say anything that would even hint of anything but loyalty to the government of which he was a part and specifically to the President.

I mean, it was well understood that Chief Norman, as Deputy Minister of Defence, was playing a key role in the defence of the country. But why I said I'm rather surprised, from my narrow perspective, that you even asked the question. It wasn't a topic of conversation at all. He was absolutely a key partner in what we were all doing.

[Question: what was his observation of the CDF.]
Brave, sometimes almost stupidly brave. They had a belief in their own invincibility, which made them very brave fighters, but they were not very well disciplined and there were groups that seemed to me to be on the periphery, if you like, of the main CDF who fought very bravely, but tended to do what they wanted to do rather than what they were broadly being told to do. They were more like a militia. I would characterize them as a militia.

Appendix IV

Observations on the Autopsy of Chief Hinga Norman, Dr Albert Joe Demby, Former Vice President of Sierra Leone

Dr Albert Joe Demby, former Vice President of the Republic of Sierra Leone, attended the autopsy of Sam Hinga Norman on 5 March 2007. He was later invited by Justice Renate Winter to write a report of his observations of the autopsy. An edited version, omitting list of those present.

Observations on Autopsy of Sam Hinga Norman

To Hon Justice Renate Winter
Vice-President of the Special Court for Sierra Leone

I write in respect of your request for my written report concerning my observations of Mr Norman's autopsy.

I travelled to Dakar (Senegal) on Friday 2nd March, 2007. Mr Sam Hinga Norman Jr., son of the late Mr Sam Hinga Norman, joined me in Dakar on Saturday the 3rd March, 2007. On Sunday the 4th March, 2007, Mr Norman Jr. and I were invited to go to the hospital to see the hospital and the room where the late Mr Hinga Norman was admitted and died.

[A list of those present then follows]

External Examination
1. The body had very pale lips, tongue, conjunctiva, soles of the feet and palms of the hands – signifying signs of severe anaemia.
2. Large blood-stained areas on the dressing over the operated right hip – signifying bleeding up to the time of his death.
3. The tongue was slightly protruded and being held between the teeth – signifying that the patient died while he was in severe pain.

Internal Examination
1. Two ante-mortem broken ribs on the left side of the chest –anterior arches of the forth and fifth ribs. Which is consistent with injuries sustained during the forceful cardiac massage.

2. Ante-mortem blood was found in the left thoracic cavity (hemothorax) which was moderately large.
3. Heart – alarming observations as stated in the autopsy report.
4. Operation area – bright red spots and tissues; signifying that they continued to bleed up to the time of the patient's death.

Comments and Observation

The Hospital:- The hospital where Mr Sam Hinga Norman was admitted and died was described by the president of Sierra Leone as: 'One of the most renowned hospitals in Senegal, where most of the Ministers and other prominent people go for medical check-ups.'

The letter from Mr Ray Cardinal, Chief of the detention at the Special Court, to the family of Mr Norman stated that Mr Norman was hospitalised at the Military Hospital known as De La Dantec in Dakar. This is a modern and well-equipped hospital. In my opinion this is not true, for he was admitted at the hospital called Aristide Le Dantec, which is a short distance away from hospital De La Dantec.

This Aristide Le Dantec hospital is in my opinion, an old colonial teaching hospital. And where Mr Norman was admitted was [and] is a prison house within this hospital compound. It is not a hospital ward, but a cubicle (cell) as there are ten such cubicles. There is no semblance of a ward as no emergency medical facilities were seen around the cubicle. In fact no nurses' room or place for them to sit and administer drugs to the patient. They do come to these cubicles, examine and change the dressings of the patient and leave. There are no emergency facilities around and if needed, one has to rush to the nearest ward, about 50 yards or so, crossing at least 3 Security Guard posts. This prison house lacks the basic medical amenities like oxygen, emergency drugs, emergency equipment etc. no wonder by the time the nurse went and brought the old outdated respirator, Mr Sam Hinga Norman had died. The lack of facilities necessitated the forceful cardiac massage and hence the broken ribs. Mr Norman died on his cubicle bed made of wood without the standard beds which can be raised or tilted etc when needed.

Patient Condition

From the condition of the patient's heart at autopsy, it gives me the impression that the patient was not examined and prepared for the operation. That such serious condition seen at autopsy would have given the cardiologist after thorough examination, to ascertain whether he was fit for such operation or not. If he was in fact examined and found fit for such operation, then what other precaution was taken? According to Dr Harding, the patient was examined by the cardiologist and the intensive care unit specialist when he collapsed on Tuesday 20th February 2007, i.e. 12 days after operation. The laboratory examination, I understand, was not even done at this hospital. It was reliably reported by Jawara, a family representative present at the bedside of Mr Norman, that he was still bleeding after the operation and that he regularly reported this unusual bleeding to Dr Harding, who usually told him not to worry. Was this continuous severe bleeding, as seen in his dresses [sic] even after laundry, which is still in the custody of the Special Court, and heavy blood-stained dressing found at the operation site during autopsy, not have been responsible for his collapse on those two occasions, i.e. 20th and 22nd February 2007 respectively? After the two pints of blood on the 20th, he came round and again collapsed on 22nd February and died.

So Mr Norman bled from the day of the operation, i.e. 8/2/07, not knowing how much blood he lost during the operation, until the day he died i.e. 14 days. During all this period his haemoglobin was tested only once and two days before he died. After that one blood transfusion of two pints, he developed High Fever and Rigor. Was his anaemia not responsible for his sudden collapse while attempting to lie on the bed for examination and [he] died a few minutes later? While we talk of his cardiac condition at autopsy, especially the recent infarction, yet I am of the view that the severe anaemia had not allowed sufficient blood to the cardiac muscles. Would the Coronary Arteries' Atheromatous and Stenotic conditions not have been detected in a well-equipped hospital? This serious condition of the heart would of been diagnosed and a decision taken before the day of the operation. The ECG report on the 20th February 2007 indicated that the Anaemia was responsible for the Anomaly. Why was the patient continuously bleeding from the day of the operation to the time of his death? In my opinion, if this patient was admitted in a well-equipped hospital all these anomalies would have been detected before it was too late.

Even if the patient had survived the collapse of the 22nd February 2007, the fractured two ribs and hemothorax was another severe complication that would have kept him in the hospital for a longer time. This was definitely preventable in a modern and well-equipped hospital.

Conclusion

While I do accept the autopsy findings, yet I have the follow remarks:

1. The hospital was not ideal to handle such cases.
2. If the hospital was indeed ideal, then Mr Norman was regarded as a prisoner or a detainee, hence kept in a cubicle without proper medical care.
3. No proper investigation was done prior to his hospitalisation or after his collapse on the 20th February 2007.
4. Two pints of blood were not sufficient for an obese person with such low haemoglobin.
5. The two weeks of post operative bleeding was definitely an indication that something was wrong and needed thorough and immediate attention. That the continuous bleeding was indeed responsible for the severe anaemia, hence

his collapse on the two occasions and even some aspects of the myocardial conditions.

In my opinion therefore, while I do still accept the autopsy findings, yet I do record here that Mr Sam Hinga Norman died due to **medical negligence and the failure of the Special Court to provide the enabling environment i.e. proper medical facilities for his treatment (hospital).**

Dr Albert J. E. Demby

Notes

Chapter 1
1. Alan Hoe interview.
2. Ibid.
3. Ibid.
4. The *Independent*, 18 January 1996.
5. Alan Hoe interview.
6. The *Independent*, 18 January 1996.
7. Alan Hoe interview.
8. Peter Flynn interview.

Chapter 2
1. The *Independent* January, 28, 1999.
2. Alastair Riddell correspondence.
3. Ibid.
4. P. Scholey, *SAS Heroes: Remarkable Soldiers, Extraordinary Men* (Botley, Oxford, Osprey Publishing, 2008), p.180.
5. Rudiger Bruns, 'Hostage of the Revolutionary United Front' [Appendix 1].
6. Ibid.
7. Alastair Riddell correspondence.
8. Rudiger Bruns, 'Hostage of the Revolutionary United Front'.
9. Ibid.

Chapter 3
1. Col Rudolph (Roelf) van Heerden interview.
2. Ibid.
3. Ibid.
4. Ibid.
5. J.Hooper, 'Executive Outcomes in Sierra Leone', *Combat & Militaria*, Vol. 3, No. 4, January, 1996, p. 14.
6. Ibid. p. 16.
7. Col Rudolph (Roelf) van Heerden interview.
8. Ibid.
9. Ibid.
10. J. Hooper, *Bloodsong: First Hand Accounts of a Modern Private Army in Action* (London, Collins 2003) p.162.
11. Fred Marafono papers.
12. President Kabbah, Statement to the Truth and Reconciliation Commission, 5 August,2003, para. 20.

13. Peter Flynn interview.
14. Fred Marafono papers.
15. Ibid.
16. Peter Flynn interview.
17. Ibid.
18. Ibid.

Chapter 4

1. Truth and Reconciliation Commission, vol. 3a, chpt. 3, para 647, http://trcsierraleone.org/drwebsite.
2. Col Rudolph (Roelf) van Heerden interview.
3. Ibid.
4. Abidjan Accord, http://www.sierra-leone.org/abidjanaccord.html.
5. Statement By President Kabbah to Peace and Reconciliation Commission, 5 August 2003, para. 20. http://www.sierra-leone.org/kabbah080503.html.
6. Ibid, para. 19.
7. Ibid, para. 19.
8. Sierra Leone News, 30 January 1997, http://www.sierra-leone.org/Archives/sinews0197.html.
9. Sierra Leone News, 3 February, http://www.sierra-leone.org/Archives/sinews0297.html.
10. Ibid, 3 February 1997.
11. Ibid, 14 February 1997.
12. Sierra Leone News, 7 March, http://www.sierra-leone.org/Archives/sinews0397.html.
13. Ibid, 6 March 1997.
14. Ibid, 25 March 1997.
15. Churchill Archives Centre, Penfold Papers, pp. 40–41.
16. Truth and Reconciliation Commission, vol. 3a, chpt. 3, para 673.
17. Churchill Archives Centre, Penfold Papers, p. 33.
18. Ibid. p. 33.
19. Ibid., p. 33.

Chapter 5

1. Truth and Reconciliation Commission, vol. 3a, chpt. 3, para 688.
2. Churchill Archives Centre, Penfold Papers, p. 34.
3. Ibid. p. 34.
4. Ibid. p. 35.
5. Sierra Leone news, 28 May 1997,http://www.sierra-leone.org/Archives/sinews0597.html.
6. Churchill Archives Centre, Penfold Papers, p. 36.
7. Ibid. p. 37.
8. Sierra Leone news, 30 May.
9. Peter Penfold interview.
10. Truth and Reconciliation Commission, vol. 3a, chpt. 3, paras 698–9 .
11. Ibid. para 696.
12. Ibid. para 700.
13. Sierra Leone news, 20 June 1997, http://www.sierra-leone.org/Archives/sinews0697.html.
14. Truth and Reconciliation Commission, vol. 3a, chpt. 3, para 704.

15. Ibid. para 741.
16. Churchill Archives Centre, Penfold Papers, p. 42.
17. Ibid. pp.41–2.
18. Truth and Reconciliation Commission, vol. 3a, chpt. 3, para 707.
19. Ibid. para 735.
20. Ibid. para 756.

Chapter 6

1. M. M. Khobe, 'The Evolution and Conduct of ECOMOG Operations in West Africa.' *Boundaries of Peace Support Operations*, Monograph 44, February 2000.
2. H. Ross, *Paddy Mayne*, p.134.
3. Fred Marafono papers.
4. Johann (Juba) Joubert interview.
5. Peter Penfold interview.
6. Sierra Leone News, 8 October 1997, http://www.sierra-leone.org/Archives/sinews1097.html.
7. Security Council Resolution – 1132.
8. Sierra Leone News, 23 October 1997.
9. Fred Marafono papers.
10. Johann (Juba) Joubert interview.
11. Tijjani Easterbrook correspondence.
12. Ibid.
13. Sierra Leone News, December 1997, http://www.sierra-leone.org/Archives/sinews1297.html.
14. Churchill Archives Centre, Penfold Papers, p. 43.
15. Ibid., p. 44.
16. Johann (Juba) Joubert interview.
17. The *Times*, May 15 1998.
18. Johann (Juba) Joubert interview.
19. Ibid.
20. Sierra Leone News, 7 January 1998, http://www.sierra-leone.org/Archives/sinews0198.html.
21. Ibid., 19 January 1998.
22. Johann (Juba) Joubert interview.
23. Ibid.
24. Peter Penfold interview.
25. Johann (Juba) Joubert interview.
26. Ibid.
27. Ibid.
28. Sierra Leone News, 17 March 1998, http://www.sierra-leone.org/Archives/sinews0398.html.
29. Tshisukka Tukayula (TT) De Abreu interview.
30. *The Sunday Times*, 10 May 1998.
31. Sierra Leone News, 11 March 1998.
32. *Newswave*, October 1998, p.23.
33. Ibid., p. 24.
34. Johann (Juba) Joubert correspondence.
35. Fred Marafono papers.

Chapter 7

1. Peter Penfold interview.
2. Churchill Archives Centre, Penfold Papers, p. 44.
3. Ibid., p. 45.
4. Ibid., p. 45.
5. Johann (Juba) Joubert interview.
6. E. Barlow, *Executive Outcomes*: *Against All Odds* (Alberton, Republic of South Africa, Galago Books, 1999) p. 275.
7. The *Times*, 9 May 1998.
8. The *Sunday Times*, 10 May 1998.
9. Johann (Juba) Joubert interview.
10. Churchill Archives Centre, Penfold papers, p. 48.
11. Hansard, 27 July 1998, vol. 317, c. 19.
12. Peter Penfold interview.
13. Peter Penfold personal papers.
14. Peter Penfold interview.
15. Ibid.
16. The *Times*, 15 May 1998 (first edition).
17. Peter Penfold interview.
18. Churchill Archives, Penfold papers, p. 49.
19. Peter Penfold interview.
20. Churchill Archives Centre, Penfold papers, pp. 48–9.
21. Ibid., p. 46.
22. Tim Spicer (3 February 2010) was happy to be included in the quote.
23. Peter Penfold interview.
24. *Hansard*, 27 July 1998, vol., 317, cc. 19–35.
25. Peter Penfold interview.
26. *Hansard*, 27 July 1998, vol., 317, cc. 19–35.
27. Churchill Archives Centre, Penfold papers, pp. 46–7.
28. *Hansard*, 27 July 1998, vol., 317, cc. 19–35.
29. Johann (Juba) Joubert interview.
30. House of Commons – Foreign Affairs – Second Report, para. 10.
31. Ibid., para. 63.
32. Ibid., para. 68.
33. Ibid., para. 42.
34. Ibid.
35. Ibid., para. 71.
36. *Hansard*, 27 July 1998, vol., 317, cc. 19–35.
37. Peter Penfold interview.
38. Ibid.

Chapter 8

1. Johann (Juba) Joubert interview.
2. Tijjani Easterbrook correspondence.
3. Johann (Juba) Joubert interview.
4. Command Sergeant Major (retired) US Special Forces.
5. Ibid.
6. Sendaba Meri's statement to Board of Inquiry, Fred Marafono papers.

7. Military contractor's statement to Board of Inquiry, Fred Marafono papers.
8. Tijjani Easterbrook correspondence.
9. Ibid.
10. Johann (Juba) Joubert interview.
11. Ibid.
12. Sierra Leone news, 19 December 1998, http://www.sierra-leone.org/Archives/sinews1298.html.
13. Sierra Leone news, 8 January 1999, http://www.sierra-leone.org/Archives/sinews0199.html.
14. General Sir David Richards' testimony at the Special Court for Sierra Leone.
15. Ibid.
16. Johann (Juba) Joubert interview.
17. Sierra Leone news, 28 April 1999, http://www.sierra-leone.org/Archives/sinews0499.html.
18. Johann (Juba) Joubert interview.
19. Fred Marafono papers.
20. Tijjani Easterbrook correspondence.
21. Johann (Juba) Joubert interview.
22. Ibid.
23. Ibid.
24. Sierra Leone news, 12 May 1999, http://www.sierra-leone.org/Archives/sinews0599.html.

Chapter 9
1. H. Ross, *Paddy Mayne: Lt Col Blair 'Paddy' Mayne, 1 SAS Regiment* (Stroud, The History Press), p. 104.
2. Ibid. p. 191.
3. Johann (Juba) Joubert interview.
4. Peter Penfold interview.
5. Ibid.
6. Sierre Leone news, 8 September 2000,http://www.sierra-leone.org/Archives/sinews0900html.
7. Ibid., 22 May 2000, http://www.sierra-leone.org/Archives/sinews0500html.
8. Ibid., 9 May 2000.
9. Ibid.
10. Ibid., 12 May 2000.
11. Ibid.
12. Ibid., 24 May 2000.
13. S. Griffin, quoted in Roberson, p. 49.
14. W. G. Roberson, 'British Military Intervention into Sierra Leone: A Case Study.' Master's thesis for Faculty of the US Army Command and General Staff College, 2007, p. 81.
15. Sierra Leone news, 15 August 2000, http://www.sierra-leone.org/Archives/sinews0800html.
16. Ibid., 12 August 2000.
17. W. Fowler, *Operation Barras: The SAS Rescue Mission, 2000* (London, Cassell, 2004), p. 124.
18. W. G. Roberson, p. 62.
19. House of Commons Library, *British defence policy since 1997.* RP08/57, 27 June 2008, pp. 58–9.
20. MoD Press Release, serial number 472.

21. Ibid.
22. Sierra Leone news, 30 October 2000, http://www.sierra-leone.org/Archives/sinews 1000html.
23. A. Forna, *The Devil that Danced on the Water: A Daughter's Memoir of Her Father, Her Family, Her Country and a Continent* (London, Flamingo, 2003), pp. 386–7.

Chapter 10
1. Florence Norman interview.
2. Norman family papers.
3. Fred Marafono papers.
4. M. Nesbitt, 'Lessons from the Sam Hinga Norman Decision of the Special Court for Sierra Leone', p. 1.
5. Sierra Leone News, 5 March 2003, http://www.sierra-leone.org/Archives/sinews0303.html.
6. P. Penfold, 'The Tangled Web of Sierra Leone's Special Court,' *Africa Analysis* No. 491, 28 April.
7. Truth & Reconciliation Commission, database, 5 October 2004.
8. Peter Penfold interview.
9. Sierra Leone News, 10 March 2003.
10. Ibid., 18 March 2003.
11. Ibid., 2 April 2003, http://www.sierra-leone.org/Archives/sinews0403html.
12. D. Dimmock, 'Washing rejects the ICC,' http://www.choike.org/.
13. P. Penfold, 'The Tangled Web of Sierra Leone's Special Court.'
14. Peter Penfold interview.
15. Ibid.
16. Norman family papers.
17. Ibid.
18. Sierra Leone News, 7 April 2003.
19. G. Sereny, *Albert Speer: His Battle with Truth*, (London, Picador), p. 573.
20. Norman family papers.
21. Ibid.
22. Alfred SamForay correspondence, 21 August 2009.
23. Norman family papers.
24. Ibid.
25. Alfred SamForay correspondence, 21 August 2009.
26. Peter Penfold interview.
27. Fred Marafono papers.
28. Roelf van Heerden interview.
29. Hinga Norman Defence Fund, Press Statement, 24 March 2003.
30. Norman family papers.
31. M. Nesbitt, 'Lessons from the Sam Hinga Norman Decision', p.12.
32. Truth & Reconciliation Commission, para., 839.
33. Fred Marafono papers.
34. Truth & Reconciliation Commission, para., 839.
35. Statute of the Special Court for Sierra Leone.
36. Norman family papers.
37. Ibid.
38. Roelf van Heerdon interview.

39. Ibid.
40. Fred Marafono papers.
41. Ibid.
42. Florence Norman interview.
43. Sam Norman Jr interview.
44. Norman family papers.
45. P. Penfold, 'The Tangled Web of Sierra Leone's Special Court.'
46. Norman family papers.
47. Ibid.
48. Ibid.
49. Fred Marafono papers.
50. Norman family papers.
51. *Newswave*, p.24.
52. Fred Marafono papers.
53. Ibid.
54. Ibid.
55. Norman family papers.
56. Ibid.
57. P. Penfold, 'The Tangled Web of Sierra Leone's Special Court'.
58. Peter Penfold interview.
59. Fred Marafono papers.
60. Special Court Press Release, 16 July 2007.
61. Norman family papers.
62. Ibid.
63. S. Kamara & M. Nijie, 'Hinga Norman Located', *Awareness Times*, p.1, http://www.sl/drwebsite/publish/article_20054822.shtml.
64. Norman family papers.
65. Ibid.
66. Ibid.
67. Ibid.
68. Lansana Jawara, 'My Recollection of Events that Led to the Death of Chief Sam Hinga Norman in Senegal', Norman family papers.
69. Ibid.
70. Ibid.

Chapter 11

1. *Newswave*, October 1998, p.23.
2. Peter Penfold interview.
3. Ibid.
4. Gen Sir David Richards' testimony at the Special Court for Sierra Leone.
5. Ibid.
6. Peter Penfold interview.
7. Dr Joe Demby's Report, Observations on Autopsy of Hinga Norman for Special Court of Sierra Leone, Peter Penfold Papers.
8. Special Court for Sierra Leone Press Release, 16 July 2007.
9. Ibid.
10. Peter Penfold interview.
11. Ibid.

12. Fred Marafono papers.
13. Doug Brooks, President of IPOA, correspondence, 2 April 2010.
14. Doug Brooks, interview by Stephen Mbogo, 'Privatising Peacekeeping', *West Africa*, Issue 4244, 18–24 September 2000, p. 21.
15. Peter Penfold interview.

Appendix 2
1. Eeben Barlow, Executive *Outcomes, p. 541.*
2. Tim Spicer, correspondence, 30 March 2010.
3. Johann(Juba) Joubert, 23 April 2010.
4. Eeben Barlow, Executive *Outcomes, p.541.*

Bibliography

Barlow, Eeben. *Executive Outcomes: Against all Odds*. Alberton, Republic of South Africa: Galago Books, 1999 (2007 edn).

Brooks, Doug. Interview by Stephen Mbogo, 'Privatising Peacekeeping', *West Africa*, Issue 4244, 18–24 September 2000.

Churchill Archives Centre. Penfold, Peter, British Diplomatic Oral History Programme, 80.

Dimmock, David. 'Washing rejects the ICC'. http://www.choike.org/.

Forna, Aminatta. *The Devil that Danced on the Water: A Daughter's Memoir of Her Father, Her Family, Her Country and a Continent*. London: Flamingo, 2003 (edn.).

Fowler, William, *Operation Barras: The SAS Rescue Mission, 2000*. London: Cassell, 2004.

Geraghty, Tony. *Guns For Hire: The Inside Story Of Freelance Soldiering*. London: Piatkus Books, 2008.

Griffin, Stuart. *Joint Operations: A Short History*. JDCC, 2005.

Hirsch, John, L. *Sierra Leone: Diamonds and the Struggle for Democracy*. International Peace Academy Occasional Paper Series, London: Lynne Rienner Publishers Inc., 2001.

Hoe, Alan. *The Quiet Professional: Major Richard J Meadows of the US Special Forces*. Lexington, Kentucky: The University Press of Kentucky, 2011.

Hooper, Jim. *Bloodsong: First Hand Accounts of a Modern Private Army in Action*. London: Collins, 2003.

Kamara, Sayoh & Nijie, Modou. 'Hinga Norman Located,' *Awareness Times*, 23 January 2007, http://www.news.sl/drwebsite/publish/article_20054822.shtml.

Khobe, Mitikishe, M. 'The Evolution and Conduct of ECOMOG Operations in West Africa.' *Monographs for the African Human Security Initiative*, 44, Boundaries of Peace Support Operations, February 2000, http://www.iss.co.za/Pubs/Monographs/No44/ECOMOG.html.

Nesbitt, Michael. 'Lessons from the Sam Hinga Norman Decision of the Special Court for Sierra Leone: How Trials and Truth Commissions can Co-exist.' *German Law Journal*, No. 10 (1 October 2007), http://www.germanlawjournal.com/.

Newswave, October 1998.

Penfold, Peter. 'The Tangled Web of Sierra Leone's Special Court,' in *Africa Analysis*. No 491, 28 April 2006.

Report of the Board of Inquiry to Determine the Cause for the Supply of Wrong Spares for the Mi-24V Helicopter Gunship SLAF001. Defence Headquarters, Armed Forces of the Republic of Sierra Leone, 15 May 1999.

Roberson, Walter Grady. *British Military Intervention into Sierra Leone: A Case Study*. Thesis for Faculty of the US Army Command and General Staff College, 2007.

Ross, Hamish. *Paddy Mayne: Lt Col Blair 'Paddy' Mayne, 1 SAS Regiment*. Stroud: The History Press, 2008 (edn.).

Select Committee on Foreign Affairs Second Report. http://www.parliament.the-stationery-office.co.uk/pa/cm199899/cmselect/cmfaff/116/11607.

Sereny, Gitta. *Albert Speer: His Battle with Truth*. London: Picador, 1996 (edn.).

Sierra Leone News. http://www.sierra-leone.org/archives.html.

Sierra Leone Truth & Reconciliation Commission: Volume 3a: Chapter 3: The Military and Political History of the Conflict. http://www.trcsierraleone.org/.

Singer, P. W. *Corporate Warriors: The Rise of the Privatized Military Industry*. Cornell University: Cornell University Press, 2003.

Spicer, Tim, *An Unorthodox Soldier: Peace and War and the Sandline Affair*. Edinburgh: Mainstream Publishing, 1999.

Taylor, Claire & Waldman, Tom. *British defence policy since 1997*. RP08/57, House of Commons Library, 2008.

U N, Security Council Committee – 1132. http://www.un.org/.

Special Court for Sierra Leone. http://www.sc-sl.org/.

Van Heerden, Roelf. As told to Andrew Hudson. *Four Ball, One Tracer: Commanding Executive Outcomes Forces in Angola and Sierra Leone*. Johannesburg: Thirty Degrees South Publishers, 2011.

Venter, Al J. *War Dog: Fighting Other People's Wars: The Modern Mercenary in Combat*. Philadelphia: Casemate, 2006.

Index